GOOD HOUSEKEEPING
STEP-BY-STEP

Microwave

COOK BOOK

GOOD HOUSEKEEPING
STEP-BY-STEP
Microwave
COOK BOOK

Cecilia Norman

Ebury Press thank Moulinex for their expert assistance in the preparation of this book. The ovens featured in the colour photographs in the book and on the cover are from the Moulinex range.

Book Club Associates
LONDON

This edition published 1983 by Book Club Associates
by arrangement with Ebury Press
National Magazine House
72 Broadwick Street
London W1V 2BP

2nd impression 1984

Design by Roger Daniels
Photography Paul Kemp

Cover photograph:
Pork Chops with Redcurrant Glaze and assorted vegetables.

Typeset by Advanced Filmsetters (Glasgow) Ltd
Printed and bound in Italy by
New Interlitho s.p.a., Milan

Contents

FOREWORD 6

INTRODUCTION 7

STOCKS AND SOUPS 19

EGGS AND CHEESE 25

FISH AND SHELLFISH 31

MEAT 43

POULTRY AND GAME 60

VEGETABLES 75

PASTA, RICE AND GRAINS 84

SAUCES 90

PUDDINGS AND DESSERTS 100

BAKING 110

CONFECTIONERY 116

JAMS AND PRESERVES 122

INDEX 126

Foreword

The purpose of this special microwave cookery book is to explain how to get the best results from the microwave oven, using step-by-step instructions on the various techniques. You will find all the information you need to understand how the microwave oven works and its effects on ingredients. It tells you which types of containers are suitable and which are not, which types of foods cook well in a microwave and which are best suited to conventional methods. All the basic techniques are explained in clear illustrations and there is advice on how to adjust the cooking times on your own microwave oven so that the recipes will work well for you.

Each recipe section has an introduction giving all the information you need to produce excellent results. Step-by-step instructions take you through the simplest and most complicated recipes. If you are not familiar with microwave cooking I suggest you read all the introductions carefully and study the various techniques. Even if you are a confirmed 'microwave cook', you may find a few extra tips that you did not know before.

This book is based on many years microwave experience and the cookery taught at my school.

Cecilia Norman

THE MICROWAVE COOKING SCHOOL
Hampstead, London

Introduction

People have odd ideas about microwave ovens. Some suppose them to be miraculous magic boxes, others wonder what on earth persuades people to pay upwards of £150 to cook a jacket potato in 5 minutes. In fact, the microwave oven has many, many attributes and, in its own way, is more versatile than a freezer.

You may not have wanted a freezer originally but if you now have one you would not part with it. You will feel the same way about your microwave oven. You may even prefer to buy a microwave oven before you own a freezer.

The microwave oven is perhaps the most useful cooking appliance so far developed, because it fits perfectly with modern lifestyles and changing eating patterns. It is equally useful for the family or single person. It can defrost, reheat or carry out prime cooking, taking the place of both the hob and conventional oven for a high proportion of their cooking tasks. It goes hand-in-hand with the freezer, enabling you to store and reheat in the serving portions required, eliminating waste and offering a choice of dishes almost to order. Combined with the refrigerator, which can store hygienically for short periods, it enables you to prepare food ahead, to be reheated quickly, safely and efficiently. The disabled and blind find it much easier to operate than a conventional cooker.

The first obvious advantage of the microwave oven is the speed with which it can produce meals: it takes only a quarter to one-fifth of normal cooking times. And because microwave cooking is so quick, using the same amount of electricity as one conventional ring, there are savings in fuel consumption. Here are a few examples of the enormous savings in cooking time:

	Average time in minutes	
	Conven-tional	Micro-wave
Baked potato	60	5
Casserole	120	45
Crumbles	45	5
Fairy cakes (6)	15	2
Fish (450 g/1 lb)	10	4
Lamb chops (2)	7	5
Plaice (4 fillets)	10	5
Roast chicken		
(1.5 kg/3½ lb)	90	25
Chicken portion	15	2
Sausages (2)	10	2
Sponge pudding	90	4

The microwave oven also considerably cuts preparation and clearing-up times, eliminating the worst washing-up chores.

Used in conjunction with a conventional cooker, a microwave oven reduces the overall cooking time. Cook some component parts of a dish by microwave and some conventionally. For instance, a special roast-beef dinner can be hastened by par-cooking the potatoes, par-cooking the joint of meat and then browning them in a hot conventional oven at the same time as you bake the Yorkshire puddings. You can then make a meringue pie or crumble in the microwave oven for dessert.

Use your microwave oven in conjunction with the freezer to store, thaw and reheat a greater selection of home-cooked or commercially prepared dishes. Garden produce can be blanched, or vegetables can be cooked and then stored in the freezer for subsequent reheating.

The microwave oven cooks in its own right too. Scrambled eggs are easy, fish dishes are fabulous and poultry cooks superbly. Vegetables retain their colour and have a marvellous crisp texture. Jams can be made in small quantities just when you feel like using up an odd amount of fruit, and the microwave oven is excellent for sauces and confectionery. It cooks pasta and rice well, and although there is no significant saving in time over conventional methods, these foods are much easier to cook in the microwave oven as the cooking can be done in the dish in which the food will be served.

The microwave oven reheats perfectly without fear of spoiling or drying up the food. Reheating times depend on the shape and density of the food and also the starting temperature—a precooked frozen meal will take longer to reach eating temperature than a meal stored in the refrigerator. But generally speaking, a room temperature meal can be reheated in 2–3 minutes.

Quick Tips for the Microwave User

There are many small tasks that the microwave oven can be used for, either before you start cooking by microwave or when using conventional methods. Try using it for softening butter, melting chocolate, dissolving gelatine and heating small quantities of liquid.

Cake making
Melt chocolate for cakes and icings. If the butter is too firm to cream with the sugar, you can soften it by putting it in the microwave oven for a few seconds; do not melt it. To avoid curdling eggs in a creamed mixture, they need to be at room temperature; if they have been stored in the refrigerator, 3 seconds in the microwave oven (not more or the eggs will burst), will take the chill off them.

Coffee
Use the oven to freshen up stale coffee beans.

Jams
Open the paper sugar carton and put the entire carton in the microwave oven. The warm sugar will then dissolve more quickly when it is stirred into the fruit.

Flowers
Dry flowers in the microwave oven and bring back the perfume to a pot-pourri.

Mayonnaise
Take the chill off the vinegar and oil before making mayonnaise.

Nuts
A lovely flavour is imparted to almonds when they are just light brown inside. You will have to cut one or two in half to test for this.

Sauces
Heat milk for making white sauces or custards. Make roux-based sauces while the foods to be sauced are being cooked conventionally.

Vegetables
If you want to lightly thaw frozen vegetables before adding them to stews, slash the packet first on top and microwave them for just a few seconds.

What are Microwaves?

Microwaves come into the same category as radio and television waves, sunlight, radar systems used in traffic control and infra-red fires. These waves are all known as non-ionising rays, which means that they do not build up in the body and are therefore not dangerous. (Ionising rays, on the other hand, do build up in the body. These include X-rays, gamma rays and cosmic rays, which are all short waves.) Microwaves travel in straight lines and are reflected by all types of metal.

There are few inner workings to a microwave oven. The main component is the magnetron, whose job it is to convert electricity into microwave energy. When you switch on, the magnetron starts to manufacture its microwaves and these invisibly enter the oven cavity and pass through the food. Every microwave oven is lined with metal, even though this may be covered by plastic or paint. So every time the microwaves reach the sides, top or bottom of the oven, they are reflected back again. They pass through the food at a rate of 2450 billion times a second, agitating the molecules in the food; these rub together causing friction, and it is the friction which heats the food. You could compare this to the warmth resulting from rubbing your hands together in cold weather. The more friction that occurs, the more cooking takes place.

When the oven is switched off or the door is opened, the microwaves disappear, but the food continues cooking until the heat inside the food diminishes.

The microwaves pass freely through glass, plastic, paper and other non-metallic materials and they are utilised by the food. Although the oven door is transparent, it is lined with perforated metal. The perforations are too tiny to allow the microwaves to pass through, ensuring that they are kept within the cooking cavity.

How microwaves work

Electric energy is converted to microwaves which are reflected by the oven's metal walls and pass straight through any non-metallic substances.

Microwaves, which are attracted to food, penetrate to a depth of about 4 cm (1½ inches). The centre of the food is cooked by conduction of heat generated in the outer layer.

Microwave Ovens and Safety

There are two kinds of microwave oven—commercial and domestic. Very large powerful ovens have to be fitted with a special electric outlet but domestic models, which do not exceed 1.5 kw input (approximately 700 watts output), may be wired to a normal 13 or 15 amp three-pin *earthed* plug. A two wire flex will not do.

Regarding safety, before leaving the factory, all microwave ovens are subjected to stringent tests and are required to satisfy the requirements of the Electrical Safety Regulations 1975 (amended 1976).

When unpacking your new oven check the doors are properly aligned and if in doubt ask for an engineer to check it over. Do not purchase a second-hand oven unless it has been approved by a microwave engineer. It may well be in first-class condition, but it is wise to have this confirmed as a new magnetron can be costly.

How Food Cooks in a Microwave Oven

In a microwave oven, all surfaces of the food are heated simultaneously to a depth of approximately 4 cm ($1\frac{1}{2}$ inches). The microwave friction causes the heat and this then spreads by conduction. Because of the pattern of microwaves in the oven, the middle of any food receives mostly waves bounced off the top of the oven cavity. Consequently the food in the middle tends to cook more by conduction, while the sides are attacked by microwaves from all directions. This means that foods that can be, should be stirred or turned so that the middle has its turn at the edge of the container.

The air in a microwave cabinet is not heated; it remains at room temperature while only the food gets hot. So it is not possible to have a crisp outside and a soft inside to food. As the food cooks, moisture is drawn to the outside and the coolness of the cavity meets the hot food so that the surface remains soft and sometimes damp. Very little browning occurs. So, for example, a baked loaf will never have a crisp, brown crust and a joint of meat may be overcooked on the outside and yet the surface will not brown. You cannot make Yorkshire puddings in the microwave oven, and meringues are hardly satisfactory.

There is a limit to the amount of food you can put in the microwave oven at any one time, so that the larger capacity of a conventional oven will sometimes produce better results than the speed of microwave cookery. For instance, a number of jacket potatoes spaced out in the conventional oven would take about an hour to cook; only half a dozen can be cooked at a time in the microwave oven, although in approximately one-quarter of the time. So if you are cooking more than 24 potatoes at once, it is better to use the conventional oven.

Making sauces

When cooking on a conventional hob the lower surface of the pan becomes heated first, so that food particles may burn unless stirred. In the microwave oven there is no direct contact between the dish and the heat, so that surface burning cannot occur. Stirring is still necessary for even cooking, but less frequently. As a result, it is easier to make good sauces by microwave than by conventional cooking on the hob.

Frying

Deep frying is not possible in the microwave oven because of the lack of control of temperature, but onions and similar items can be browned well in a small amount of fat. Special browning dishes or plates are obtainable as optional extras. These are useful for searing and browning. Choose a browning dish which has a lid when you are going to start a dish by browning, for example chicken pieces or meat, and then finish by adding a sauce. Use the lid to keep in the moisture and the heat and prevent any splattering.

Boiling, poaching and steaming

Milk will boil over in the microwave oven just as it does on the hob, but if the LOW setting is used, there is less chance of this happening. On LOW you can also simmer and poach. For poaching, simmering or boiling three-quarters cover with cling film and stir through the gap. Cooking starchy foods like potatoes or rice is much easier as the water will not bubble up and force off the lid as it often does on a conventional hob. Steaming in the microwave oven is easy; no extra water is required, you just cover the dish with a lid or cling film and the food cooks in its own moisture. You should steam with a loose cover of cling film and a corner folded back so that the odd puff of steam can make its escape.

Grilling

A simple microwave oven is not suitable for grilling but there are a number of ovens on the market with grills and hot air devices for browning and searing, and browning dishes which help sear and brown the food. A microwave oven fitted with a grill is, of course, more difficult to clean. But if

Microwave Cooking Techniques

searing only is needed, (which would be the equivalent of cooking in a frying pan), use a browning dish. Or cook the food by microwave and finish by browning under a conventional grill.

Baking
Microwaves can be used for making cakes, but they will not brown. This does not matter if dark ingredients such as chocolate or black treacle are used or if the surface of the cake is to be covered with icing. Making pastry is not successful. Microwaves are attracted to fat and sugar, so that the interior of the pastry is inclined to scorch while the outside layer remains unaffected by the heat.

Browning and coating
Although the microwave oven doesn't sear, if ingredients would normally change colour during cooking, such as syrups, they will do the same in the microwave oven. Nuts will roast and become brown inside and honey in a recipe is a particularly good browning ingredient. Where dark ingredients are used the food will achieve a deeper hue: use dark brown sugar, molasses, treacle, rich beef stock cubes, yeast extract, tomato purée, soy sauce, red wine, chocolate, cocoa and coffee essence to darken otherwise light foods.

Coatings can often improve the appearance of microwave-cooked food. Cakes can be iced or piped decoratively with whipped cream. Savoury dishes can be covered in browned crumbs; these are even better if turmeric or paprika is included when melting the butter. There are also a number of proprietary browning agents for use with the microwave oven.

Once you have discovered how easy it is to cook by microwave, you will become accustomed to the differences in colour. You will find that the improvement in the texture and taste of many of the foods, plus the convenience and speed of cooking, will outweigh any resistance you may have to its appearance.

All foods completely enclosed in a skin must be pricked or scored, cut or shelled before cooking. Otherwise the water molecules inside, which turn to steam, will burst and cause splattering.

Microwaves are also attracted to fat, to water and to bones. Ingredients with a high fat content, such as cheese and egg yolks, overcook rapidly causing separation, curdling and toughening. Microwave these ingredients for a short time only or on a LOW setting.

Microwaves cook first round the outside of the food, unless it is so large that it covers the entire shelf. All ovens have a slightly uneven cooking pattern, with what are known as 'hot spots'. For even cooking, food must therefore be stirred or somehow repositioned during cooking. To test your oven for hot spots, arrange nine similar cups or glasses each containing the same amount of water at the same temperature on the oven shelf. Microwave on HIGH and those that boil first indicate the positions of the hot spots. If there is one particular place, either avoid putting the food in this part or make sure that you stir or turn.

Foods that cannot be stirred because it would spoil the arrangement, and which similarly cannot be repositioned or turned over, can be evenly cooked by turning the dish. This is usually necessary even when the oven is fitted with a turntable. The recommended number of turns is given in the individual recipes.

Positioning and repositioning
Place thinner parts of food portions in the centre and thicker parts around the outside of the dish. When several portions are being cooked in one dish and they are of similar size, they should be arranged in a single layer and repositioned during cooking so that those in the middle, receiving less microwaves, can change places with those on the outside, which will be receiving more.

Turning over
Single items thicker than 6 cm (2½ inches) will cook more evenly if they are turned over once during cooking, because the microwave signal is stronger towards the upper part of the oven. This is particularly important when the food is not covered. When turning food over, reposition so that the outside parts are placed in the centre of the dish.

Stirring and whisking
Stirring is necessary in exactly the same way as it is when cooking conventionally. Stir from the outside towards the centre so that all the food is equally mixed. Whisking ensures even mixing to prevent lumpy sauces. It is specially important when the sauce contains critical ingredients such as eggs.

Covering with a lid or cling film
Always cover food if a moist, even heat is required, so that the steam is trapped. The food then cooks by steam as well as by microwave.

Covering is particularly important to prevent evaporation when only a small amount of liquid is used. Use a lid or cling film if stirring is necessary.

When the food is fairly liquid, three-quarters covering is often sufficient; tightly cover, then pull back one corner of the cling film. You can then insert the spoon to stir through the gap. Use cling film for complete covering only when the food is being reheated or cooked for a very short time, or if the food is being microwaved on LOW. When food is microwaved on HIGH or lengthy cooking periods are necessary, the cling film must be vented. When removing cling film peel it from the side furthest away from you so that the steam is directed away from your face.

Covering with paper
Use greaseproof or non-stick paper for covering to prevent food from becoming soggy or if a considerable amount of repositioning or turning is necessary. The paper may blow about in the microwave oven if it is fitted with a fan, so secure it with a wooden cocktail stick or lightly tuck the ends of the paper

underneath the dish. The latter method is only suitable for short time cooking as paper underneath dishes can catch fire. When covering for long periods, split open a roasting bag and tuck it completely underneath the dish.

When thawing or cooking food where heating will cause surface moisture, or when you wish to absorb any splattering of fat, use absorbent kitchen paper.

Shielding
To prevent parts of unstirrable foods becoming over-cooked,

cover vulnerable areas with small smooth pieces of foil pressed close to the food. Secure it with cocktail sticks if there is any possibility of it being blown off. Foil must not touch the interior lining of the oven or it will damage the magnetron. If preferred, overwrap with cling film.

Standing time
When food is removed from the microwave oven a standing time is often allowed so that any uneven heat can equalise itself. This is part of the cooking process and should not be omitted. If a standing time is specified in the recipe, cover the food with a tent of foil when it is removed from the oven and allow the standing time indicated in the recipe. This is usually equal to the cooking time but not always.

Use of thermometers and humidity detectors
A special microwave thermometer can be left in meat and poultry during cooking. Ordinary meat thermometers are not suitable and must not be used. A microwave meat thermometer is not usually suitable for use in syrups and jams, as the maximum reading is not high enough for boiling sugar.

A special microwave cooking thermometer is a probe which plugs into a socket inside the microwave oven. To use it, insert it into the thickest part of the meat or the centre of a pudding. The maximum internal temperature for perfect cooking is then pre-set on

the control panel of the microwave oven and the microwaves are shut off automatically when the food is ready. This method of testing is not always accurate since, if the probe is pushed into a fatty part of the food, the reading may not be correct. Microwave thermometers are also inclined to be inaccurate when used in thin pieces of food.

Some ovens have a humidity detector which determines when the food is cooked. To use this the food must be completely covered with cling film; the detector then picks up the first puff of steam emitted through the cling film and calculates how long the food will require. These are excellent provided instructions are followed carefully and the quantities recommended are used, but these too occasionally allow some overcooking.

If you are using a thermometer or probe to determine when the food is cooked, follow the chart below.

Baby food	35°C (95°F)
Beverages	70°C (160°F)
Meat	
Beef	50–70°C (120–160°F)
Casseroles	65°C (150°F)
Lamb	80–85°C (175–180°F)
Pork	80–85°C (175–180°F)
Veal	80°C (175°F)
Soups	70°C (160°F)
Vegetable	
Casseroles	65°C (150°F)

Stacking
Plated meals can be stacked with up to three plates, one above the other. There must be an air space between each plate and microwave stacking rings are ideal for this purpose. The top plate must be covered. It makes no difference to the heating if the others are also covered. Mix the foods vertically so that the meat and various vegetables alternate throughout the stack.

Containers for Microwave Cooking

Cooking times

Cooking time in the microwave oven is in direct relation to the amount of food being cooked. A small quantity will cook much faster than a large, though it is not always necessary to double the amount of cooking time when doubling the quantity; there is a saving of time overall when larger amounts are being cooked. If one quantity or one item takes 1 minute, two quantities or two items which are similar in size will take only 1¾ minutes. As a rough guide increase the time by about half when the recipe is being doubled.

The cooking time given in recipes is always the lowest reasonable time, to ensure that you do not overcook. When timing always take into account any further instructions, such as 'cook until tender' or 'until thickened'. Under-cooked food can be rectified, burnt food cannot.

Size of food portions

Small even-shaped portions will cook more successfully than large or uneven pieces. This is because the microwave signal penetrates to a depth of 2.5–4 cm (1–1½ inches), but after this the signal becomes weaker and cooking continues by conduction.

Starting temperatures

The colder the food, the longer the cooking time will be. The food temperature varies from refrigerator to refrigerator and likewise with the freezer. Non-frozen foods should be at room temperature, otherwise cooking times will be affected.

The one material which cannot be used in a microwave oven is metal. So ordinary saucepans and iron casseroles, or any container with a metallic trim of any description, are out. Otherwise you can choose from a wide range of ceramic, glass, wood, paper and plastic materials to suit your purpose. The shape of the container also affects the cooking speed.

Foods which are going to reach a very high temperature, such as those with a high sugar or fat content, must be cooked in dishes which can withstand these temperatures. Ovenglass is always a good choice, but some specialist microwave cooking ware can also be used. Re-usable plastics are extremely useful provided the food is not going to become too hot, and wood and straw can also be used in certain circumstances. A list of useful containers and the best way to use them is given in the chart on pages 13 to 15.

Browning dishes

Microwave browning dishes, such as those produced by Corning, are white in colour but underneath you may notice a grey sheen. This is a special coating which attracts the microwaves. When the dish or plate is put into the microwave oven empty and heated for a few minutes, the surface becomes as hot as a frying pan. Unfortunately these browning dishes do not hold the heat for long and, once food is added, the browning capability diminishes fairly rapidly. The browning dish has four small feet which raise it just above the oven shelf; this is to prevent damage to the shelf, but be guided by the manufacturer's instructions.

The browning dish can be used as a serving dish but take care not to scratch the surface. Browning dishes need not and should not be scoured, clean with a cloth and a paste made with bicarbonate of soda and water.

A browning plate is flat, surrounded by a groove. This is ideal when browning sausages or fatty foods. You can then have maximum heat while the surplus fat drains away.

Testing containers

To test if it is safe to use a certain dish in the microwave oven (excluding metal), put the dish in the microwave oven. Place a jug or glass half-filled with cold water either in or beside the dish. Microwave on HIGH for 1–2 minutes. If the dish remains cool and the water is hot, the dish is very suitable for microwaving. If the dish is slightly warm and the water is hot, the dish will also be suitable for microwaving but for shorter periods. If the dish becomes hot but the water remains cool, the dish is unsuitable for use in the microwave oven because it will absorb microwaves and could subsequently break. Dishes suitable for the microwave oven do not become hot as a result of the microwaves, but from the heat of the food being cooked in them. If cooking is for a prolonged period the dish will become very hot, so it is essential to use oven gloves to protect your hands.

Shapes of containers

A ring-shaped container will always give the best results as the microwave energy can enter from both sides as well as the top, giving more even cooking. Round containers will usually give better results than square or rectangular ones as there are no corners where over-cooking can take place. A straight-sided container is better than one with sloping sides because the depth is more even throughout. The depth of the container is equally important. Foods cooked in deep dishes cook more slowly than those in shallow dishes—choose the depth of the dish as a way of speeding up or slowing down cooking.

Microwave Cookware

Cookware	Uses	Advantages	Comments
Absorbent kitchen paper	Covering foods which splatter. Underneath foods which absorb moisture, eg thawing bread.	Easily disposable.	Take care not to use patterned side against food as colour comes off.
Brown paper bags	Poultry.	Holds in the heat but doesn't make food too soft; absorbs fat splashes.	
Cardboard chocolate and candy boxes	Making biscuits and cakes.	Interesting shapes often unobtainable in other materials.	Do not use if there is any metallic trimming or lettering. Line with cling film.
China cups, plates and dishes	Reheating.	Attractive for serving, saves washing-up.	Suitable for reheating only. Do not use metal-trimmed china.
Chinette	Reheating.	This is the only paper suitable for use in the microwave that will not 'give' when containing hot food.	Not re-usable.
Cling film	Covering vegetables, fish and meat dishes. Lining cake dishes.	Traps heat for faster cooking. Forms an excellent seal and is disposable. Saves washing-up.	Do not overstretch. Remove carefully to avoid steam burns. Fit loosely over the dish. Wrap double for the freezer. For prolonged cooking turn back a corner after covering.
Coffee pots	Reheating beverages.		Avoid jugs with metal trim and those with plastic handles and handles held by metal screws.

Microwave Cookware (continued)

Cookware	Uses	Advantages	Comments
Cooking bags	Convenience foods.	Save washing-up.	Slit on top to prevent bursting.
Corning Ware	All microwave cookery.	Interchangeable between conventional and microwave ovens, freezer and grill.	Guaranteed safe under the grill. Can be used in the freezer.
Glass ceramics	Casseroles, sauces and cakes.	Interchangeable between conventional and microwave ovens.	Avoid metal-trimmed dishes and plates.
Glass jugs, heatproof	Heating liquids.		Always use a size larger than required. Do not freeze in narrow-necked jugs.
Glass, ovenproof bowls and casseroles	Bowls for sauces, custards and soups; casseroles for stews and desserts.	Easy to wash, practically unbreakable and transparent.	Avoid metal-trimmed glass. Use lids as required. Choose a larger size than you think may be needed.
Greaseproof paper	Covering foods which might pop or splutter, eg fish, chicken and baked beans.	Keeps in some of the steam while allowing the food to crisp.	Use a piece larger than the cooking dish. Secure with a wooden cocktail stick to prevent the paper blowing about in the oven.
Microwave browning dish or plate	Searing and sealing meat, floured fish and dry fried eggs.	Suitable for all foods where a heat-sealed surface is necessary.	Do not overheat. Use the lid when directed. Clean with bicarbonate of soda and a damp soft cloth.
Natural shells	Fish starters.	Attractive.	Suitable for short cooking only.
Ovenable paper-board	Casseroles, individual pies and cakes.	Can also be used in the conventional oven up to 200°C (400°F) mark 6.	Not suitable for use under the grill.
Ovenproof porcelain dishes	Cakes, pies and tarts.	Attractive for serving.	Cooking is sometimes slower. Avoid any metal trimming.
Paper cups	Heating drinks.	Easily disposable.	Do not use for heating oil or sugar.
Paper napkins	Heating burgers and doughnuts, warming rolls, thawing bread.	Absorb hot fat and moisture. Do not stick as much as kitchen paper.	Avoid the soft, coloured types. Do not use under dishes during prolonged cooking.
Paper plates	Reheating dry foods.	Easily disposable.	Not suitable for large quantities of food. Short-term heating only, the plates tend to lose rigidity on heating. Use double for serving.
Plastic boxes	Initial thawing blocks of food.		Freeze with the lid on but remove lid before microwaving. Most will not withstand temperatures above 80°C (180°F) so do not freeze foods with high sugar content unless box is recommended by the manufacturer for microwave use.
Plastic cups	Heating drinks.	Disposable.	Do not boil liquid or plastic will melt.
Polypropylene bowls	Puddings, sauces and soups.	Re-usable many times. Boilable, but scar if used with hot fat or syrups.	Avoid pouring hot syrup or fat into the base. Do not use supplied lids in the microwave oven as they may be forced off by steam.

Cookware	Uses	Advantages	Comments
Polystyrene foam dishes	Warming food and drinks.	Disposable and easy to hold.	Will melt at high temperatures. Do not use for foods with high sugar or fat content.
Polythene bags, standard quality	Brief thawing of small quantities of food from the freezer. Proving yeast doughs.	Convenient for freezer to microwave.	Remove all metal ties. Will not withstand high temperatures, so use for initial thawing only. Will not support weight of warm contents.
Polythene bags, double thickness	Freezing, thawing, and warming.		Do not use metal ties.
Pottery cups, plates	Cooking and reheating.		Test before using for the first time (see page 12). Avoid metal-trimmed and metallic-glazed pottery. Unglazed pottery may absorb moisture and become hot.
Pyrex (see Glass, ovenproof)			
Racks, suitable for microwave	Roasting meat and thawing where passage of air round food required.		Choose only specially made racks. Not suitable under grill.
Roasting bags	Softening potatoes, roasting, cooking vegetables.	Hasten cooking. Aid browning.	Do not use metal ties. Remove from the oven carefully as bags are likely to burst. When liquid accumulates during cooking, place bag in a dish. Do not completely seal.
Straw baskets	Warming rolls.	Attractive for serving.	Will become brittle if heated on too many occasions or for too long.
Thermoplastics	Most forms of cooking.	Easy to clean, versatile, usable in conventional ovens and freezer.	Follow the manufacturer's instructions for use.
Toughened glass	Reheating beverages, dissolving gelatine.	Transparent. Easy to wash.	Use oven gloves to remove from the oven as can become warm by conduction.
Waxed paper	Covering food.	Prevents splattering.	
Waxed paper cartons	Reheating drinks.	Suitable for freezer to microwave.	Open carton before heating. Do not heat for too long or the carton may burst and the wax melt.
Waxed paper plates	Reheating most foods.	Do not absorb moisture.	Do not heat for long or the wax may melt.
Wine glasses	Desserts, drinks.	Attractive for serving.	Use for warming only. Delicate glasses may crack.
Wooden boards, baskets	Warming rolls.	Attractive for serving.	Wood absorbs moisture and may warp if heated for too long. No metal staples or handles in the wood.

General Look on the bottom of your normal dishes. There will sometimes be a note that the utensil is suitable for use in the microwave oven.

You should not use plastic containers that have tightly fitting lids. Do not balance lids on the tops of containers as they will be sucked down.

Heat Controls on a Microwave Oven

There are so many different microwave ovens on the market that it would be impossible to describe the heat controls on them all. However some of the old models have only a single control which is HIGH. Others have HIGH and LOW control, the LOW one being for defrosting. Others have variable controls enabling you to move through the entire power range from HIGH, which is full power, to VERY LOW which is the equivalent of a keep hot control.

In this book when food is said to be cooked on HIGH, that indicates maximum output of microwave energy and is between 600 and 700 watts. MEDIUM indicates about 60% of full power, ie 420 watts on a 700-watt oven. LOW indicates about 35% of full power. Until oven markings are standardised you may find indicators differ from this basis.

Choosing your power setting

Most recipes can be cooked on HIGH, including vegetables, beverages, fish and bacon. Use the HIGH setting for reheating.

The MEDIUM setting can be used for all the above except when using the browning dish, which has to be on HIGH. Use the MEDIUM setting for casseroles when you have insufficient time to spare to cook on a lower setting.

Use a LOW setting for most defrosting, cooking egg and cheese mixtures, melting cheese, for casseroles using less tender meat and for softening butter.

If your oven has a WARM setting, use this for raising yeast doughs and keeping food hot. With frozen food you will have to almost double thawing times.

On some ovens the lower settings are a definite change of wattage, while on others the lower settings operate on a pulsing system so that the microwaves are on for some seconds and then switched off for a longer period of time. You can hear this on and off clicking if you listen carefully. You can make soufflés only if your oven has a LOW setting which is a continuous low wattage.

Checking your oven output

Before using any of the recipes in this book you must ascertain the output of your oven, otherwise this will affect the descriptions HIGH, MEDIUM or LOW and their timings. The output of an oven is usually about half the input. Thus if your oven is rated 1.3 kw the likely output of energy will be 600 watts. Half of the energy is used in the conversion of the electricity for microwave use.

If your oven output on HIGH is 400–450 watts you will have to allow 35% more cooking time. For ovens rated between 500 and 550 watts you need to add about 20%. These are of course only approximations. If your oven is new, look on the back or in the handbook and it will give the manufacturer's rating.

A simple, though not foolproof, test for measuring the output of your oven is as follows:

Testing your oven's output

1 Put 1 litre (35 fl oz) water in a large ovenglass measuring jug. Record the temperature (T1).

2 Microwave on HIGH without covering for exactly 2 minutes. Immediately record the temperature (T2).

3 Subtract the first reading from the second reading (T2 minus T1) equals T3.

4 Multiply the answer (T3) by 19.5 for a Fahrenheit reading or 35 for a Celsius reading. Example: T1 = 58°F, T2 = 86°F, T2−T1 = 28. 28 × 19.5 = 546. Output therefore 546 watts.

Thawing and Reheating Frozen Foods

Commercially packed foods are often frozen on polystyrene trays or in metal dishes. Remove the food from a metal dish and place in a microwave-suitable dish; remove a polystyrene tray as soon as possible because it prevents the microwaves from getting through the base to thaw the meat.

Because microwaves tend to heat round the outside of the food more than in the centre, you may find that the outside areas, particularly of meat, will begin to cook before the centre is thawed. Overheating on the edges will be much less on the DEFROST setting.

Remember to place blocks of food in the microwave oven ice-side up; cover where possible and break up lumps as soon as they can be separated. Push still-frozen parts towards the outside of the dish, stirring as soon as it is possible. Plated cooked frozen food can be reheated direct from frozen. Raw foods should be thawed before cooking starts.

Reheating

Reheat most dishes, covered, on HIGH. If possible stir during cooking to distribute the heat evenly. Turn dishes which cannot be stirred and microwave for half the time on HIGH and half on LOW. Arrange the food on plates with the thick or dense parts towards the outside and the thin or more delicate parts towards the inside and try to arrange the food in an even layer.

To test whether food is sufficiently reheated, feel the bottom of the plate or dish. This should not become hot until the food is hot. Be careful when reheating sugary items such as jam doughnuts because the microwaves reach the hot sugary filling first and you may burn your mouth. Take care also not to overcook food which is already well cooked, as cooking will continue during the reheating process. A little sauce added to meat will provide just that little extra moisture to prevent it from drying out.

Minestrone (page 22)

Convenience Foods

At one time or another, even the die-hard cook has to resort to using convenience foods. Take advantage of your microwave oven to speed preparation even further. Many manufacturers give microwave cooking instructions on their packages and cans. Since metal can rarely be used in the microwave oven, you must empty the food from the cans into a serving dish or plate before heating. Although foil dishes not more than 2 cm ($\frac{3}{4}$ inch) deep can be used in the microwave oven, provided they are filled with food and the metal does not touch the sides of the oven, they slow down the cooking or reheating times. Cooked pies and pastries should be removed from foil dishes and reheated on a piece of absorbent kitchen paper. To maintain greater crispness place this kitchen paper on a roasting rack. Use the kitchen paper and roasting rack method for thawing bread, rolls, cakes and puddings as well.

If you do not have a roasting rack elevate the bread on an upturned dish or bowl. To maintain the crispy base on a pizza brush the underneath with vegetable oil and reheat on a partly heated browning dish. Boil-in-bags must be slit and placed on a serving plate or dish before thawing and reheating.

Eggs Peperonata (page 30)
in a Pyrex quiche dish from the
Corningware bakeware range

Beverages

The microwave oven is faster than a kettle for boiling small quantities of water and better than a saucepan for heating milk because there is no possibility of overheated milk solids sticking to the sides of the container. If you like the feel of a saucepan you can obtain one made entirely of ovenproof glass, or a glass or pottery jug, or a cup or glass for single servings, will do. Drinks are hotter if prepared and heated in a cup, as the cup itself will heat as the liquid is warming.

Most drinks will reheat satisfactorily, although there is nothing like a fresh cup of tea. There is no need to put both the cup and the saucer into the microwave oven but until you are able to judge exactly how long reheating or cooking will take, it is a good idea to leave both there in case it boils over. The overflow will then be contained within the saucer, making it easier to clear up.

Coffee
Coffee made with freshly ground beans can be made several hours ahead and strained into a microwave-suitable jug. There are also available coffee makers specifically designed for use in the microwave oven; these usually produce filter coffee. For instant coffee, heat the water in a jug or cup, then add the granules. An average cup of black coffee takes not less than 1 minute to reheat on HIGH. Two cups black coffee take $2\frac{1}{2}$–$2\frac{3}{4}$ minutes on HIGH. 600 ml (1 pint) black coffee takes $4\frac{1}{4}$–$4\frac{3}{4}$ minutes to heat on HIGH. 1.1 litres (2 pints) black coffee take 7–$7\frac{1}{2}$ minutes to reheat on HIGH.

Water for tea, instant drinks or soups
150 ml ($\frac{1}{4}$ pint) cold water takes $1\frac{3}{4}$–$2\frac{1}{4}$ minutes to reach boiling point on HIGH. Two cups will take 3–$4\frac{3}{4}$ minutes; 600 ml (1 pint) will take 5–7 minutes; 900 ml ($1\frac{1}{2}$ pints) will take 8–10 minutes. Timings will vary depending on the starting temperature, the container and how many cups or mugs the larger quantities are divided between.

When drinks are only being reheated and it is not necessary to reach boiling point, less time will be required. Leave drinks to stand for a few seconds before stirring in sugar, powdered milk or coffee granules, and stir before serving.

Milk
Take care when heating milk in the microwave oven as it boils over easily. One cup will take $1\frac{3}{4}$–$2\frac{3}{4}$ minutes to reach drinking temperature on HIGH. 300 ml ($\frac{1}{2}$ pint) milk takes $2\frac{1}{2}$–4 minutes; 600 ml (1 pint) takes 4–5 minutes. Stay near the microwave oven when heating milk and if you see it boiling up in the cup or container, quickly open the door.

Average drinking temperature is 150–160°F (65–70°C).

Defrosting frozen concentrated orange and grapefruit juice

1
Dip the unopened container into hot water to loosen the block.

2
Remove the collar and lid and tip the block of frozen concentrate into a jug.

3
Microwave on HIGH for 1–$1\frac{1}{2}$ minutes, breaking the block into lumps with a plastic spatula as soon as it is possible. Stir frequently during thawing.

4
As soon as only a few lumps remain, stir well, then leave at room temperature until completely defrosted.

Supper Menu for 4 people

4 plaice fillets, total weight about 450 g (1 lb) with 300 ml ($\frac{1}{2}$ pint) parsley pouring sauce (see page 92)
four 175 g (6 oz) baked jacket potatoes (see chart page 77)
4 tomatoes
100 g (4 oz) green peas

Golden Pudding (see page 102)

40 minutes before serving
1 Prepare the pudding basin and put the syrup in the base. Make up the mixture, cover and set aside.
2 Make the parsley sauce and add the parsley. Cover and set aside.
3 Prepare the potatoes. Microwave on HIGH for 12–14 minutes turning over halfway through the cooking time.
4 Meanwhile, place the fish in a shallow dish. Season; cover loosely.
5 Halve the tomatoes and arrange around the edge of a shallow dish. Season; top each with knob of butter.
6 When the potatoes are cooked, wrap each in foil to retain its heat.
7 Cook the peas in a small bowl, adding 30 ml (2 tbsp) salted water. Cover with cling film and microwave on HIGH for 3 minutes or until cooked. Shake the bowl once during the cooking time.
8 Microwave the fish on HIGH for 3–4 minutes, turning the dish three times during cooking. Remove the cover, pour over the parsley sauce, recover and reheat on HIGH for 2 minutes until hot.
9 Drain the peas, place in the centre of the dish of tomatoes. Microwave on HIGH for 3 minutes.
10 Remove the cover from the fish and the peas and tomatoes. Unwrap the potatoes and add a knob of butter or margarine. Serve hot.
11 While eating the main course, cook the pudding. Spoon mixture into pudding basin and microwave on HIGH for 3$\frac{1}{2}$ minutes only. Leave to stand for 5–10 minutes; serve hot.

Dinner Party Menu for 4 people

Smoked Salmon, Cucumber and Prawn Toasts (see page 41. Use half the quantity of the topping and follow the timing in the recipe)
Marinated Chicken in Teriyaki Sauce (see page 68)
275 g (10 oz) Saffron Rice (see page 87)
450 g (1 lb) sliced courgettes (see chart page 76)
green salad with French dressing
Fresh Pineapple Flambé (see page 106)
coffee
Chocolate Truffles (see page 118)

In the morning
1 Make the hollandaise sauce for the smoked salmon, cucumber and prawn toasts. Cover with cling film and leave to cool.
2 Dice the cucumber. Thaw the prawns. Prepare the smoked salmon strips. Cover all with cling film and refrigerate.
3 Cook the saffron rice by the all-in-one method (see page 87). adding a pinch of saffron. Cool and refrigerate.
4 Prepare and slice the courgettes. Place in a suitable serving dish, add 30 ml (2 tbsp) water and a sprinkling of nutmeg. Cover with cling film and refrigerate.
5 Make a French dressing, cover and set aside.
6 Prepare the salad ingredients, place in a salad bowl, cover and refrigerate.
7 Prepare the fresh pineapple slices, cover with cling film and refrigerate.

2 hours before cooking
8 Prepare the marinade for the chicken in a roasting bag. Add the chicken and leave, turning the chicken occasionally.

40 minutes before serving
9 Microwave the chicken.
10 Meanwhile, finish making the topping for the smoked salmon, cucumber and prawn toasts. Cut out 8 rounds of bread but only measuring 5.5 cm (2$\frac{1}{2}$ inches). Toast, butter and complete the toppings for the toasts.
11 When the chicken is cooked, remove from the oven and leave to

stand for 10 minutes.
12 Meanwhile, microwave the courgettes on HIGH for about 8 minutes until tender. Shake the dish once or twice during the cooking time.
13 Test to see if the chicken is cooked. Slit the roasting bag down the centre, remove the chicken to a warm serving dish and cover with foil. Complete the chicken sauce. Pour over the chicken and recover with foil.
14 Drain the courgettes, add a little butter if wished and cover with cling film.
15 Serve the smoked salmon, cucumber and prawn toasts, allowing 2 toasts each.
16 While eating the starter, reheat the rice, covered with cling film, on HIGH for 5 minutes, stirring before serving.
17 Serve the chicken, courgettes, rice and dress the salad.
18 Cook and serve the pineapple flambé.
19 Make fresh coffee or reheat pre-prepared coffee. Serve with the truffles.

CHAPTER ONE

Stocks and Soups

All soups are tasty when freshly microwaved but are even better when they are cooked ahead, refrigerated for several hours and reheated. Add the final garnish after reheating.

Most soups can be cooked on HIGH but it is advisable to reheat on LOW those which are thickened with egg and cream liaisons. There is no need to reheat all the soup at once—a single serving reheated in a bowl will be hot in 2–3 minutes. When reheating, stir as soon as bubbles appear round the edges, then continue microwaving until they reappear and stir again. This is to avoid the possibility of your swallowing a mouthful of searing hot soup followed by a cold one.

Most soups are suitable for freezer storage so make full use of the freezer–microwave oven combination for quick meals. Freeze in the serving quantities you are likely to need. A practical method of freezing is to pour the cold soup into a freezer bag resting upright in the bowl you will eventually use for serving. (Make sure that the bowl is freezer-proof before using this method.) Only two thirds fill the bag and seal it loosely at the top. Freeze until the soup is solid, then seal tightly and remove from the bowl.

To thaw, dip the bag in hot water and transfer the frozen soup to the bowl. Microwave on HIGH unless the soup has been thickened with egg, breaking up the lumps as soon as possible. If there is egg in the soup, microwave on LOW.

When there is limited freezer space it may be more practical to freeze in boxes, because they can be stacked. For thawing I usually remove the lid and up-turn the box in a bowl. Choose one that allows plenty of room for the soup to spread as it thaws. A few seconds in the microwave oven will soon loosen the block, making it easy to lift away the box. Some plastic boxes may be unsuitable for this method, particularly if the soup has a high fat content. Never try to thaw in the bag or box.

To hasten reheating, three-quarters cover the bowl with cling film as soon as the frozen block of soup has separated into lumps. Thawing of soups is slow—a single serving will take at least 6 minutes to reheat on a HIGH setting. Large quantities are best thawed in a saucepan.

Stocks

It really is worth making your own stock if you enjoy wholesome soups and sauces. While stock cubes are very good they do tend to add a similar flavour to every dish they are used in. Homemade stock makes use of the skins and bones that would otherwise be wasted and the only added expense is the fuel, which is considerably reduced in microwave cookery. Fish stocks are easy and trouble-free to prepare in the microwave and the fishy odour is less likely to permeate the kitchen. See Rolled Plaice Fillets in Lemon and Caper Sauce (page 37) for method.

To make stock in a microwave oven a choice of settings is important. Not only does the MEDIUM setting prevent boiling over, but it also gives you a much better, richer stock.

Beef stock is not totally successful as it takes about 2 hours to cook in the microwave oven and even then it will not be as rich as when conventionally cooked. Considerable condensation occurs during this lengthy period and may run all over the oven shelf.

Chicken stock is much easier and is well worthwhile. Cut up the carcass and put into a 2.8-litre (5-pint) ovenproof glass mixing bowl with any bones and skin. You can use the carcass and bones left over from cooked chicken, duck or turkey if you wish, or raw ones. Add a bay leaf or bouquet garni, salt and pepper and generously cover with water (as there is less evaporation when cooking by microwave you need less liquid than with the saucepan method).

Three-quarters cover the bowl with cling film to hold in some of the heat and microwave on HIGH until the stock boils. If possible reduce the setting to MEDIUM for the remaining time. If your oven has no MEDIUM setting, continue cooking on HIGH. To reduce the likelihood of boiling over make only small quantities of chicken stock on the HIGH setting. A large bowl half-filled will yield about 600 ml (1 pint) stock and takes about 45 minutes to prepare. Strain, cool and remove the fat before using. Make larger quantities conventionally.

Packet Soup Mixes

Spinach Soup

550 g (1¼ lb) fresh spinach
40 g (1½ oz) butter or block
   margarine
40 g (1½ oz) plain flour
450 ml (¾ pint) milk
150 ml (¼ pint) chicken stock
nutmeg
salt and freshly ground pepper
1 egg yolk
45 ml (3 tbsp) double cream

Reconstitute soup mixes in a large bowl according to the directions on the packet but reduce the liquid by 30–45 ml (2–3 tbsp). Three-quarters cover with cling film and microwave on HIGH until boiling, stirring occasionally. 600 ml (1 pint) soup will take about 6 minutes, 900 ml (1½ pints) 8 minutes. Stir again and cook for a further 1–2 minutes.

Clear soups with particles of vegetable or pasta should be cooked for a further 5–10 minutes on LOW.

Reheating other soups
Canned soups require reheating only. Dilute condensed soups with water as usual (not milk). Heat individual portions uncovered. Larger amounts should be reheated in a large bowl three-quarters covered with cling film; stir occasionally during reheating and again just before serving and garnishing.

Reheating one individual bowl will take 2 minutes, two individual bowls 4 minutes, one large five-serving bowl 10 minutes. These times will vary according to whether the soup is clear, thick or contains vegetables or meat.

The probe temperature should be set at 70°C/160°F.

1

Thoroughly wash the spinach and remove the thick stems. Discard any yellow or bruised leaves.

2

Put the spinach leaves in a large roasting bag and close loosely. Stand the bag upright on the oven shelf and microwave on HIGH for 5 minutes or until the spinach is well packed down and cooked.

3

Carefully open the bag and tip the spinach and juices into a food processor or blender and blend to a smooth purée.

4

Put the butter in a 2.8-litre (5-pint) ovenproof glass bowl and microwave on HIGH for 45 seconds or until melted.

5

Stir in the flour. Microwave on HIGH for 30 seconds or until the surface looks puffy.

6

Using a whisk blend in the milk. Microwave on HIGH for 2 minutes. Whisk thoroughly and continue to microwave on HIGH for 2 minutes, whisking every 30 seconds until thick.

7

Beat the spinach into the sauce and add the stock. Season with nutmeg, salt and pepper. Reheat on HIGH for 3 minutes.

8

Stir the egg yolk into the double cream and add to the soup, mixing them together thoroughly.

9

Pour back into the bowl and microwave on HIGH for 30 seconds. Stir before serving.

Serves 4–6.

Tomato Soup

1 medium onion, skinned and
   quartered
900 ml (1½ pints) tomato juice
450 ml (¾ pint) beef stock
25 g (1 oz) butter or margarine,
   softened
30 ml (2 tbsp) plain flour
1 egg yolk
30 ml (2 tbsp) double cream
salt and freshly ground pepper
1 slice cooked beetroot,
   optional

1

Put the onion into a 2.8-litre
(5-pint) ovenproof glass bowl.
Cover with cling film, pulling back
one corner to vent, and microwave
on HIGH for 3 minutes or until the
onion is soft.

2

Stir in the tomato juice, water and
beef stock. Three-quarters cover
with cling film and microwave on
HIGH for 6 minutes or until the
liquid boils round the edges. Stir
and microwave on HIGH for a
further minute.

3

While the soup is cooking blend
the butter and flour in a small bowl
until a soft paste is formed.

4

As soon as the soup is ready,
quickly add the flour paste (*beurre
manié*) in five or six pieces (it
will slither easily down the sides of
the hot mixing bowl). Carefully
remove the cling film and beat
thoroughly with a balloon whisk.
Remove the onion. Microwave on
HIGH for 1 minute.

5

Blend the egg yolk and double
cream together and add 30–45 ml
(2–3 tbsp) of the hot soup.

6

Return this mixture to the soup
and stir thoroughly. Season to
taste with salt and pepper and add
the beetroot.

7

Microwave on HIGH for 4 minutes
or until the soup is very hot but
not boiling. Stir occasionally
during cooking. Cover and leave
for 5 minutes; stir well before
serving.

Serves 6.

Cream of Mushroom Soup

225 g (8 oz) button mushrooms, finely chopped
$\frac{1}{4}$ onion, skinned
600 ml (1 pint) hot chicken stock
300 ml ($\frac{1}{2}$ pint) milk
40 g ($1\frac{1}{2}$ oz) butter or margarine, softened
40 g ($1\frac{1}{2}$ oz) plain flour
salt and freshly ground pepper
15 ml (1 tbsp) fresh lemon juice

1

Put the mushrooms and the piece of onion in a 2.8-litre (5-pint) ovenproof glass bowl, three-quarters cover with cling film and microwave on HIGH for 4 minutes or until the mushrooms are soft. Stir occasionally during cooking.

2

Without removing the covering, add the stock and microwave on HIGH for 5 minutes. Cool slightly.

3

Discard the onion and purée the soup in a blender until it is smooth and creamy.

4

Pour the soup back into the bowl, add the milk and microwave on HIGH for 6 minutes or until boiling. Stir twice during cooking.

5

While the soup is reheating blend the butter with the flour to form a soft paste.

6

Add the flour and butter paste to the boiling soup in several pieces, sliding it in down the side of the hot bowl. Beat vigorously with a balloon whisk. Season to taste with salt and pepper.

7

Return the bowl of soup to the microwave oven and microwave on HIGH for 2 minutes or until the soup is bubbling. Beat again, then stir in the lemon juice

Serves 4.

Minestrone

2 small leeks, trimmed
1 carrot, peeled and cut into 0.5 cm ($\frac{1}{4}$ inch) dice
2 celery stalks, trimmed and finely sliced
25 g (1 oz) butter or margarine
30 ml (2 tbsp) tomato purée
shake of garlic powder
2.5 ml ($\frac{1}{2}$ level tsp) dried basil
213-g (7.5-oz) can cannellini beans, drained
salt and freshly ground pepper
50 g (2 oz) short-cut macaroni
25 g (1 oz) Parmesan, grated

1

Cut the leeks in half lengthways, then cut each piece in half and finely slice lengthways again. Wash thoroughly in a bowl of cold water. Drain.

2

Put the prepared leeks, carrots and celery into a 2.8-litre (5-pint) ovenproof glass bowl and add the butter, tomato purée, garlic powder and basil. Three-quarters cover with cling film and microwave on HIGH for 15 minutes or until the carrots begin to soften. Stir two or three times during cooking.

3

Stir in 1 litre ($1\frac{3}{4}$ pints) boiling water, the beans and season with salt and pepper. Microwave on HIGH for 10 minutes or until the vegetables are soft, stirring once during cooking.

4

Add the macaroni. Stir thoroughly and microwave on HIGH for 5 minutes or until the pasta is tender. Stir once during cooking. Leave to stand for 5 minutes, then stir in the cheese or serve the soup offering the cheese separately.

Serves 5–6.

Note A can of baked beans can be used instead of cannellini.

Puréed Courgette Soup

450 g (1 lb) firm courgettes,
  topped, tailed and finely
  sliced
125 g (4 oz) onion, skinned and
  very finely chopped or
  minced
300 ml ($\frac{1}{2}$ pint) hot chicken
  stock
thyme sprig
5 ml (1 tsp) chopped chives
15 g ($\frac{1}{2}$ oz) butter or
  margarine, softened
15 g ($\frac{1}{2}$ oz) plain flour
450 ml ($\frac{3}{4}$ pint) milk
salt and freshly ground pepper

1

Mix the courgettes and onion together in a 2.8-litre (5-pint) ovenproof glass mixing bowl. Three-quarters cover with cling film and microwave on HIGH for 5 minutes or until the courgettes are steaming. Stir two or three times during cooking.

2

Add the hot chicken stock, sprig of thyme and chives and microwave on HIGH for 10 minutes, stirring occasionally.

3

Carefully remove the cling film, take out the thyme, then purée the mixture in a blender.

4

Pour back into the bowl, return to the microwave oven and microwave on HIGH for 2 minutes or until boiling.

5

While the purée is reheating blend the softened butter with the flour to form a soft paste. Add to the purée in small pieces allowing them to slide down the side of the hot bowl. Then beat them in thoroughly with a balloon whisk.

6

Add the milk and microwave on HIGH for 4 minutes, stirring once during cooking. Season to taste with salt and pepper. Serve hot or cold.

Serves 4.

French Onion Soup

450 g (1 lb) onions, skinned,
  and very finely sliced
50 g (2 oz) butter or block
  margarine
15 ml (1 level tbsp) plain flour
900 ml (1$\frac{1}{2}$ pints) beef stock
150 ml ($\frac{1}{4}$ pint) red wine
5 ml (1 tsp) Worcestershire
  sauce
salt and freshly ground pepper
4–6 slices French bread,
  toasted
50 g (2 oz) Cheddar cheese,
  grated

1

Put the onions and butter in a 2.8-litre (5-pint) ovenproof glass bowl and microwave on HIGH for 12 minutes. Stir occasionally during cooking.

2

Stir in the flour, then add the stock, wine and Worcestershire sauce. Three-quarters cover with cling film and microwave on HIGH for 5 minutes or until the soup begins to thicken. Stir occasionally during cooking.

3

Reduce the setting and microwave on LOW for 10 minutes.

4

Remove the bowl from the microwave oven and leave to stand. Arrange the slices of toast on a plate and sprinkle thickly with cheese. Microwave on LOW for 1$\frac{1}{2}$ minutes or until the cheese begins to melt.

5

Serve the soup, topping each portion with a slice of cheesy toast.

Serves 4–6.

Note The soup will be even better if stored in the refrigerator for 24 hours before reheating.

Chinese Chicken and Mushroom Soup

125 g (4 oz) cooked chicken
    breast meat, skinned
175 g (6 oz) button mushrooms
125 g (4 oz) bean sprouts,
    washed
900 ml (1½ pints) chicken stock
5 ml (1 level tsp) arrowroot
15 ml (1 tbsp) dry sherry
5 ml (1 tsp) soy sauce
salt and freshly ground pepper

1

Shred the cooked chicken finely.
Cut off and discard the ends of the
mushroom stalks and slice the caps
finely.

2

Put the chicken, sliced mushrooms
and bean sprouts in a 2.8-litre
(5-pint) ovenproof glass bowl and
stir in the stock. Three-quarters
cover with cling film and
microwave on HIGH for 15
minutes, stirring two or three
times during cooking.

3

Blend the arrowroot, sherry and
soy sauce together and mix with
30 ml (2 tbsp) of the hot soup.
Pour the mixture back into the
soup and stir thoroughly.
Microwave on HIGH for 5 minutes,
stirring once during cooking.
Season to taste with salt and
pepper and stir before serving.

Serves 4.

Note If desired add 15–30 ml
(1–2 tbsp) cooked rice during the
last 5 minutes cooking.

Vichyssoise

15 ml (1 tbsp) vegetable oil
1 medium onion, skinned and
    finely chopped
350 g (12 oz) potatoes, peeled
    and diced
350 g (12 oz) leeks, trimmed
    and finely shredded
750 ml (1¼ pints) chicken stock
salt and freshly ground pepper
30 ml (2 tbsp) soured or double
    cream
15 ml (1 tbsp) chopped fresh
    parsley

1

Combine the oil and onion in a
2.8-litre (5-pint) ovenproof glass
bowl and microwave on HIGH for
3 minutes or until soft. Stir once.

2

Add the potatoes and leeks to the
onion. Three-quarters cover and
microwave on HIGH for 5 minutes,
stirring every minute

3

Add half the stock, three-quarters
cover and microwave on HIGH for
4 minutes or until boiling.

4

Microwave on HIGH for a further
10 minutes or until the vegetables
are soft. Cool slightly.

5

Purée in a blender, add the
remaining stock and season.

6

To reheat the soup, microwave on
HIGH for 3 minutes or until
bubbling, stirring occasionally.

7

Just before serving stir in the
soured or double cream. Garnish
with chopped parsley.

Serves 6.

Golden Croûtons

2 slices white bread, crusts
    removed
butter or block margarine
paprika

1

Butter the bread on both sides
and cut each slice into 16 equal-
sized squares.

2

Spread the croûtons out on a sheet
of greaseproof paper on the oven
shelf and sprinkle with paprika.

3

Microwave on HIGH for 2 minutes
until the croûtons are firm but not
crisp. Reposition during cooking
(the croûtons will crisp during a
standing time of 1–2 minutes).

4

Top each bowl of soup with 3
or 4 of the crisp, golden croûtons.

Serves 4.

Note It is essential to reposition
the croûtons during cooking
otherwise undisturbed pieces may
overcook and burn.

CHAPTER TWO

Eggs and Cheese

Cooking eggs in the microwave oven is quick and successful and you will find it leaves you without those eggy pans to scour. Give yourself a little time to get used to the cooking methods because eggs react differently when cooked by microwave from when cooked by conventional methods.

Eggs cannot be boiled in the microwave oven because they are encased in a shell. The intense build-up of steam inside makes them burst, splattering all over the oven cavity. But you can coddle eggs with the help of your microwave oven. Do not attempt to reheat a whole hard-boiled egg even without the shell as it may explode in your face as you cut into it.

When eggs are cooked by conventional methods, the whites harden before the yolks; in the microwave oven, the yolks harden before the whites. This is because microwaves are attracted to fat and the yolk has a fat content while the white does not. When the whites and yolks are beaten together, eg for scrambled eggs, there is no need to take special care and they can be cooked on HIGH. Stir frequently with a fork, drawing the sides to the middle, and do not overcook. Scrambling in the microwave oven gives a greater volume than conventional scrambling because the egg does not dry in the base of the saucepan and less moisture is driven off. Scrambled eggs are ready to eat when just moist; remember they continue cooking after removal from the oven so take care not to overcook.

A measuring jug is the easiest container to use for scrambled eggs. Microwaves cook more rapidly in a circular container and if the diameter is narrow the scrambled egg will cook with less stirring. Alternatively, an egg can be scrambled quite easily on a plate, or for a single serving I recommend a cereal or soup bowl.

When poaching, cooking without water on a plate, or in the browning dish, lightly prick the outer membrane of the yolk with a cocktail stick or the tip of a sharp knife and microwave on LOW. The first few times you may find that the yolk breaks and oozes through. This indicates that you have inserted the knife too deeply but you will soon master the technique.

Using the browning dish

For nice crisp-fried eggs or eggs and bacon use the browning dish. A very lightly done egg can be cooked in the buttered browning dish simply by covering with a lid and leaving for a few moments. There will be no need to prick the yolk if cooking this way. Sometimes when eggs are poached in water or broken and cooked whole in a bed of other ingredients, such as chopped spinach, pricking is not imperative. These dishes are often cooked on MEDIUM or LOW, covered with cling film or a lid.

Egg dishes such as custards which are normally cooked in a water bath or in a double saucepan can be cooked equally well in the microwave oven. Use a LOW setting or sit the dish in a larger dish of water and microwave on HIGH. Stir thin custard sauces frequently and reposition and turn the dishes of baked custards. Test for cooking in the usual way—a sauce should just coat the back of a spoon. To test 'set' custards insert the tip of a table knife into the custard about 2.5 cm (1 inch) from the edge. When cooked no juices will rise to the top. The centre will be soft but not runny and will cook by conduction of the heat from the outer edges during standing time.

Of course eggs are used in many other ways in cooking, such as in cakes, for binding and for coating, and no special care need be taken then. In cake making it is important to use eggs at room temperature. If you normally keep them in the refrigerator you can put the whole egg, unshelled, in the microwave oven, set on HIGH and count up to 3. The chill will be off and no harm done. The microwave oven cannot produce a traditional dry crisp meringue but soft meringues and meringue toppings are easy to cook.

Cheese is another delicate, high protein food. It becomes stringy when overcooked, be it conventionally or by microwave, so cook egg and cheese mixtures gently and slowly using the LOW setting. Cheese can be melted on a HIGH setting if it is being used as a topping for a snack.

Scrambled Eggs

2–6 eggs
small knob–25 g (1 oz) butter
or margarine
30 ml (2 tbsp)–75 ml (5 tbsp)
milk or milk and water
salt and freshly ground pepper
to taste

1

Put the butter in a bowl or jug and microwave on HIGH for 45 seconds until melted. Add the milk or milk and water, salt, pepper and eggs and beat lightly together.

2

Microwave on HIGH until the egg is just set and slightly moist in the middle. Stir every 30 seconds during cooking, drawing the edges to the middle.

3

Leave to stand for 1–2 minutes before serving. Serve on hot buttered toast.

Serves 1–4.

Poached Eggs

1–4 eggs
75 ml (5 tbsp)–450 ml ($\frac{3}{4}$ pint)
boiling water
1.25 ml ($\frac{1}{4}$ tsp)–5 ml (1 tsp)
vinegar or lemon juice
salt

1

If cooking only 1 egg, put the boiling water, vinegar or lemon juice and a pinch of salt into a cereal bowl. If cooking more than 1 egg, put these ingredients in a 23-cm (9-inch) round shallow dish. Microwave on HIGH for $1\frac{1}{2}$–2 minutes or until the water boils. Break each egg on to a saucer and slide it into the water.

2

Cover loosely with cling film and microwave on MEDIUM for the required cooking time.

3

Leave to stand for 1 minute before uncovering (the egg will continue to cook during standing time). Remove from the water using a slotted spoon and serve on hot buttered toast.

Serves 1–4.

Although up to 4 eggs can be poached at a time in a large shallow dish the shape of the eggs will be better if they are individually cooked in cereal bowls. The yolk and white are likely to cook at the same time if the eggs are poached on MEDIUM setting. If your oven is fitted only with a HIGH and DEFROST setting, after the water has come back to the boil, microwave a single egg on LOW and 2, 3 or 4 eggs on HIGH, reducing the cooking time by three-quarters and following with an equal rest period.

Scrambled Eggs

Eggs	Milk or mixture of milk and water	Butter or margarine	Seasoning	Cooking time
2	30 ml (2 tbsp)	small knob	salt and freshly	$1\frac{1}{2}$–2 mins
4	60 ml (4 tbsp)	15 g ($\frac{1}{2}$ oz)	ground pepper	$2\frac{1}{2}$–3 mins
6	75 ml (5 tbsp)	25 g (1 oz)	to taste	$3\frac{1}{2}$–4 mins

Poached Eggs

Eggs	Boiling water	Vinegar or lemon juice	Cooking time
1	75 ml (5 tbsp)	1.25 ml ($\frac{1}{4}$ tsp)	45 secs
2	300 ml ($\frac{1}{2}$ pint)	2.5 ml ($\frac{1}{2}$ tsp)	$1\frac{1}{2}$ mins
3	300 ml ($\frac{1}{2}$ pint)	2.5 ml ($\frac{1}{2}$ tsp)	2 mins
4	450 ml ($\frac{3}{4}$ pint)	5 ml (1 tsp)	$2\frac{1}{2}$ mins

Micro-fried Egg

knob of butter
1 egg

1

Preheat the browning dish for 3–4 minutes, slightly less than the maximum recommended by the manufacturer.

2

Add a knob of butter and, using oven gloves, tilt the browning dish so that it is evenly coated.

3

While the dish is heating, break the egg into a saucer and pierce the yolk with the tip of a sharp knife.

4

When the buttered browning dish is hot, slip the egg in as quickly as possible.

5

Cover and microwave on HIGH until the egg is nearly cooked. Leave to stand for 30 seconds before serving.
   If cooking more than 1 egg at a time, break the eggs into the corners of the dish.

For nice crisp, buttered eggs use the browning dish.

Egg and Bacon in a Browning Dish

1 egg
knob of butter or block
   margarine
2 rashers back or streaky
   bacon, rinded

1

Preheat the browning dish to the maximum recommended by the manufacturer. While the browning dish is heating, break the egg into a saucer and prick through the outer membrane of the yolk with the tip of a sharp knife. Snip the bacon fat at intervals.

2

When the browning dish is ready add the butter and quickly put in the bacon rashers, arranging them round the edge of the dish. Microwave on HIGH for 30 seconds, then turn rashers over.

3

Slide the egg into the centre of the dish, then cover with the lid and microwave on HIGH for 30 seconds or until the egg is nearly cooked. Leave to stand, covered, for 1 minute before serving.

Serves 1.

Note For 2 eggs and 4 rashers bacon, increase the cooking time to 45 seconds in steps 3 and 4.

Egg and Bacon in an Ordinary Dish

2 rashers back or streaky
   bacon, rinded
1 egg

1

Snip the bacon fat at intervals so that it will lie flat on the dish. Arrange the bacon rashers on either side of a shallow dish and cover with absorbent kitchen paper. Microwave on HIGH for $1\frac{1}{2}$ minutes or until the bacon is almost cooked.

2

Break the egg into a saucer and pierce through the outer membrane of the yolk with the tip of a sharp knife.

3

Slide the egg between the bacon rashers, cover with cling film and microwave on HIGH for 45 seconds or until the egg is nearly cooked.

4

Leave to stand for 1–2 minutes before removing the cling film.

Serves 1.

Note It is better to cook the egg and bacon in a dish rather than a plate so that the cling film is not in direct contact with the egg yolk.

Baked Eggs with Frankfurters and Mushrooms

knob of butter or block
  margarine
three 50-g (2-oz) frankfurters,
  cut into 1-cm (½-inch) slices
75 g (3 oz) button mushrooms,
  roughly chopped
salt and freshly ground pepper
4 eggs
150 ml (¼ pint) double cream

1

Put the butter in a 23-cm (9-inch) round shallow dish and microwave on HIGH for 45 seconds or until melted.

2

Add the frankfurters and mushrooms and microwave on HIGH for 4 minutes or until the mushrooms are soft. Stir two or three times during cooking. Drain. Season with pepper and add salt sparingly.

3

Leaving a border of frankfurter mushroom mixture, make four wells in the mixture and break an egg into each.

4

Pour the cream evenly over the mixture, being sure to coat the eggs completely. Reduce the setting, cover and microwave on LOW for 7 minutes or until the egg whites are on the point of setting. Give the dish a quarter-turn three times during cooking.

5

Leave to stand for 5 minutes before uncovering to enable the eggs to finish cooking.

Serves 4.

Note For variation, substitute any variety of salami or chopped ham.

Welsh Rarebit

30 ml (2 tbsp) milk
1 egg yolk
1.25 ml (¼ level tsp) mustard
  powder
pinch of pepper
125 g (4 oz) Cheddar cheese,
  grated
2 slices bread
butter

1

In a medium bowl blend the milk and egg yolk together. Then add the mustard and pepper and mix thoroughly.

2

Gently stir in the grated cheese and microwave on LOW for 1½ minutes or until the cheese is partially melted. Stir twice during cooking (under rather than over-cook or the cheese will become stringy).

3

Toast and lightly butter the bread and leave the grill switched on.

4

Pile half the cheese mixture on to each slice of toast and quickly brown under the grill.

Serves 2.

Note Double the mixture for 4 servings, microwaving on LOW for about 3 minutes. If you prefer not to brown the cheese, top the Welsh rarebit with sliced tomatoes, mushrooms, strips of ham or chopped corned beef. To cook sliced tomatoes and mushrooms, see pages 76 to 77.

Spanish Omelette

15 g ($\frac{1}{2}$ oz) butter or block
    margarine
$\frac{1}{2}$ small green pepper, seeded
    and thinly sliced
$\frac{1}{2}$ small red pepper, seeded and
    thinly sliced
1 small onion, skinned and
    chopped
1 small potato, cooked and
    diced
3 eggs
30 ml (2 tbsp) milk or water
salt and freshly ground pepper

1

Put the butter in a 21.6-cm
(8$\frac{1}{2}$-inch) shallow pie dish and
microwave on HIGH for 45 seconds
until melted.

2

Add the green and red peppers and
onion, cover with cling film and
microwave on HIGH for 3 minutes
until soft.

3

Add the diced, cooked potato to
the vegetables in the pie dish and
stir to mix.

4

Beat the eggs, milk or water and
seasoning together and pour into
the dish. Cover loosely with cling
film and microwave on LOW for a
further 3 minutes, until the
omelette is set.

5

Carefully remove the cling film and
brown quickly under a hot grill.

Serves 2.

Note You can vary the filling by,
instead of potato in step 2, adding
grated cheese, cooked mushroom
slices, chopped ham, cooked
chopped bacon or tuna fish.

Puffy Omelette

15 g ($\frac{1}{2}$ oz) butter or block
    margarine
3 eggs, separated
45 ml (3 tbsp) milk
1.25 ml ($\frac{1}{4}$ level tsp) salt
1.25 ml ($\frac{1}{4}$ level tsp) white
    pepper

1

Put the butter in a 23-cm (9-inch)
round dish and microwave on
HIGH for 45 seconds or until
melted. Tilt the dish so that the
surface is completely covered with
butter.

2

In a large bowl lightly beat the egg
yolks, milk, salt and pepper
together. Using clean beaters and a
grease-free bowl, whisk the egg
whites until stiff.

3

Stir 15 ml (1 tbsp) of the egg whites
into the milk mixture, then fold in
the remainder (do not overmix).
Pour into the buttered dish and
microwave on LOW for 5 minutes
or until the foam is only just set.
Quickly and without causing a
draught, open the oven door and
give the dish a quarter-turn three
times during cooking.

4

While the omelette is cooking,
light the grill and heat to
maximum. After the omelette is
cooked leave to stand for a minute,
then slide on to a flameproof
plate, folding over at the same
time. Brown under the grill.

Serves 2.

Eggs Peperonata

15 ml (1 tbsp) vegetable oil
2 large onions, skinned and finely chopped
5 ml (1 level tsp) plain flour
450 g (1 lb) tomatoes, skinned and sliced
1 red pepper, seeded and thinly sliced into rings
1 green pepper, seeded and thinly sliced into rings
salt and freshly ground pepper
4 eggs

1

Combine the oil and onion in a 27-cm (10½-inch) round shallow dish and microwave on HIGH for 3 minutes or until the onion is soft. Stir occasionally during cooking.

2

Stir in the flour, then add the tomatoes and peppers and season with salt and pepper.

3

Three-quarters cover with cling film and microwave on HIGH for 7 minutes or until the peppers are soft. Stir gently occasionally during cooking.

4

Make four wells in the vegetable mixture and arrange a slice of red or green pepper in each. Break an egg into each well.

5

Completely cover with cling film and microwave on LOW for 7 minutes or until the egg white is on the point of setting. Give the dish a quarter-turn three times during cooking. Leave to stand for 5 minutes before removing the cover. Serve a portion of peperonata with each egg.

Serves 4.

Crispy Hot Cheese Sandwich

4 slices bread
2 slices processed cheese
butter or margarine

1

Preheat the browning dish to maximum according to the manufacturer's instructions.

2

Meanwhile sandwich the bread with the cheese, then spread the butter on the outside of the sandwiches.

3

Immediately the browning dish is ready, put in the sandwiches, pressing down with a fish slice. Leave for 15 seconds then turn over and microwave on HIGH for 10 seconds or until cheese has melted. Do not cover during cooking. Serve immediately.

Serves 2.

Note One sandwich can be cooked in the same way.

Ham and Cheese Snack

2 slices Gruyère cheese
4 slices ham
½ egg, beaten
15 g (½ oz) rusks, finely crushed

1

Sandwich the cheese between two slices of ham, then dip in the beaten egg and coat with the crumbs.

2

Put on small individual plates, cover with greaseproof paper and microwave each on HIGH for 1 minute or until the cheese is melted.

Serves 2.

Note For a really convenient snack use square slices of ham which are available in vacuum packs.

CHAPTER THREE

Fish and Shellfish

Fish fillets, cutlets and whole fish can all be cooked by microwave and served simply or dressed up with sauces. Use the microwave oven for all methods of fish cookery except frying. Deep frying in the microwave oven is extremely dangerous and shallow frying is not possible, but you can simulate frying by coating fish in egg and crumbs and microwaving in 15 ml (1 tbsp) oil.

Fish tastes excellent when cooked by microwave because it retains its natural juices. It cooks fast and reheats well and so is a good stand-by for latecomers or when you want to prepare a dinner party starter which can be done in advance. But be sure not to overcook fish in the microwave oven as cooking continues during a brief standing time.

Cooking whole fish
To cook whole fish, first slash the skin in several places to prevent it bursting. Place in a dish in a single layer, overlapping the thinner parts and arranging them towards the centre. Insert small pieces of cling film between overlapping parts to keep them separate. When cooking more than two fish use a square or oblong dish and move the outside fish to the middle halfway through cooking. Large fish should also be turned over once during cooking. Cover the heads and tails with small pieces of smooth foil as soon as they are cooked. As a general guide allow about 4 minutes per 450 g (1 lb).

Whole fish which are too big to fit into the oven straight can be curved into a round dish or cooked directly on a turntable. Loosely join the head and tail with string. Remember you cannot straighten the fish once it is cooked.

Cutlets and pieces
To cook cutlets or large pieces of fish, arrange them in a single layer of even thickness. Arrange any thin parts towards the centre and overlapping. Keep overlapping parts separated with small pieces of cling film. Cover cutlets during cooking because the parts near the bone cook quickly and splatter.

Fillets can be cooked flat or they can be rolled, which enables you to cook more pieces at once. Fillets and small pieces of fish should be repositioned or gently stirred during cooking.

Shellfish
Shellfish can also be cooked by microwave but timing is important as overcooking causes them to toughen. Test frequently to see whether they are done. If cooking lobster, kill it first; death may not be immediate in the microwave oven as it is not possible to get a large enough container of boiling water inside.

Thawing fish and shellfish
Frozen fish and shellfish should be thawed before cooking by microwave. Remove the fish from the wrapper and put in a dish or on a plate. Microwave on LOW, turning and repositioning the fish frequently. Fillets should be separated as soon as the top one softens. While waiting for the centre parts to thaw, the edges may start to cook; so as soon as the edges are pliable, finish thawing in cold water.

Fillets and steaks
It is easy to see when fillets or steaks are thawed because the glassy appearance disappears, but it is more difficult to judge whole fish, since you cannot see into the centre. Pierce with a skewer in the thickest part and if there is resistance allow more time.

Small pieces, such as shelled scallops, should be arranged in a circle and covered with absorbent kitchen paper. Remove any that are nearly thawed to avoid accidental cooking. Complete thawing in cold water.

Boil-in-the-bag fish
Boil-in-the-bag fish should have the bag pierced before cooking.

Crumbed fish fillets
Although it isn't possible to fry in the microwave oven, fish coated in golden crumbs will be very appetising indeed.

Cooking fish
Fresh fish is so tasty when cooked simply that a sauce may seem unnecessary. Garnish plain fish with chopped fresh parsley, chives, lemon wedges, watercress sprigs, browned breadcrumbs or a savoury butter.

Baked Fish

1 whole fish up to 900 g (2 lb) in weight, cleaned
salt and freshly ground pepper
butter, softened

1

Slash the skin 3 times on each side to allow for even cooking. Rub salt and pepper into the skin. Spread both sides with butter, about 25 g (1 oz) to a 450 g (1 lb) fish.

2

Place in a shallow dish in which the fish just fits. Cover with cling film and microwave on HIGH for 3 minutes per 450 g (1 lb) or until the fish is tender.

3

After 3 minutes, turn the fish over and reposition it, if possible. Cover the head and tail with smooth pieces of foil to prevent them from becoming dry and brittle. Be careful to place the foil so that it will stay within the perimeter of the dish. To test, insert a fork into the thickest part of the fish. If it does not flake easily allow a little longer cooking time. Garnish and serve.

Serves 1–2.

Note This recipe is suitable for Dover sole, whiting, mackerel, mullet, trout, carp, bream or haddock. It is not suitable for plaice and lemon sole.

Baked Whole Flat Fish

1 large plaice or lemon sole weighing 400 g (14 oz) after cleaning
butter, softened, or soft margarine
salt and freshly ground pepper

1

Slash the skin 3 times on each side to allow even cooking. Butter the black skin of the fish and place this side down in a shallow dish in which the fish just fits.

2

Season the fish with salt and pepper and butter liberally over the white skin.

3

Without covering, microwave on HIGH for 2 minutes or until the tail end is cooked. Give the dish a half-turn.

4

Cover the cooked end of the tail with a small piece of foil and microwave on HIGH for 1 minute or until the wide end is cooked. To test, insert the tip of a sharp knife into one of the slits in the skin and through to the underside of the dish. The flesh should be white. Garnish and serve.

Serves 1.

Note The plaice is left uncovered because the skin, which may be tough to eat, protects the delicate flesh, keeping it moist and flavoursome. Remove the skin before serving if you wish.

Baking Two Large Fish

2 whole fish up to 900 g (2 lb) in weight, cleaned

1

Prepare the fish as in step 1 of Baked Fish (left). Arrange each fish in 2 identical shallow oblong dishes. Cover with cling film. Place the dishes one on top of the other at right angles. Microwave on HIGH for 1 minute.

2

Reverse the dishes top to bottom, giving each a quarter-turn. Cover the tail ends, if cooked, with smooth pieces of foil. Continue to cook, reversing the dishes every 2 minutes for a further 7 minutes or until both fish are cooked. Calculate the cooking time at about 4 minutes to 450 g (1 lb) total fish weight.

Baking four fish
Three-quarters cook the first pair and set them aside while completely cooking the second pair. Remove the dishes from the oven and complete the cooking of the first pair. Garnish and serve.

Kipper Pâté (page 36) and Smoked Salmon, Cucumber and Prawn Toasts (page 41)

Baked White Fish Cutlets, Steaks or Fillets

cutlets, steaks or fillets of cod,
    haddock, plaice, sole, coley,
    whiting, hake, carp or John
    Dory
salt and white pepper
butter or margarine (optional)
lemon juice (optional)

1

Season the fish to taste with salt
and white pepper, butter if desired
and sprinkle with lemon juice if
liked.

2

Arrange in a single layer in a
shallow dish. Place the thicker
parts of fillets towards the outside,
overlapping the thin ends and
separating them with cling film or
non-stick paper.

3

Cover the dish loosely with cling
film or greaseproof paper and
microwave on HIGH for 4 minutes
per 450 g (1 lb).

4

Turn cutlets and steaks over and
reposition three times during
cooking. For fillets, give the dish a
quarter-turn three times during
cooking.

**Fresh Salmon with Sauce
Maltaise (page 38) in a
Corningware French white dish**

Baked Smoked Haddock, Cod or Kippers

smoked haddock (on the bone,
    filleted or golden cutlets), or
    smoked cod or kippers

1

Wash the fish and place skin side
down in a shallow dish. Cover
loosely with cling film.

2

Microwave on HIGH for 4 minutes
per 450 g (1 lb) giving the dish a
quarter-turn three times during
cooking.

3

Test the fish and if it does not flake
easily, allow a little longer cooking
time. Leave to stand for 5 minutes
before uncovering.

Note Kipper fillets and golden
cutlets may be cooked in two
layers separated with cling film in
the same dish, and repositioned
during cooking.

Baked Smoked Mackerel, Trout or Eel

whole or filleted smoked
    mackerel, trout or eel
lemon juice (optional)
butter, softened, or soft
    margarine

1

Put the fish into a shallow dish that
just fits them. Overlap the tails or
thinner parts, separating them
with cling film, to make an even
layer of fish.

2

Sprinkle with lemon juice if liked
and spread with softened butter
allowing about 15 g ($\frac{1}{2}$ oz) to 450 g
(1 lb) fish.

3

Cover loosely with cling film and
microwave on HIGH for 2 minutes
or until hot. Serve the fish with the
juices from the dish poured over.

Note If you prefer smoked fish to
taste less salty, place a few
tablespoons of water in the dish
before starting to cook. These are
ready to eat cold and simply need
re-heating.

Browned Baked Fish

whole fish up to 225 g (8 oz)
   weight such as trout,
   mackerel, herring or mullet
butter or block margarine
salt and freshly ground pepper

1

For one 225-g (8-oz) fish preheat a small browning dish according to the manufacturer's instructions, adding about 15 g ($\frac{1}{2}$ oz) butter for the last 30 seconds.

2

Meanwhile cut the skin 3 times on each side of the fish. Rub with salt and pepper.

3

Without removing the dish from the oven, turn the fish quickly in the brown, sizzling butter. Microwave, uncovered, on HIGH for 2 minutes.

4

Turn the fish over carefully and reposition. Microwave on HIGH for 1 minute or until cooked. For 2 fish allow 4–5 minutes cooking, turning once. For 4 fish allow 7–8 minutes cooking; turn and reposition after 3 minutes.

Browned Cutlets, Steaks or Fillets

fillets of fish up to 225 g (8 oz)
   weight such as cod, haddock,
   coley, whiting, plaice or sole,
   washed and patted dry
butter or block margarine
seasoned flour for coating

1

Preheat a browning dish according to the manufacturer's instructions adding about 15 g ($\frac{1}{2}$ oz) butter for the last 30 seconds. Meanwhile, lightly coat the fillets in seasoned flour.

2

Turn the fish quickly in the brown sizzling butter then, with the skin sides uppermost if appropriate, microwave, uncovered, on HIGH, cooking thin fillets for 1 minute, cutlets and steaks for 2 minutes.

3

Turn the fish over carefully and reposition. Microwave on HIGH for 2 minutes or until tender.

Poached Whole Fish

450–900 g (1–2 lb) fish
1–2 sticks celery, washed and
   sliced
1 small onion, skinned and
   sliced
1 carrot, peeled and sliced
1 large tomato, skinned and
   seeded (optional)
chopped fresh herbs such as
   parsley, chervil, dill
salt and freshly ground pepper
30 ml (2 tbsp) fresh lemon or
   lime juice, or flavoured
   vinegar
60 ml (4 tbsp) water, cider or
   wine

1

Wash the fish and dry on absorbent kitchen paper. Put the prepared vegetables and herbs into a dish that the fish will just fit. Season the fish and place on top of the vegetables.

2

Add the lemon or lime juice or flavoured vinegar and water, cider or wine. Cover loosely with cling film and microwave on HIGH for 5–7 minutes or until tender, turning the fish after 3 minutes cooking. Leave covered to stand for 3 minutes before serving.

3

The vegetables can be served with the fish or puréed in a blender and reheated with a knob of butter to serve as a sauce.

Note *For white fish cutlets, steaks and fillets,* add milk or water and a little butter for the liquid. When strained from the fish after cooking, the liquid can be used in making a sauce.
   Suitable for whole fish up to 900 g (2 lb) weight after cleaning. Choose fish such as trout, mackerel, whiting, bream, mullet, halibut, haddock, bass, brill, herring, carp or turbot. The method is also suitable for cutlets, steaks and fillets such as cod, haddock, hake, carp, salmon, huss (rock salmon), John Dory, plaice and sole.

Crispy Crumbed Fillets

450 g (1 lb) fish fillets, such as
   cod, haddock, whiting, plaice,
   coley
15 ml (1 tbsp) vegetable oil
25 g (1 oz) butter or block
   margarine
salt and freshly ground pepper
1 egg, beaten
golden crumbs

1

Cut the fish into portions that will
fit easily into the dish allowing
room for quick turning over.

2

Sprinkle the fillets with salt and
pepper, dip in beaten egg and
golden crumbs and pat with a knife
to press the crumbs well into the
surface.

3

Preheat the browning dish to
maximum according to the
manufacturer's instructions,
adding the oil and butter during
the last 30 seconds.

4

As soon as the dish is hot use oven
gloves to tilt the dish so that the
surface is evenly coated with fat.

5

Quickly put the fish into the
prepared browning dish, placing
the best-looking side downwards.
Microwave on HIGH for 2 minutes
then turn the fish over, giving the
dish a half-turn at the same time.
Cook for a further 2 minutes or
until the fish is cooked. Drain.

Micro-fried Fish

15 ml (1 tbsp) vegetable oil
450 g (1 lb) crumbed fish fillets

1

Put 15 ml (1 tbsp) vegetable oil in a
large shallow dish and microwave
on HIGH for 1 minute.

2

Add the prepared fillets
remembering that the side that is
placed underneath will be the one
that shows when the fish is served
up and will be the better side.
Microwave on HIGH allowing
about 4 minutes per 450 g (1 lb).

3

Turn the fish over and give the dish
a half-turn once during cooking.

Note The coating on crumbed
fish cooked in an ordinary dish will
be acceptable but not crisp.
Commercially crumbed fish is not
suitable as the coating tends to fall
off once the fish is thawed.

Fish Fingers

15 ml (1 tbsp) vegetable oil
frozen fish fingers

1

Preheat a browning dish to
maximum according to the
manufacturer's instructions,
adding the oil during the last 20
seconds.

2

Using oven gloves quickly tilt the
dish to completely coat the surface
with the oil and put in the fish
fingers. Microwave on HIGH for 20
seconds per fish finger, then flip
the fish fingers over, repositioning
them in the dish, and microwave
on HIGH for a further 10–15
seconds (the length of time
depends on the starting
temperature of the fish).

3

Leave to stand for 2–3 minutes
before serving.

Note Starting temperatures of
frozen fish vary, so watch the
cooking carefully. Undercooking
can be remedied—overcooking
cannot!
   Fish fingers can be cooked from
frozen in the microwave oven on a
well greased ordinary plate—but
they will not be crisp. 10 fish
fingers will take about 3 minutes
on HIGH, 4 fish fingers take about
2 minutes. A better result is
obtained using the browning dish.

Mackerel à l'Orange

25 g (1 oz) butter
1 medium orange, peeled,
    segmented and chopped
2 sprigs of mint
two 175-g (6-oz) mackerel,
    cleaned
salt and freshly ground pepper

1

Put the butter in a shallow dish which will just take the fish arranged in a single layer and microwave on HIGH for 1 minute or until melted.

2

Stir in the chopped orange and the mint. Cover with greaseproof paper and microwave on HIGH for 2 minutes, stirring after 1 minute.

3

Slash the skin of the mackerel in two or three places and season with salt and pepper.

4

Place in the dish side by side, cover with greaseproof paper and microwave on HIGH for 2 minutes.

5

Turn the mackerel over, re-cover and microwave on HIGH for 2 minutes or until the fish is cooked.

6

To serve, remove the sprigs of mint and spoon the orange over the fish.

Serves 2.

Note Trout are also very good cooked this way.

To cook 4 fish, double the quantities allowing half to three-quarters as much time again at each stage of cooking. When turning them over, reposition so that the outside fish are placed in the middle.

Kipper Pâté

450 g (1 lb) kipper fillets
125 g (4 oz) unsalted butter at
    room temperature
30 ml (2 tbsp) lemon juice
5 ml (1 level tsp) paprika
30 ml (2 tbsp) double cream
freshly ground black pepper
black olives and lemon slices,
    to garnish

1

Arrange the kipper fillets in a shallow dish (this can be done in a double layer provided they are separated by a sheet of cling film), or cut up the fillets to fit the dish.

2

Cover the dish and microwave on HIGH for 3–4 minutes or until the fish is cooked. Give the dish a half-turn halfway through cooking. Remove the skin and any bones from the fish.

3

Cut the butter into four pieces, and purée with the fish, the lemon juice and paprika in a blender or food processor. Then quickly blend in the double cream and pepper to taste.

4

Spoon the mixture into individual or one large serving dish and decorate with black olives and lemon slices. Chill.

5

Remove from the refrigerator about 30 minutes before serving. Serve with thin slices of freshly toasted brown bread.

Serves 6–8.

Note Kipper pâté freezes well without the garnish.

Smoked Fish
à la Crème

750 g (1½ lb) smoked haddock or
   cod fillet
25 g (1 oz) butter or margarine,
   softened
15 g (½ oz) plain flour
300 ml (½ pint) milk
125 ml (4 fl oz) double cream
15 ml (1 tbsp) chopped fresh
   parsley, or 5 ml (1 level tsp)
   dried parsley
2 hard-boiled eggs, chopped
freshly ground pepper
salt (optional)

1

Cut up the fish fillet if necessary
and put in a dish in which it just
fits. Cover loosely with cling film
and microwave on HIGH for 6
minutes or until cooked. Give the
dish a quarter-turn during
cooking.

2

While the fish is cooking blend the
butter and flour together in a small
bowl to form a soft paste.

3

Remove the fish from the dish.
Flake the flesh and discard all skin
and bones.

4

Stir the milk and cream into the
juices left in the dish and
microwave on HIGH for 4 minutes
or until boiling, stirring twice
during cooking.

5

Gradually add the liquid to the
flour and butter paste, beating
thoroughly, then stir in the
parsley. Microwave on HIGH for 1
minute or until the sauce thickens
and just boils. Stir twice during
cooking.

6

Stir the flaked fish and the hard-
boiled eggs into the sauce and
microwave on LOW for 4 minutes
or until reheated. Stir occasionally
during cooking.

7

Season with pepper, adding salt
only if necessary. Serve with
vegetables of your choice.

Serves 4.

Note If you are cooking whole
smoked haddock remember that a
750 g (1½ lb) fish will yield only
about 450 g (1 lb) edible flesh.
Always reheat fish in sauce dishes
on a LOW setting.

Soused Herrings

4 herrings, filleted
salt and freshly ground pepper
150 ml (¼ pint) wine vinegar
6 peppercorns
2 bay leaves
1 onion, skinned and very
   thinly sliced

1

Put the fillets flat and skin side
down on a board. Sprinkle the flesh
side with salt and pepper.

2

Roll up the fish starting from the
head end and secure with wooden
cocktail sticks. Arrange in a single
layer in a shallow square or round
dish.

3

Combine the vinegar, 150 ml (¼
pint) water, the peppercorns, bay
leaves and onion rings in a jug and
microwave on HIGH for 2 minutes
or until the mixture boils.

4

Pour over the herrings, cover and
microwave on HIGH for 5 minutes
or until the fish is cooked. Give the
dish a half-turn halfway through
cooking.

5

Turn the fish over carefully in the
liquid, cover and leave to cool
before refrigerating.

Serves 4.

Note You can also use this recipe
for small mackerel. Larger fillets
can be cut in two lengthways and
rolled up in the same way. They
can be kept in the refrigerator for
up to 4 days.

Rolled Plaice Fillets in Lemon and Caper Sauce

900 g (2 lb) plaice fillets
salt and freshly ground pepper
25 g (1 oz) butter or block
 margarine
30 ml (2 level tbsp) plain flour
15 ml (1 tbsp) lemon juice
15 ml (1 tbsp) capers
2 egg yolks
chopped fresh parsley and
 lemon wedges to garnish

1

To make a quick fish stock: skin the plaice and put them in a medium jug or bowl. Just cover with water and microwave on HIGH until the mixture boils. Stir, reduce the setting and microwave on LOW for 5 minutes. Strain.

2

Cut the fillets of plaice in half lengthways and season lightly with salt and pepper. Roll up head to tail and arrange in a shallow dish. Cover and microwave on HIGH for 4 minutes, then reposition the fish and microwave on HIGH for 2 minutes or until the fish is just cooked. Spoon the juices from the plaice into a measuring jug. Set the fish aside, covered, while making the sauce.

3

Make the juices up to 225 ml (8 fl oz) with the prepared fish stock. Put the butter in a large jug or bowl and microwave on HIGH for 45 seconds or until melted. Stir in the flour, then add the fish juices and stock.

4

Add the lemon juice and capers and season to taste with salt and pepper. Microwave on HIGH for 1 minute, then stir and continue microwaving until the mixture boils and thickens slightly.

5

Beat the egg yolks with 15 ml (1 tbsp) cold water and stir into the sauce. Reduce the setting and microwave on LOW for 2 minutes, or until the sauce thickens. Stir once during cooking.

6

Pour the sauce over the fish and without covering microwave on HIGH for 1 minute or until reheated. Serve hot, garnished with chopped fresh parsley and lemon wedges.

Serves 4–5.

Note For stronger flavoured fish stocks, add bones, heads if they are small, herbs, small pieces of onion, celery, carrot, and some salt and pepper. The bones and skin from 900 g (2 lb) fish, well covered with cold water, will take about 5 minutes on HIGH to reach boiling point. Reduce the setting to LOW for the remainder of cooking time. The bowl should not be more than one-third full and should be left uncovered.

Fresh Salmon with Sauce Maltaise

four 125–175 g (4–6 oz) slices
 fresh salmon
salt and freshly ground pepper
40 g (1½ oz) butter, softened

For the sauce maltaise
1 small orange
125 g (4 oz) unsalted butter
60 ml (4 tbsp) double cream
3 egg yolks
1.25 ml (¼ level tsp) salt
1.25 ml (¼ level tsp) white
 pepper

1

Season the salmon with salt and pepper and spread on both sides with butter.

2

Arrange in a single layer in a narrow dish, the ends tucked inwards towards the centre.

3

Cover with greaseproof paper (salmon tends to pop during cooking) and microwave on LOW for 8–12 minutes or until the fish is just cooked. Turn the fish over and give the dish a half-turn, halfway through cooking.

4

Cover the dish tightly and leave to stand while preparing the sauce.

Aromatic Poached Halibut Steaks

For the court bouillon
200 ml (7½ fl oz) dry white wine
1 medium carrot, peeled and finely chopped
1 celery stick, scraped and finely chopped
1 medium onion, skinned and finely chopped
2 bay leaves

6 crushed peppercorns
4 sprigs parsley
5 ml (1 level tsp) salt
grated rind of 1 lemon
5 ml (1 tsp) lemon juice

four to six 2.5-cm (1-inch) thick halibut steaks, about 900 g (2 lb), cut from the tail end of the fish

5

To prepare the sauce, cut 1 slice from the orange and reserve for garnishing. Finely grate the rind from the orange and squeeze out the juice. Put the butter in a medium bowl and microwave on HIGH for 1 minute or until melted.

6

Add the orange rind and juice and the remaining ingredients and whisk until smooth.

7

Microwave on HIGH for 1 minute, beating briskly with a balloon whisk every 15 seconds. Continue to cook on LOW for 2–3 minutes or until the sauce thickens, whisking frequently.

8

Pour a little sauce over the top of each cutlet. Then garnish with the orange slice.

Note Remember to beat the sauce frequently and vigorously to ensure emulsification and prevent curdling. Do not attempt to make a smaller quantity of sauce as the timing, which is critical, will be too short to control. The sauce may be frozen and thawed gently in the microwave oven, beating frequently. The consistency of the sauce depends upon the size of the orange used.

1

Put all the court bouillon ingredients with 450 ml (¾ pint) water into a large deep casserole. Cover with the lid and microwave on HIGH for 8 minutes or until the liquid is boiling.

2

Uncover and gently lower in the fish steaks. Replace the lid and microwave on HIGH for 3 minutes or until the liquid starts to bubble.

3

Continue microwaving on HIGH for 1–2 minutes or until the liquid bubbles again. Give the dish a half-turn halfway through cooking. Microwave on HIGH for a further 1 minute or until the flesh can easily be separated from the bone and is opaque in the centre.

4

Replace the lid after testing and leave to stand for 5 minutes. Remove the fish carefully with a slotted spoon. Serve hot with melted butter.

5

The fish is equally delicious cold and if serving this way, it should be left in the liquid until it is completely cold, then well drained and served with mayonnaise.

Serves 4–6.

Note This recipe is equally good when cooking expensive cuts such as salmon or cheaper cuts such as cod or haddock steaks. It improves the flavour of frozen fish steaks too; these should be thawed and drained before adding to the bouillon.

Fish Balls in Cucumber Sauce

450 g (1 lb) white fish fillet, minced
2 medium onions, skinned and grated or finely chopped
1 small carrot, peeled and grated
50 g (2 oz) fresh white breadcrumbs
2.5–5 ml ($\frac{1}{2}$–1 level tsp) salt
1.25 ml ($\frac{1}{4}$ level tsp) white pepper
1 egg, size 2, beaten

For the sauce
1 small cucumber, topped, tailed but not peeled, then puréed in a blender or finely chopped
about 225 ml (7$\frac{1}{2}$ fl oz) fish or chicken stock
50 g (2 oz) butter or block margarine
1 small garlic clove, skinned and crushed
50 g (2 oz) plain flour
1.25 ml (1 level tsp) ground bay leaf
30 ml (2 tbsp) double cream
salt and freshly ground pepper

1

To make the fish balls combine the minced fish, onions, carrot, breadcrumbs, salt and pepper and bind with the beaten egg.

2

Divide the fish mixture into 16 pieces and form into balls, using wet cold hands.

3

Arrange the fish balls in a large shallow dish. Cover and microwave on HIGH for 6 minutes, repositioning and turning the balls over once halfway through cooking.

4

To make the sauce, measure the cucumber purée and make up to 600 ml (1 pint) with stock.

5

Put the butter in a medium bowl, add the garlic and microwave on HIGH for 45 seconds or until the butter is melted. Add the flour, ground bay leaf and the cucumber liquid.

6

Microwave on HIGH for 3 minutes or until the sauce thickens, whisking twice during cooking. Stir in the cream and season to taste with the salt and pepper.

7

Pour over the fish and without covering, microwave on LOW for 8 minutes or until reheated. Give the dish a half-turn halfway through cooking.

Serves 6–8.

Note If wished, the fish balls can be prepared in advance. Arrange in the dish, cover and refrigerate. Bring back to room temperature before cooking.

Lobster Thermidor

40 g (1$\frac{1}{2}$ oz) butter
1 small onion, skinned and finely chopped
2 small or 1 large lobster, cooked, or 350 g (12 oz) cooked lobster meat
45 ml (3 tbsp) dry white wine
5 ml (1 level tsp) French mustard
300 ml ($\frac{1}{2}$ pint) Béchamel Sauce, coating consistency (page 93)
90 ml (6 level tbsp) grated Gruyère cheese
30 ml (2 level tbsp) grated Parmesan cheese
1 egg yolk

1

Put the butter and onion in a large shallow dish and microwave on HIGH for 2 minutes until the onion is softened.

2

Stir in the lobster meat, wine and mustard and microwave on HIGH for 2 minutes, stirring gently once during cooking.

3

Put the Béchamel sauce into a large jug and microwave on HIGH for 2 minutes or until thoroughly hot. Beat in half the cheeses and the yolk.

4

Pour into the lobster mixture and stir well. Cover with greaseproof paper and microwave on HIGH for 1 minute then continue on LOW if necessary, until the mixture is thoroughly hot.

5

Divide the mixture between the four lobster shell halves or put into individual flameproof dishes. Sprinkle with the remaining cheeses and brown under the grill.

Serves 4.

Note Crabmeat can be used in the same way.

Scampi Walewska

450 g (1 lb) shelled raw scampi
  or frozen scampi tails
45 ml (3 tbsp) medium sherry

For the sauce
25 g (1 oz) butter or block
  margarine
25 g (1 oz) plain flour
150 ml ($\frac{1}{4}$ pint) milk
25 g (1 oz) Parmesan cheese,
  grated
2 egg yolks
30 ml (2 tbsp) single cream
1.25 ml ($\frac{1}{4}$ level tsp) salt
1.25 ml ($\frac{1}{4}$ level tsp) pepper

1

If using frozen scampi, thaw it and drain well on absorbent kitchen paper. Pat dry.

2

Arrange the scampi in an even layer in a 23-cm (9-inch) shallow dish, leaving a well in the middle.

3

Spoon the sherry evenly over the scampi. Cover with cling film, lifting up a corner to leave a tiny gap. Microwave on HIGH for $3\frac{1}{2}$ minutes, giving the dish a quarter-turn four times during cooking. Leave covered while preparing the sauce.

4

Put the butter in a medium bowl and microwave on HIGH for 30 seconds or until melted.

5

Stir in the flour and microwave on HIGH for 20 seconds or until the mixture is puffy.

6

Stir in the milk and microwave on HIGH for 2 minutes, whisking frequently until the sauce thickens.

7

Measure the sauce and make up to 300 ml ($\frac{1}{2}$ pint) with the juices from the scampi, adding extra milk if necessary. Stir in the cheese.

8

Blend the egg yolks with the cream, stir into the sauce and season with the salt and pepper. Microwave on HIGH for 45 seconds, whisking thoroughly every 15 seconds.

9

Spread the scampi out evenly in the cooking dish or transfer to a hot, microwave-suitable serving dish. Pour over the sauce and microwave on LOW for 2 minutes or until reheated. Serve with freshly boiled rice.

Serves 2–3.

Note This delightful sauce is equally good with cooked scallops, shrimps or prawns.

Smoked Salmon, Cucumber and Prawn Toasts

125 g (4 oz) unsalted butter
75 ml (5 tbsp) double cream
3 egg yolks, slightly beaten
30 ml (2 tbsp) lemon juice
salt and freshly ground pepper
125 g (4 oz) piece cucumber,
  finely diced and well drained
125 g (4 oz) cooked peeled
  prawns, thawed and well
  drained
50 g (2 oz) smoked salmon, cut
  into thin strips
8 slices brown or white bread
butter or margarine
paprika to garnish

1

Put the butter into a 900-ml ($1\frac{1}{2}$-pint) bowl and microwave on HIGH for 1 minute or until melted.

2

Add the cream, egg yolks and lemon juice and whisk until smooth.

3

Reduce the setting and microwave on LOW for 3 minutes or until the sauce obviously thickens, whisking every 30 seconds during cooking. Continue beating for about 20 seconds, when it will thicken further. Cover the surface with cling film and leave to cool.

4

Season to taste with salt and pepper (do not add too much salt as the salmon is salty). Stir in the cucumber, prawns and a third of the smoked salmon.

5

Using an 8–10 cm (3–4 inch) cutter or upturned glass, cut out a round from each slice of bread.

6

Toast and lightly butter the bread rounds and top with the prawn and cucumber mixture, arranging remaining salmon strips on top.

Makes 8.

Trout with Almonds

50 g (2 oz) butter or block
   margarine
four 225 g (8 oz) trout, cleaned
salt and freshly ground pepper
50 g (2 oz) flaked almonds
lemon wedges, parsley or
   watercress sprigs to garnish

1

Preheat a browning dish according
to the manufacturer's instructions,
adding the butter for the last
30 seconds.

2

Meanwhile wipe the trout to dry
them. Cut through the skin 3 times
on each side. Rub in salt and
pepper and set aside.

3

When the browning dish is hot and
the butter brown and sizzling,
quickly add the almonds; stir them
around to colour and coat with the
butter. Remove the almonds on to
absorbent kitchen paper using a
slotted spoon.

4

Reheat the dish with the browned
butter in it for 30 seconds. Turn
the trout quickly in the butter to
coat each side and microwave on
HIGH for 3 minutes. Carefully turn
the trout over, repositioning them,
and microwave on HIGH for 4
minutes or until cooked.

5

Serve the trout with the almonds
scattered over them and garnished
with lemon wedges and parsley or
watercress sprigs.

Serves 4.

Family Fish Pie

900 g (2 lb) white fish fillet,
   skinned, such as coley, cod,
   haddock
pinch of grated nutmeg
salt and freshly ground pepper
700 g (1½ lb) potatoes
25 g (1 oz) butter or block
   margarine
60 ml (4 tbsp) milk

For the sauce
about 300 ml (½ pint) milk
40 g (1½ oz) butter or block
   margarine
40 g (1½ oz) plain flour
1.25 ml (¼ level tsp) made
   English mustard
75 g (3 oz) Cheddar cheese,
   grated
salt and freshly ground pepper
paprika to garnish

1

Put the fish, 65 ml (2½ fl oz) water,
nutmeg and salt into a casserole.
Cover with cling film and
microwave on HIGH for 7 minutes
or until cooked.

2

Strain the liquid from the fish into
a measure. Flake the fish, removing
any bones.

3

Cook the potatoes (see page 77).
When they are tender, strain them
well and mash until smooth. Beat in
the butter, milk, and salt and
pepper to taste.

4

For the sauce, add milk to the fish
liquid in the measure to make
450 ml (¾ pint). Make a basic white
sauce (see page 91). When it is
cooked stir in the mustard, cheese
and the flaked fish. Add salt and
pepper to taste.

5

Spread the fish in a 1.1-litre
(2-pint) pie dish and cover it with
the potato, forking up the surface.
Sprinkle paprika over the potato.

6

To reheat the pie, microwave on
HIGH for 5 minutes or until hot.

Serves 4.

Note The pie freezes well.
Individual pies are very useful.

CHAPTER FOUR

Meat

Meat is still the most popular main course and it is an excellent stand-by for snacks, quick burgers or suppers. Cooking by microwave is fast and clean, but meat is expensive and to get the best results it is worth studying the effect of microwave cooking on different cuts.

Meat does not tenderise well when cooked in the microwave oven, so always buy the best cuts that you can afford. Tougher cuts will be better if you tenderise the meat first by marinating, by sprinkling with meat tenderising powder (a natural product made from pawpaw), by beating with a cleaver, or by chopping or mincing. On the whole, casserole cuts are not suitable for cooking in the microwave oven.

When fatty meats are microwaved, the melted fat is quickly drawn out and separates, settling in the cooking dish. This makes it an ideal way of cooking for slimmers. Always remove the fat as it oozes out of the meat as fat attracts the microwaves to itself, drawing them away from the meat. If much melted fat is left for long, spattering will occur.

Another factor governing how the meat cooks is the shape. Choose as even a shape as possible when purchasing joints. Since microwaves cook more powerfully on the uppermost side of a large mass, turn the meat over halfway through cooking. Microwaves also have a greater cooking effect to a depth of about 2.5 cm (1 inch), so the inside of pieces thicker than this will cook more slowly than the outside.

Cooking times will vary with the size, shape and starting temperature of the meat, together with the tenderness factor and fat and water content. I have given my preferred power settings but there is no reason for you to adhere rigidly to these—for you may be in a hurry and wish to cook entirely on HIGH when speed is more important than tender results. Perhaps you have a lot of cooking to do and do not want to monopolise the oven with just one piece of meat. Not every oven has variable controls (a selection of power settings) and you may have to use a HIGH/LOW combination, instead of MEDIUM or MEDIUM HIGH and you will find advice on this in your manufacturer's handbook.

Microwave cooking is faster than conventional cooking but because there is no dry heat, some meats will not brown. These can be brushed with a coloured sauce or condiment or be cooked in a dark-coloured gravy.

Roasting Joints
Choose even, compact shapes. They should have a thin layering of fat or you will find that the part near the thickest band of fat cooks too quickly. Larger joints will brown because of the longer cooking time and a more pronounced browning can be obtained by raising the joint so that it is in the upper part of the oven. Small joints can be brushed with a sauce or with brown or red coloured spices.

Lean joints can be roasted by any of the methods but fatty meat must be microwaved on a rack so that the melted fat can be removed easily during cooking.

Apart from the mini-roast, the best textured joint is that which is partially microwaved and finished in the conventional oven. However you will find that there is less shrinkage when joints are cooked entirely by microwave.

Roast Beef
If you like beef rare it is better to choose a joint of not more than 12 cm (5 inches) in diameter. Of course some of the family might prefer well-done meat and the microwave oven copes well with this; simply microwave the joint on HIGH and reduce the cooking time correspondingly. The outside will be well done and the inside under done. Another way of cooking some parts rare and others well done is to buy a joint (without bone) and shape it thinner at one end—the thinner end will be the well-done one. A MEDIUM setting achieves more even cooking throughout the joint.

The mini-roast (see page 50), utilising the browning dish, produces a specially succulent joint and so it may be better to roast two of these consecutively than one large joint.

Beef Pot Roasts
Pot roasts can be cooked in the microwave oven but there is no

substantial reduction in the cooking time compared with conventional cooking. If you have no other means of cooking here is what you should do. Tenderise the joint before starting by marinating, rubbing with tenderising powder or piercing deeply with a fork or skewer. Put the joint in a roasting bag in a shallow dish. Pour in no more than 150 ml ($\frac{1}{4}$ pint) water and the flavouring vegetables and seasoning. Close the bag partially with a large elastic band or tie loosely with string, leaving a hole for the steam to escape. Microwave on LOW, carefully turning over the bag and joint halfway through cooking. Give the dish a quarter-turn three times during cooking. Allow about 45 minutes per 450 g (1 lb) beef. Leave the joint to stand for 20 minutes before removing from the bag.

Roast Lamb

The top half of a leg of lamb can be roasted in the same way as beef. Large joints of lamb with the bone in cook successfully because the bone traps the heat; this causes the surrounding meat to cook more quickly, helping the meat in the centre of the joint to catch up with the outsides. If there is no bone, joints of smaller weights cook best.

When roasting the knuckle end, shield the bone with smoothed foil as soon as this part is cooked. (Make sure the foil does not touch the oven linings.) A whole leg of lamb may be too long to fit into the microwave oven, so ask your butcher to partially snap the bone. Then you can fold it back and tie it to the upper part with string. Or buy a knuckle and fillet end.

Shoulder of lamb should be roasted with the fatty side down for the first part of the cooking time, then turned.

A crown roast is an excellent microwave choice. Your butcher will prepare the meat for you if you don't wish to do it yourself. Stuff according to your favourite recipe and microwave on MEDIUM for 9–10 minutes per 450 g (1 lb). Shield the tips of the bones with foil and overwrap with cling film. Allow a 20 minute standing time after cooking.

Roast Veal

Roast only rolled joints as others cook unevenly. Veal contains very little fat and dries out quickly.

Brush the joint with oil, then put in a roasting bag, adding a few cloves. Partially seal with an elastic band or string and put the bag in a shallow dish. Microwave on HIGH for the first 5 minutes, then reduce to LOW. Turn the bag and the joint over carefully halfway through cooking. A microwave thermometer or probe can be inserted through the bag into the joint—but make sure the dish can be turned if a probe is in position.

Roast Pork

This is the only joint that should be salted before cooking. To obtain a crisper crackling, slash through the skin at 2.5-cm (1-inch) intervals and rub liberally with salt.

Steaks

Frying steak is so expensive that it really is better to cook steaks conventionally. The browning dish gives passable results but there is only a fractional saving of time on cooking and washing-up. Cook as for chops and follow the timings given on the chart (page 46). Strips and thin slices of fillet steak used in stir-fry and sauced speciality dishes are always well done and in these cases the browning dish is most satisfactory.

Chops

Choose chops 2–2.5 cm ($\frac{3}{4}$–1 inch) thick and if more than one is being cooked, select chops of uniform weight and size.

Both lamb and pork chops can be cooked by microwave. Use the browning dish for lamb chops unless they are being sauced but pork chops can be cooked with or without the browning dish. If there is kidney attached to a pork chop there is no need to remove it, but make certain that the kidney is pricked with the tip of a sharp knife and covered with greaseproof paper to prevent its skin popping and causing spattering during cooking.

Mince

Mince is the most versatile of meats. It is cheap, tender and can be easily divided into the quantities required. Fresh mince does not keep well and should be refrigerated or frozen after purchase. Frozen mince should be thawed before use.

Meat loaves, meat sauces, burgers and meat balls are all good

stand-bys and mince can be made to go further when mixed with other ingredients such as breadcrumbs or rice.

Minced veal is leaner than lamb or beef. Par-cook fatty mince in a plastic colander over a large ovenproof glass bowl so that the melted fat can trickle through the holes and be drawn off. Stir the meat once during cooking and allow about 3 minutes per 450 g (1 lb) on HIGH. To fully brown mince allow 4 minutes. Mince browns during a standing time if this is allowed. Remember when the fat has gone the weight of the meat will be correspondingly less, so that lean mince may be more economical. 450 g (1 lb) average minced beef weighs about 275 g (10 oz) after browning.

Ground meat is finer than mince and produces a more substantial meat loaf. The best mince is the one you make yourself though setting up the machine may be tedious. Fine chopping can be carried out in the food processor but do not overchop or the finished meat balls, burgers or loaf will be too solid.

Meat loaf cooks quickly and uniformly on a HIGH setting if a ring mould is used. You can utilise a cake ring mould for this. Meat cooked in a ring mould will cook one-third quicker than in a loaf tin. Leave a standing time of 5–10 minutes after cooking.

When making long meat loaves you may find that the ends cook before the middle is ready. Shield these ends with foil as soon as they are cooked and continue microwaving until the centre catches up. Cooking half the time on MEDIUM or HIGH and the remainder on LOW eliminates this problem. Always give the dishes a half-turn once during cooking, even when a turntable is used.

Meat Balls

Arrange meat balls in a circle in a round, square or oblong dish; turn them over and reposition two or three times during cooking. Giving the dish a turn occasionally also helps. Meat balls cooked without sauce will darken but not brown on the top. When cooking in a sauce, baste to keep them moist.

Offal

Liver and kidneys are so well and quickly cooked in the microwave oven, that it would seem ludicrous to cook them any other way. Remove the sinewy vessels and inedible parts in the usual way and remove the skin if you can. If this proves too fiddly, make sure the liver or kidneys are cut into slices or pieces. As long as these two popular meats are covered during cooking, splattering will be controlled. Do not be alarmed if you hear popping noises, as this is quite usual.

Sweetbreads must be soaked in cold salted water for at least 1 hour before cooking. Carefully cut out any tubes, fat and membrane to prevent damage to the sweetbreads. Then blanch them for 5 minutes in the microwave oven in a large bowl of salted boiling water acidulated with lemon juice. Drain, rinse in cold water and press out excess moisture with a clean dry cloth. Continue according to your favourite recipe.

Tongues cured by the butcher must be soaked for several hours. Immerse in plenty of boiling water in a covered casserole, adding herbs and seasoning. If the tongue is large, you will have to curve it. Allow 20 minutes per 450 g (1 lb) on HIGH or 50 minutes per 450 g (1 lb) on LOW. The LOW setting is better if you have time to spare.

Bacon

There are many ways of microwaving bacon and it depends on how much trouble you wish to take, but the basic rule is cover in some way to prevent splattering. Complete covering reduces the smells but the bacon will not be very crisp. A light covering with absorbent kitchen or greaseproof paper works well, but the paper must be removed immediately after cooking, otherwise the bacon sticks to the paper. This is especially true of unsmoked, sweetcure bacon because of its sugar content. Do not overcook bacon or it will become brittle.

When cooking several rashers, overlap the fat and lean. Snip the rind if any before cooking, to prevent the bacon from curling. Microwave on HIGH allowing about 30 seconds per rasher.

For 6 or more rashers use a preheated browning dish or tray, putting a few fatty bacon trimmings in during the last minute or so of preheating. The melted fat acts as a coating to the dish or tray so that the bacon rashers will not stick. When the dish is hot, arrange the bacon in a single layer and microwave on HIGH, turning the rashers once during cooking.

For quantities between 225 g and 450 g (8 oz and 1 lb), overlap the slices on a rack over a shallow dish, cover with greaseproof paper and microwave on HIGH for about 12 minutes per 450 g (1 lb), giving the dish a quarter-turn three times during cooking.

Bacon or Ham Joints (Rolled and Tied)

Select unsmoked rather than smoked bacon joints. Salty joints tend to go crisp on the outer edges. To keep the joint moist remove the wrappings and cook in a roasting bag. Seal loosely with an elastic band or string and place the bag in a shallow dish. Microwave on HIGH for 5 minutes, turning the bag and joint over and reducing the setting to MEDIUM or LOW for the remaining cooking time (see the charts) when the thermometer should register 70°C/165°F. Tent loosely with foil and leave to stand for 10 minutes until the temperature reaches 75°C/170°F.

Cooked 'Ready to Eat' Bacon Joints

These joints require reheating only. Remove the wrapping and put the joint in a covered casserole, adding 15 ml (1 tbsp) water, or in a roasting bag loosely secured with a large elastic band or string leaving a 2.5 cm (1 inch) gap. Place in a shallow dish.

Microwave on LOW giving the dish a half-turn halfway through the reheating period. Allow about 20 minutes per 450 g (1 lb). If using a meat thermometer to test the temperature it will read 55°C/130°F when the joint is ready. Leave in the covered casserole or the roasting bag for 10 minutes, during which time the temperature should rise to 60°C/140°F.

Sausages

Sausages can be cooked in the microwave oven but they will not brown or crisp unless the browning dish or tray is used. Prick the sausages thoroughly and reposition and turn them over during the cooking period.

An ordinary dish is a suitable utensil when the sausages are to be cut up after cooking for use in risottos or stews, but take care—the pallid colour can belie the overcooked condition of the inside which may resemble a dried-up sponge.

Use the microwave oven to take the chill off sausages and par-cook before frying or grilling conventionally. The browning dish will produce even crisper sausages if they are not refrigerator-cold when put into the preheated dish.

Cooking Meat

JOINTS Roast	Per 450 g (1 lb): Underdone on MEDIUM 11–13 minutes, on HIGH 6–7 minutes; Medium rare on MEDIUM 13–15 minutes, on HIGH 7–8 minutes; Well done on MEDIUM 15–17 minutes, on HIGH 8½–9 minutes. Allow 15–20 minutes standing time.
STEAKS	1–2 minutes for 1 steak; 2–3 minutes for 3 steaks, depending on how rare they are to be served.
CHOPS Lamb	In pre-heated browning dish 1½ minutes on HIGH, then further 1½–2 minutes on MEDIUM.
Pork	Cook pork chops on HIGH. 1 average-sized chop will take 4–4½ minutes. 2 chops: 5–5½ minutes. 3 chops: 6–7 minutes. 4 chops: 6½–8 minutes. Allow standing time of 2 minutes for 1 chop, 3–5 minutes for more. Much will depend on the shape of the chop.
CUBED MEATS	Cooking time will entirely depend on quality and toughness of the meat, which should be cooked on as low a setting as possible.
VEAL Escalopes	2 minutes per escalope on HIGH, depending on size.
Roast	Microwave on HIGH for 9 minutes per 450 g (1 lb) or 11 minutes on MEDIUM. Better results will be obtained if the first part of the cooking is carried out on HIGH, and the second period on MEDIUM.
POT ROAST	Microwave on LOW with 150 ml (¼ pint) water in roasting bag with vegetables and seasoning for 45 minutes per 450 g (1 lb). Allow 20 minutes standing time.
KIDNEY	8 minutes per 450 g (1 lb) on HIGH.
LIVER	6–8 minutes per 450 g (1 lb) on HIGH.
SAUSAGES	2 sausages: 2½ minutes in browning dish. 4 sausages: 4 minutes in browning dish.
BACON	1 rasher: 30 seconds–1 minute on HIGH. 450 g (1 lb): 12–14 minutes on HIGH.

Thawing Meat

For frozen pieces of meat as well as whole joints, the microwave is an ideal defroster. This enables you to choose your main course not more than an hour before the meal time. But, of course, if you do remember to get it out of the freezer the night before, dinner will be all the quicker.

Some meat dishes will be better cooked conventionally or partially by conventional means, but the recipes included in this chapter should satisfy the discerning eater. Although large joints can be partially thawed on a MEDIUM setting I recommend thawing on LOW. This reduces the likelihood of the joint cooking on the edges before thawing is complete. There is no absolute rule about unwrapping prior to thawing, but you will find it less messy if you are able to remove the polystyrene tray if there is one. Joints that are packaged completely in plastic film may be thawed initially without unwrapping but this should only be for long enough to enable you easily to peel away the wrapping. You should be able to do this after about one-quarter of the total thawing time.

Thawing Note In very round terms smaller pieces of any type of meat take between 6 and 10 minutes per 450 g (1 lb) followed by a standing time of about 10 minutes. Large pieces including joints need a standing time halfway through thawing as well as after the indicated timing. Beefburgers, mince, etc. take 16–20 minutes per 450 g (1 lb) to thaw.

	Thawing on LOW
BACON **Packet of rashers**	One 225 g (8 oz) pack 2 minutes. Put the packet in the microwave oven and microwave on LOW for 10 seconds. Turn over and microwave on LOW for a further 10 seconds. Leave to stand until the packet can be flexed slightly, open and separate the rashers. As soon as the slices can be separated the bacon is ready to cook. No standing time is necessary.
CHOPS **Lamb**	8–10 minutes. Separate during thawing and place bones to centre. Shield if necessary. Turn over once. Allow to stand for 5–10 minutes.
Pork	As for lamb.
CUBED MEATS	6–8 minutes per 450 g (1 lb). Stir three times. Standing time 10–15 minutes.
JOINTS **Roast**	Total microwave time 7–10 minutes per 450 g (1 lb). It is best to thaw for 3 minutes, then turn over and thaw for further 3 minutes, rest for 10 minutes, continue microwaving on LOW for 3 minutes, give a further 20 minutes rest, then continue microwaving for a last 2 minutes per 450 g (1 lb) with a final 2 minutes per 450 g (1 lb) resting time.
KIDNEY	6–9 minutes per 450 g (1 lb). Separate during thawing. Leave to stand for 5 minutes.
LIVER	8–10 minutes per 450 g (1 lb). Separate during thawing. Leave to stand for 5 minutes.
SAUSAGES	4–6 minutes per 450 g (1 lb).
STEAKS	As for chops. Reposition sides to middle during thawing.
VEAL **Escalopes**	As for chops. Take great care to shield warmed parts.
Roast	As for joints above.

Thawing Large Joints

1

Put the packaged joint, polystyrene tray underneath, in a large shallow dish. Microwave on LOW for the first period (see chart).

2

Remove the polystyrene tray and wrappings. Put an upturned, undecorated saucer or rack in the dish.

3

Turn the joint over and put on the saucer or rack and microwave on LOW for the second period.

4

Shield with small pieces of smooth foil any parts of the joint that seem warm to the touch.

5

Without altering the position of the shielding foil, turn the joint over and allow a 10 minute standing time. Mop up any juices with absorbent kitchen paper.

6

Microwave on LOW for a third period, shielding warm parts with foil as before. Continue to mop up any juices with kitchen paper.

7

Turn the joint over and leave to stand for 20 minutes, then remove the foil.

8

Insert a skewer into the joint. Under firm pressure it should pass all the way through if the joint is completely thawed. Allow a standing time equal to the thawing time.

Thawing Chops and Steaks

1

Remove from the package and put on a rack over a shallow dish. Single chops or steaks can be thawed on an upturned undecorated saucer.

2

Microwave on LOW, separating the pieces as soon as possible. Arrange the meat thicker parts towards the outside.

3

Shield the edges with small, smooth pieces of foil, making sure that the foil cannot touch the oven lining.

4

Turn the meat over, reposition and shield where necessary. To test whether the meat is thawed, frequently press the surface of the meat with the fingers.

5

Remove the pieces when they are cold but not icy to the touch and a skewer inserted through the top surface can be pushed through to the underside. Leave to stand for 5–10 minutes to complete thawing.

Mini Roast (page 50)

Thawing Raw Cubed Meat

1

Put the package in a dish in the microwave oven and microwave on LOW long enough to enable you to unwrap the package.

2

Spread the unwrapped meat in a large shallow baking dish and microwave on LOW for as long as it takes for the surface of the meat to give to the touch. Stir three times during this period, pushing the frozen pieces to the outside.

3

Using absorbent kitchen paper, mop up any liquid which oozes out or pour it off if you wish to save it for use in sauces, gravies or stews.

4

Leave to stand for 10–15 minutes or until a piece can be speared with a fork. If the meat is to be cooked by microwave, prick all pieces thoroughly to help to tenderise.

Note If you are using free-flowing cubes you have the advantage of being able to thaw the exact quantity you require. Small amounts are often sold on polystyrene trays and although it is permissible to start thawing on these, they do slow the process down.

Lamb, Aubergine and Red Pepper Kebabs (page 53)

Thawing Mince

1

To thaw an entire package:
Put the wrapped package on the oven shelf and microwave on LOW until the top surface softens. Turn the package over and microwave on LOW until the upper surface softens again.

2

Remove the wrappings, scrape off the thawed parts and put them in a dish. Turn the frozen section into another dish and microwave on LOW, breaking up the pieces and stirring as it becomes possible.

3

As soon as any parts soften remove them from the dish. Leave to stand for 5–10 minutes until the lumps can be flattened with a fork.

Note If the frozen mince you are using is not the quantity needed for your recipe, thaw on the lowest microwave setting and break away the semi-thawed parts for immediate use, returning the rest to the freezer immediately.

Thin burgers can be cooked from frozen. Burgers over 0.5 cm ($\frac{1}{4}$ inch) thick should be thawed on the lowest setting. Arrange in a circle on the oven shelf or a plate and turn over and reposition frequently.

Meat Gravy

**cooking juices from the joint
beef stock
15 ml (1 level tbsp) cornflour
gravy browning, optional
salt and freshly ground pepper**

1

Collect the meat cooking juices from the joint and pour into a large measuring jug. Remove any fat.

2

Make up to 450 ml ($\frac{3}{4}$ pint) with beef stock. Microwave on HIGH for 3 minutes or until boiling.

3

Blend the cornflour with a little water and stir into the stock.

4

Microwave on HIGH for 3 minutes until the gravy thickens. Stir once during cooking. Add a few drops of gravy browning for a darker colour if wished. Season to taste.

Serves 6.

Note If you prefer a slightly thicker gravy add an extra 5 ml (1 level tsp) cornflour.

Mini Roast

900-g (2-lb) rolled joint of
    roasting beef (top-side or
    similar), 15–18 cm (6–7 inches
    across)
vegetable oil
Meat Gravy (page 49)

1

Cut the joint in half lengthwise,
then re-shape each piece to a small
joint not more than 7.5 cm (3
inches) in diameter.

2

Tie with string at 1-cm ($\frac{1}{2}$-inch)
intervals. Cook the joints one at a
time. Each joint will serve three.
Brush the ends of the joints with
oil. Heat a browning dish to
maximum according to the
manufacturer's instruction
booklet.

3

Using tongs quickly put the beef,
end up, into the dish and seal the
end. Turn it and seal the other end.

4

Lay the joint on its fatty side (only
one side of the beef will have a
covering of fat due to the way it has
been divided) and seal. Quickly
turn the beef to seal the leaner
side. Then microwave on HIGH for
4 minutes, turning the joint over
halfway through cooking.

5

Transfer to a heated serving dish,
tent with foil and leave to stand for
3 minutes before carving.

6

Meanwhile wipe out the browning
dish and reheat for 3 minutes, then
cook the second joint. Serve with
gravy and vegetables of your
choice.

Serves 6.

Note A microwaved mini-roast is
roast beef at its best since there is
no chance of some parts being
overcooked while others are rare.
4 minutes cooking gives a rare
roast; for medium rare, microwave
for up to 5 minutes. Further
cooking will cause the outer edge
to be overdone.

Chops in the Browning Dish

Pork loin or spare rib chops, or
    lamb chops, trimmed
oil, salted butter or block
    margarine
salt and freshly ground black
    pepper

1

Dab the chops with absorbent
kitchen paper to remove excess
moisture.

2

Brush all surfaces with oil, salted
butter or block margarine. Preheat
the browning dish or tray to the
maximum recommended by the
manufacturer.

3

Quickly press the chops on to the
hot surface, bone ends towards the
middle. Microwave on HIGH for 1
minute, then immediately turn the
chops over keeping the bone ends
towards the middle.

4

For lamb chops reduce the setting
to MEDIUM and continue cooking.
Complete cooking pork chops on
HIGH. Give the dish a half-turn
once during cooking.

5

Test with the tip of a sharp knife.
With lamb the juices should run
clear and the flesh should be
opaque. Pork must not have any
pink colour showing inside.

6

Leave to stand for 3–5 minutes
before serving. Season to taste and
serve on heated plates.

Steaks in the Browning Dish

good quality lean beef steak
25 g (1 oz) butter or block
   margarine
parsley butter to garnish

1

Feel the steaks and if they are cold to the touch put them on a plate and microwave on LOW for 1 minute just to take off the chill.

2

To seal steaks in the microwave oven, preheat the browning dish to maximum according to the manufacturer's instructions. Add the butter or block margarine during the last 30 seconds. When the butter is dark brown add the steaks, pressing them flat with a fish slice.

3

Immediately turn the steaks over and microwave on HIGH for 1 minute. Cook the steaks according to personal taste (see chart on page 46), giving the dish a half-turn after a further minute. Serve garnished with parsley butter.

Cubed steak
Tender cuts of beef, lamb and pork are all suitable for microwave cooking. They can be browned first in a browning dish, used in stir-fry recipes, for kebabs or served with a sauce.

Beef Stroganoff

550 g (1¼ lb) fillet steak, cut in
   thin strips
75 g (3 oz) butter or block
   margarine
1 large onion, skinned and
   finely chopped
175 g (6 oz) button mushrooms,
   wiped and finely sliced
15 ml (1 level tbsp) plain flour
142-ml (5-fl oz) carton soured
   cream
salt and freshly ground pepper

1

Preheat a browning dish according to the manufacturer's instructions, adding 25 g (1 oz) butter during the last 20 seconds.

2

When the butter is brown and without removing the dish from the oven, add half the steak strips, turning and pressing them flat against the surface with a fish slice.

3

Microwave on HIGH for 30 seconds or until sealed all over. Remove the meat and set aside.

4

Carefully wipe out the hot browning dish with a thick wad of absorbent kitchen paper and heat it again for 2 minutes, adding 7 g (¼ oz) butter towards the end. Seal the remaining meat as before. Remove and set aside with the other steak strips.

5

Using the same dish or another suitable casserole, combine the remaining 50 g (2 oz) butter with the onion. Stir well, partially cover with cling film and microwave on HIGH for 3 minutes. Mix in the sliced mushrooms and microwave for 1 minute or until the onion and mushrooms are soft.

6

Stir in the flour and microwave on HIGH for 1 minute, stirring briskly two or three times during cooking.

7

Beat in the soured cream, any juices from the meat and salt and pepper to taste. Cover and microwave on HIGH for 1 minute or until hot. Stir occasionally during cooking.

8

Stir all the strips of steak into the sauce then cover and microwave on HIGH for 2 minutes or until the meat is reheated and cooked to taste. Stir once during reheating, paying particular attention to the sauce around the edges. Serve with boiled potatoes or rice, spinach or broccoli and carrots if you wish.

Serves 4–6.

Note The sauce can also be used for coating whole or sliced steaks that have been completely cooked in the conventional way. The sauce is sufficient for coating 6–8 steaks.

Italian Meat Balls

65 g (2½ oz) dry bread, crusts
   removed
450 g (1 lb) lean beef, freshly
   minced
1 small onion, skinned and
   minced
½ garlic clove, skinned and
   crushed
25 g (1 oz) Cheddar cheese,
   grated
30 ml (2 tbsp) chopped parsley
2 eggs
salt and freshly ground pepper
225 g (8 oz) tagliatelle
5 ml (1 tsp) vegetable oil

1

Soak the bread in cold water for 5
minutes, then squeeze dry and
mash in a large bowl.

2

Add the minced beef, onion, garlic,
cheese, parsley and eggs and season
to taste. Knead the ingredients
until well blended.

3

Divide the mixture into sixteen
and shape into 4-cm (1½-inch) balls
(they will be very soft).

4

Arrange in a single layer in a
shallow dish and, without
covering, microwave on HIGH for
5 minutes or until half cooked.
Give the dish a quarter-turn three
times during this period.

5

Drain away any fat that may have
gathered in the dish. Cover the
meat balls and set aside while
making the sauce.

For the sauce
1 medium onion, skinned and
   finely chopped
3 bacon rinds
25 g (1 oz) plain flour
300 ml (½ pint) tomato juice
1 beef stock cube, crumbled
1 bay leaf, crumbled
2.5 ml (½ level tsp) sugar
salt and freshly ground pepper

6

To make the sauce, put the onion
and bacon rinds in a medium bowl
and microwave on HIGH for 2
minutes or until the onion is soft.
Stir in the flour and microwave on
HIGH for 1 minute, stirring after
30 seconds. Add the tomato juice,
beef stock cube, bay leaf and sugar
and microwave on HIGH for 2
minutes. Stir in 150 ml (¼ pint) hot
water and microwave on HIGH for
3 minutes until the sauce thickens.
Add salt and pepper to taste.

7

Reposition the meat balls, taking
care that they do not break as they
are very soft, and strain the sauce
over the meat. Microwave on
HIGH for 3 minutes or until the
meat balls are fully cooked. Cover.

8

Prepare the pasta. See Cooking
Noodles (page 85). Drain the pasta
and arrange in a border around the
meat. Serve with courgettes and
mushrooms, if you wish.

Serves 4–6.

Chilli Con Carne

450 g (1 lb) lean minced beef
1 medium onion, skinned and
   finely chopped
1 green pepper, seeded and
   finely chopped
396-g (14-oz) can tomatoes,
   with their juice
396-g (14-oz) can kidney beans,
   drained
142-ml (5-oz) can tomato purée
10 ml (2 level tsp) chilli
   seasoning
2.5 ml (½ level tsp) cumin
2.5 ml (½ level tsp) salt
1.25 ml (¼ level tsp) pepper

1

Mix the beef, onion and green
pepper in a large casserole. Stir
thoroughly, cover and microwave
on HIGH for 8 minutes or until the
meat changes colour. Stir twice
during cooking, making sure that
the beef pieces are well broken up.

2

Add all the remaining ingredients
and 125 ml (4 fl oz) water. Stir.
Cover and microwave on HIGH for
10 minutes, then reduce the setting
and microwave on LOW for 1
hour. Stir occasionally during
cooking. Serve with garlic bread or
toast and a green salad.

Serves 6–8.

Note Half this quantity will take
about 40 minutes in all. Chilli con
carne can be cooked entirely on a
HIGH setting: when all ingredients
have been added microwave on
HIGH for 25 minutes. This method
is perfectly suitable if the Chilli con
carne can be prepared 24 hours in
advance. To reheat, cover and
microwave on HIGH for 5 minutes
or until thoroughly hot. Stir
occasionally during reheating.

Beefburgers

450 g (1 lb) beef, freshly minced
small piece of onion, skinned
    and grated
1 egg
few drops of Worcestershire
    sauce
5 ml (1 level tsp) salt
freshly ground pepper
2.5 ml ($\frac{1}{2}$ level tsp) mixed dried
    herbs
15 g ($\frac{1}{2}$ oz) butter

1

Mix all ingredients except the
butter thoroughly together. Shape
into four burgers.

2

Preheat a large browning dish to
maximum according to the
manufacturer's instructions,
adding the butter during the last
30 seconds.

3

Immediately press the beefburgers
flat on to the hot surface and
microwave on HIGH for 5 minutes
or until just cooked, turning the
burgers over and repositioning
after 3 minutes. Serve with Quick
Tomato Sauce (see page 93),
creamed potato and shredded
cabbage if you wish. Or serve in
burger buns topped with pickles,
onion rings and tomato on lettuce
lined plates.

Serves 4.

Note The burgers can be covered
for the last 2 minutes if preferred.
Reduce the cooking time to just
over 3 minutes for 2 burgers or 1$\frac{3}{4}$
minutes for 1 burger.

Lamb, Aubergine and Red Pepper Kebabs

900 g (2 lb) boned leg of lamb,
    trimmed and cut into 2-cm
    ($\frac{3}{4}$-inch) cubes
2 medium aubergines, halved
    lengthwise and cut into 2-cm
    ($\frac{3}{4}$-inch) slices
2 red peppers, seeded and cut
    into 4-cm (1$\frac{1}{2}$-inch) pieces
2 small onions, skinned and cut
    into 8 wedges

For the marinade
25 g (1 oz) butter
1 small onion, skinned and
    finely chopped
$\frac{1}{2}$ green pepper, seeded and
    finely chopped
1 celery stick, finely chopped
1 garlic clove, crushed
226-g (8-oz) can tomatoes
120 ml (8 level tbsp) tomato
    purée
30 ml (2 level tbsp) soft dark
    brown sugar
7.5 ml (1$\frac{1}{2}$ tsp) lemon juice
2.5 ml ($\frac{1}{2}$ level tsp) salt
2.5 ml ($\frac{1}{2}$ tsp) Tabasco sauce

1

Make the marinade. Put the butter,
onion, green pepper, celery and
garlic into a large bowl, cover and
microwave on HIGH for 8 minutes,
stirring occasionally.

2

Add all the remaining marinade
ingredients plus 75 ml (5 tbsp)
water and microwave on HIGH for
5 minutes or until boiling. Reduce
the setting and microwave on LOW
for 10 minutes. Leave to cool. The
marinade should be of a thick sauce
consistency. Add another 30–45 ml
(2–3 tbsp) water if you prefer.

3

Stir in the lamb and mix well.
Cover and chill for at least 4 hours.

4

Put the aubergines, red peppers
and onion wedges into a bowl, add
30 ml (2 tbsp) water, cover and
microwave on HIGH for 3 minutes
or until the vegetables are slightly
soft. Drain. Cover and set aside
until the lamb is ready to cook.

5

Thread the lamb, aubergine,
pepper and onion pieces on to
wooden skewers.

6

Arrange in a double layer on a
roasting rack in a shallow dish.
Microwave on HIGH for 6 minutes,
then reposition so that the inside
kebabs are moved to the outside of
the dish. Spoon the marinade over
the kebabs and microwave on
HIGH for 15 minutes or until the
lamb is cooked. Reposition the
kebabs twice during this cooking
period. Transfer to a hot dish.

7

The thin sauce which you will find
in the bottom of the dish can be
reheated and served separately.

Serves 4–6.

Lamb and Artichoke Gratin

700 g (1½ lb) lean lamb, freshly minced
salt and freshly ground pepper
juice of 1 lime
20 ml (4 level tsp) plain flour
60 ml (4 tbsp) dry white wine
397-g (14-oz) can artichoke hearts, drained
15 ml (1 level tbsp) grated Parmesan cheese
30 ml (2 level tbsp) fresh breadcrumbs

1
Spread the meat out in a 23-cm (9-inch) round shallow ovenproof glass dish, season with salt and pepper and sprinkle with the lime juice. Leave for 2 hours. Microwave on HIGH for 10 minutes or until the meat is just cooked. Stir and break up the lumps two or three times during cooking.

2
Mix the flour and wine together and pour over the meat. Stir thoroughly and microwave on HIGH for 2 minutes or until the mixture thickens slightly.

3
Chop the artichokes and spread over the meat. Sprinkle with the Parmesan cheese and the breadcrumbs, preferably mixed together. Microwave on HIGH for 2 minutes, then give the dish a half-turn and microwave on HIGH for a further 2 minutes or until the artichokes are hot. Brown under the grill.

Serves 4.

Lamb Chops Paprika

four 175-g (6-oz) lamb chops, trimmed
30 ml (2 level tbsp) seasoned flour
15 g (½ oz) butter or block margarine
1 red pepper, seeded and cut into rings
1 medium onion, skinned and finely sliced
15 ml (1 level tbsp) paprika
salt and freshly ground pepper
150 ml (¼ pint) double cream

1
Coat the chops lightly in seasoned flour. Preheat the browning dish to maximum according to manufacturer's instructions, adding the butter during the last 15 seconds.

2
Quickly put the chops into the sizzling butter and turn them over. Microwave on HIGH for 3 minutes. Turn the chops over and reposition, then add the red pepper and onion. Cover and microwave on HIGH for 6 minutes, repositioning the chops once.

3
Sprinkle the chops with the paprika, salt and pepper and microwave on HIGH for 2 minutes.

4
Stir in the cream round the sides of the dish and, without covering, microwave on HIGH for 2 minutes until the sauce is hot. Stir once.

Serves 4.

Note If browning is not important, cook in a casserole.

Pork Fillet with Cashew Nuts

25 g (1 oz) butter or block margarine
450 g (1 lb) pork fillet, thinly sliced
4 sticks of celery, trimmed and thinly sliced
grated rind and juice of 1 orange
150 ml (¼ pint) chicken stock
salt and freshly ground pepper
15 ml (1 level tbsp) cornflour
50 g (2 oz) cashew nuts

1
Preheat the browning dish to maximum according to the manufacturer's instructions, adding the butter for the last 30 seconds, without removing the dish from the oven.

2
Immediately add the pork slices and stir quickly. Microwave on HIGH for 2 minutes. Add the celery slices and stir. Microwave on HIGH for a further 2 minutes.

3
Add the orange rind and juice, stock and seasoning and cook for 2 minutes on HIGH. Blend the cornflour to a paste with a little water and stir into the juices. Add the cashew nuts and microwave on HIGH for 2 minutes or until the juices have thickened. Serve with rice and a crisp side salad.

Serves 4.

Pork Chop on a Plate

225-g (8-oz) pork chop
vegetable oil

1

Trim away excess fat and brush one side of the chop with vegetable oil.

2

Put the chop oily side down on a plate and cover with greaseproof paper to prevent splattering.

3

Microwave on HIGH for 2 minutes or until cooked. Test with the point of a sharp knife.

4

Season to taste and leave for 2 minutes before serving with apple sauce, a jacket baked potato and baked beans if you wish.

Serves 1.

Note Trimming will probably remove 40 g (1½ oz) from the original weight. Cooking times are variable, depending on size of chop, amount of fat, and so on.

Granny's Pork Chops in Cider

40 g (1½ oz) butter or block
   margarine
four 175-g (6-oz) pork chops,
   trimmed
salt and freshly ground pepper
45 ml (3 level tbsp) plain flour
3 green dessert apples, each
   peeled, cored and cut into 8
   wedges
200 ml (7 fl oz) dry or extra dry
   cider

1

Preheat a large browning dish according to the manufacturer's instructions adding the butter in 2 pieces during the last 30 seconds.

2

Meanwhile season the chops and coat with flour. Reserve the remaining flour. When the browning dish is hot and the butter dark brown and sizzling, quickly add the chops, pressing them down with a fish slice.

3

Turn the chops over quickly to seal the other side. Microwave on HIGH for 5 minutes, repositioning and turning the chops over halfway through cooking. Remove the chops and set aside.

4

Stir the prepared apples into the butter left in the dish. Cover and microwave on HIGH for 3 minutes or until the apples are tender. Stir once during cooking. Stir in the remaining flour and mix in the cider.

5

Arrange the chops on top of the apples, browner side down. Cover with the lid and microwave on HIGH for 8 minutes or until the chops are cooked. Turn the chops over and reposition halfway through the cooking time.

6

Serve the chops browner side up, garnished with a few pieces of apple, and pour the sauce over. Serve with potatoes and cabbage, if you wish.

Serves 4.

Note To cook the chops without the browning dish, pre-cook the chops on HIGH for 5 minutes without additional fat. Remove from the dish while melting the butter and cooking the apples.

Pork Chops with Redcurrant Glaze

4 pork chops, 2–2.5 cm
  ($\frac{3}{4}$–1-inch) thick
15 g ($\frac{1}{2}$ oz) butter or block
  margarine
salt and freshly ground pepper
60 ml (4 tbsp) redcurrant jelly
15 ml (1 tbsp) red wine vinegar
2.5 ml ($\frac{1}{2}$ level tsp) French
  mustard

1

Trim any excess fat from the chops
and pat dry to remove any excess
moisture. Preheat the browning
dish to maximum according to
manufacturer's instructions,
adding the butter for the
last 30 seconds.

2

Without removing the browning
dish from the oven quickly press
the chops on to the hot surface,
placing the bony ends towards the
centre of the dish. Microwave on
HIGH for 3 minutes, then turn the
chops over and reposition.

3

Continue to microwave on HIGH
for 6 minutes or until the chops are
tender—and until there is no trace
of pink inside. Give the dish a half
turn once during cooking. Leave to
stand, covered, for 5 minutes
before serving. Season to taste.

4

Meanwhile put the redcurrant
jelly, vinegar and mustard in a
large measuring jug, stir and
microwave on HIGH for 3$\frac{1}{2}$
minutes or until syrupy. Pour the
glaze over the chops and serve.

Serves 4.

Veal Escalopes in Onion and Cream Sauce

4 veal escalopes, each about
  100 g (4 oz)
salt and freshly ground pepper
25 g (1 oz) butter or block
  margarine

For the sauce
1 medium onion, skinned and
  finely chopped
25 g (1 oz) butter or block
  margarine
90 ml (6 tbsp) dry white wine
150 ml ($\frac{1}{4}$ pint) double cream
salt
1.25 ml ($\frac{1}{4}$ tsp) lemon juice

1

Flatten the veal cutlets to 0.25 cm
($\frac{1}{8}$ inch) thick. Dry with absorbent
kitchen paper, and season.

2

Put the butter in a large shallow
dish, cover lightly and microwave
on HIGH for 3 minutes or until
foaming.

3

Quickly remove the covering, add
the escalopes and microwave on
HIGH for 2 minutes. Turn over and
reposition the escalopes and
microwave on HIGH for 1$\frac{1}{2}$
minutes or until just cooked.
Drain, then cover and set aside.

4

Make the sauce. Put the onion and
butter in another dish. Microwave
on HIGH for 2 minutes or until the
onion is soft, stirring once during
cooking.

5

Stir in the wine and microwave on
HIGH for 1 minute or until boiling.

6

Add the cream, salt to taste and
microwave on HIGH for 2 minutes
or until boiling, stirring twice
during cooking. Allow to cool
slightly, then purée the sauce in a
blender and stir in the lemon juice.

7

Pour the sauce over the veal.
Without covering, microwave on
LOW for 2 minutes or until
reheated. Take care not to
overheat the sauce or it will
curdle. Serve with rice or new
potatoes and green beans or
spinach, if you wish.

Serves 4.

Note The veal can be sealed first
in a frying pan if preferred. If 4
escalopes are too large to make a
single layer in the dish, cook 2 at a
time. Add half the butter for the
first 2, add the remaining butter
and microwave until foaming.
Reheat all the escalopes in the
sauce.

Sautéed Veal or Pork Escalopes

Kidneys in Madeira

4 veal or pork escalopes, each about 100 g (4 oz), trimmed and flattened
25 g (1 oz) butter or block margarine
30 ml (2 tbsp) brandy

8 lamb's kidneys, about 450 g (1 lb)
30 ml (2 tbsp) Madeira
25 g (1 oz) butter or block margarine
1 garlic clove, skinned and crushed
15 ml (1 tbsp) chopped fresh parsley
2.5 ml ($\frac{1}{2}$ tsp) Worcestershire sauce
2.5 ml ($\frac{1}{2}$ level tsp) mustard powder
5 ml (1 level tsp) cornflour

For micro-fried crumbs
50 g (2 oz) butter or block margarine
50 g (2 oz) fresh breadcrumbs

1

Heat the butter or margarine in a shallow dish on HIGH for 3 minutes or until foaming.

2

Add the escalopes and microwave on HIGH for 2 minutes. Turn over, reposition the escalopes and microwave on HIGH for 1$\frac{1}{2}$ minutes or until cooked.

3

Put the brandy in a glass and warm in the microwave on HIGH for 5 seconds, then pour over the veal in the dish and flambé. While the flames are leaping, swirl the escalopes round in the sauce.

Serves 4.

1

Skin the kidneys and cut in half horizontally. Remove the core with scissors or a sharp knife.

2

Put the kidneys into a small bowl, add the Madeira and stir well. Leave to stand for 15 minutes, stirring occasionally.

3

Put the butter in a casserole and microwave on HIGH for 5 seconds or until very soft but not melted. Mix the garlic, parsley, Worcestershire sauce and mustard powder into the butter.

4

Drain the kidneys, reserving the Madeira juices, and stir into the flavoured butter, turning the kidneys so that they are well coated. Cover and microwave on HIGH for 4$\frac{1}{2}$ minutes or until the kidneys are cooked (do not overcook). Stir, turn over and re-arrange the kidneys twice during cooking.

5

Remove the kidneys to a warm serving dish with a slotted spoon.

6

Stir the cornflour into the reserved Madeira and pour into the kidney juices in the casserole (there is no need to cover the dish). Microwave on HIGH for 1 minute or until the sauce thickens, stirring once during cooking. Pour the sauce over the kidneys.

7

To prepare the fried crumbs put the butter into a shallow dish and microwave on HIGH for 1 minute or until foaming.

8

Sprinkle the breadcrumbs evenly over the surface, then stir and microwave on HIGH for 1 minute. Stir once more, then microwave on HIGH for 2–2$\frac{1}{2}$ minutes or until the butter is absorbed and the breadcrumbs are slightly coloured.

9

To serve, put the crumbs into a small dish and hand round separately. Serve with Soft Sautéed Potatoes (see page 82) and green beans, if you wish.

Serves 4.

Note Escalopes can also be cooked by dipping in beaten egg and golden crumbs. Microwave in 15 ml (1 tbsp) oil. Turn the escalopes over halfway through cooking.

Note The micro-fried crumbs can be prepared in advance and reheated for a few seconds just before serving.

Liver and Onions

4–6 rashers streaky bacon, rinded
450 g (1 lb) lamb's liver, thinly sliced
25 g (1 oz) butter or block margarine
2 medium onions, skinned and chopped
30 ml (2 level tbsp) fresh breadcrumbs (optional)
150 ml ($\frac{1}{4}$ pint) hot beef stock
1 bay leaf

1

Cook the bacon as instructed on page 46 and set aside.

2

Wash the liver in cold water and cut out any inedible membranes. Pat dry on kitchen paper.

3

Put the butter or margarine in a flameproof casserole and microwave on HIGH for 45 seconds or until melted.

4

Stir in the onions and microwave on HIGH for 3 minutes until the onions are soft, stirring once during cooking.

5

Add the liver and turn the pieces to coat with the onion mixture. Sprinkle with the breadcrumbs, if wished. Pour over the stock, add the bayleaf and lay the bacon rashers on top.

6

Cover and microwave on HIGH for 3 minutes. Reposition the liver, recover and microwave on HIGH for $3\frac{1}{2}$ minutes or until tender. Brown under the grill, if wished.

Serves 4.

Gammon Steaks

125-g (4-oz) gammon steak
10 ml (2 tsp) honey
1.25 ml ($\frac{1}{4}$ level tsp) French mustard

1

Remove the rind and snip around the edges at 1-cm ($\frac{1}{2}$-inch) intervals to prevent the steak curling. Put on a dish or plate and cover with greaseproof paper.

2

Microwave on HIGH for 2 minutes. Brush with honey and mustard and cook for a further 30 seconds or until just cooked. Do not overcook. Leave to stand for 3 minutes during which time the gammon will finish cooking. Gammon steaks tend to 'pop' during cooking.

3

Transfer to a warm plate and garnish with pineapple, peaches, mandarin segments or apple rings.

Serves 1.

Note A 175-g (6-oz) gammon steak will take $2\frac{1}{2}$–3 minutes. Two gammon steaks will take approximately $4\frac{1}{2}$ minutes. If cooking more than 1 steak at the same time, give the dish a quarter-turn three times during cooking even if your oven is fitted with a turntable.

Sausages in the Browning Dish

4 large pork or beef sausages prepared mustard or prepared sauce to serve

1

First put the sausages on a plate and microwave on LOW for 10 seconds or until they are no longer cold to the touch. To take the chill off a pack of 4 (not frozen) sausages, leave in the wrapping and turn the package over after 5 seconds. Remove the wrapping and separate the sausages. Prick them thoroughly.

2

Preheat a large browning dish to the maximum recommended by the manufacturer, adding a small knob of butter or block margarine during the last 30 seconds.

3

Put the sausages in the dish, moving them quickly around with tongs. Microwave on HIGH, for 3 minutes or until cooked, repositioning and turning the sausages over once during cooking. Serve with mustard or sauce, if wished.

Note If more than 4 large sausages are being cooked, it is better to drain the fat from the browning dish and reheat for 2 minutes before cooking another batch. There will be no need to add any extra fat.

Sausage and Bacon Rolls

12 rashers streaky bacon
350 g (12 oz) sausagemeat

1

Remove the rind and stretch the bacon with the back of a knife.

2

Divide the sausagemeat into 12 even portions and shape into small barrels.

3

Place a sausage barrel on one end of each rasher of bacon and roll up so that the bacon is coiled around the sausage leaving no gap.

4

Arrange in a shallow dish seam sides underneath and microwave on HIGH for 10 minutes or until the sausagemeat is cooked. Reposition the bacon rolls twice during cooking making sure that those in the centre are pushed to the outside and vice versa. Drain on kitchen paper. Brown under a hot grill if wished.

Serves 4.

Tomato Meat Loaf with Rich Brown Sauce

550 g (1¼ lb) lean beef, freshly minced
1 medium onion, skinned and finely chopped
50 g (2 oz) fresh breadcrumbs
396-g (14-oz) can tomatoes, well drained
1 egg, beaten
10 ml (2 level tsp) salt
2.5 ml (½ level tsp) black pepper
2.5 ml (½ level tsp) dried basil
1.25 ml (¼ tsp) Worcestershire sauce
150 ml (¼ pint) Rich Brown Sauce (see page 95)

1

Combine all the ingredients except the rich brown sauce in a mixing bowl. Mix well.

2

Press the mixture evenly into a 1-litre (1¾-pint) ring mould.

3

Microwave on HIGH for 10 minutes or until the inside edge of the meat is just cooked. Give the dish a quarter-turn four times during cooking. Turn out on to a hot serving dish.

4

Put the sauce in a sauceboat or measuring jug and microwave on HIGH for 1 minute or until heated, stirring occasionally. Pour the sauce over the meat and serve at once.

Serves 6–8.

Sausages with Green Beans

8 large pork sausages, pricked
25 g (1 oz) butter or block margarine
1 large onion, skinned and thinly sliced
225 g (8 oz) French beans, trimmed and cut into 5 cm (2 inch) pieces
150 ml (¼ pint) beef stock
15 ml (1 level tbsp) mild prepared mustard
salt and freshly ground pepper

1

Preheat a browning dish to maximum according to the manufacturer's instructions, adding 15 g (½ oz) of the butter for the last 30 seconds.

2

Without removing the browning dish from the oven, quickly put 4 of the sausages on to the hot surface and move them around quickly using a pair of tongs. Microwave on HIGH for 1 minute then remove the sausages and set aside.

3

Drain the fat from the browning dish and reheat on HIGH for 2 minutes. Add the remaining sausages turning on the hot surface and moving them around quickly. Microwave on HIGH for 1 minute then remove the sausages and set aside.

4

Add the remaining butter to the browning dish with the onion and beans and microwave on HIGH for 2 minutes. Return the sausages to the dish, add the stock, mustard and seasoning. Cover and microwave on HIGH for 7 minutes until the sausages are cooked and the beans tender. Stir and reposition once during the cooking time.

Serves 4.

CHAPTER FIVE

Poultry and Game

Poultry can be cooked successfully in the microwave oven whether it is cut into pieces or whole. The only exception is a large whole turkey. Although the average microwave oven cavity is large enough to contain a well shaped 8 kg (18 lb) turkey, the cooking process would be extremely uneven and turning the bird would present problems. The largest recommended size is 5.6 kg (12 lb).

Boiling chickens should be avoided unless they are to be used for stock, soup or in minced dishes as they are likely to be tough. Roasting chickens, spring chickens and poussins produce excellent, flavoursome results.

Duck is always tougher and more chewy than chicken and so should be cooked for the majority of the time on a LOW setting. Although poultry does not brown appreciably in the microwave, duck flesh darkens as it cools, so that if you are preparing it for the freezer, the colour will be just right when the dish is reheated. And if freshly cooked duck is served with a sauce it will look even more appetising.

Duck is fatty and the fat should be spooned away during cooking. For this reason, it is best to cook a duck on a rack in a shallow dish, either cut up and cooked as quarters or roasted whole. Goose can be even fattier than duck and is usually roasted whole.

Prepare pheasant and other game birds in the usual way for cooking by microwave. Rabbit can be substituted for chicken in casseroles or where cooked meat is required in recipes.

Roast chicken
Fresh, young, free-range chickens produce the best flavour and the most tender flesh. They are identifiable by their skin, which should be smooth with a light creamy colour. Roasting chickens are best for cooking by microwave as it is almost impossible to tenderise a boiling fowl in the short cooking time. If the bird appears to have pockets of yellow fat, it may be unsuitable for microwaving as you will have to be continually spooning away the surplus melted fat as it accumulates. These fatty birds also shrink considerably while cooking.

There are various methods of microwave-roasting poultry. Chicken may be roasted either directly in a dish covered with a piece of greaseproof paper, or on an upturned, undecorated saucer in a dish, or on a special microwave roasting rack. The dish method is the easiest; the upturned saucer method is useful for an even-shaped bird although you may find that the saucer tends to stick to the dish. The roasting rack is a good idea if you have storage space for the rack when not in use and you do not object to the extra washing-up.

Roasting bags are good for cooking lean birds but are unsuitable for fatty poultry. Cooking in a roasting bag enhances browning, although microwaved chicken will never be as brown as conventionally roasted chicken, and the skin will remain moist. Roasting bags must never be sealed with the metal tag; the best way of closing the bag is to use a large elastic band leaving a wide gap.

Chicken may be cooked on HIGH, MEDIUM or LOW setting depending upon the dish you are cooking and the oven-to-table time you are able to allow. When chicken is cooked on HIGH, you will find that the leg and wing tips tend to overcook. These can be covered with small smooth pieces of foil halfway through cooking provided that the foil does not touch the sides or top of the oven. When the chicken is cooked on MEDIUM or in a roasting bag, shielding is not always necessary. Poultry can be roasted with stuffing loosely packed in the neck end only. If the stuffing is mainly sausage meat, it is advisable to microwave on MEDIUM or LOW to ensure that the stuffing cooks thoroughly. If you like the poultry to be browned, wipe with kitchen paper, then rub with butter and a colouring agent.

Except when using a roasting bag, a chicken should be cooked breast-side down for the first half of the cooking time. Large birds will cook more evenly if they are cooked for a quarter of the time on each of the four sides. Give the dish a turn occasionally.

Testing for doneness
If your oven is not fitted with a probe, use a microwave meat thermometer, or an ordinary meat

thermometer immediately the chicken is removed from the microwave oven. If the chicken is not 'tented' the temperature will not rise appreciably during standing time, so that you must cook to 85° C/185° F. The stuffing will register about 75° C/165° F depending on the content. Be sure to position the thermometer correctly (not into a bone).

To test for cooking without using a thermometer, insert the tip of a sharp knife close to the bone between the thigh and the body—if cooked no pink will remain and the juices will run clear. When the bone is twisted the leg should come away easily.

Chicken pieces

Chicken pieces are a useful standby particularly when one person requires just a quick supper. The sizes of chicken pieces vary considerably and those which are partially boned or boneless will cook much more quickly. On average a boneless chicken breast or drumstick will take 2–3 minutes while a quarter of a 1.5-kg (3¼-lb) chicken will take about 6 minutes.

If you remove the skin from chicken pieces, flavours and seasoning will penetrate the flesh better. Chicken with the skin on will take fractionally longer to cook. The shape of the chicken piece can make a difference to the timing so it is essential to test frequently whether it is cooked. The temperature of chicken pieces when tested with a thermometer does not always give a true reading, so test by twisting to see if the bone will move easily. The temperature does not rise appreciably after the chicken is removed from the microwave oven.

Because of the short cooking time, chicken pieces do not brown well but good results can be obtained using the browning dish or by coating in some way.

Chicken pieces should be thoroughly thawed before use; see chart on page 63. Cooking times must be adjusted according to weight, shape and number of pieces. Smaller, quicker-cooking quarters should be removed as soon as they are ready. Cook chicken pieces on HIGH.

Poultry pieces in sauce

Poultry can be cut into quarters or smaller pieces and be roasted either partly or fully before being finished with a sauce. The advantage of this is that there is no need to carve at the table and, if only one person wishes to eat, the other portions may be refrigerated or frozen for reheating later. Most of the sauces can be reheated with the poultry. A second advantage in cooking poultry when cut up is that it is possible to obtain very even results because the pieces can be repositioned and turned over much more easily than a whole bird.

Should you want to cook any of the following recipes using a single joint, remember to cut the cooking times down by at least two-thirds. Poultry portions can be tested with a meat thermometer but this is not entirely reliable since the thinner parts will cook before the thicker parts. Be sure to insert the point of the thermometer into the thickest part.

A 1.6-kg (3½-lb) chicken cut into 8–12 pieces will take 18–24 minutes to cook. The pieces should be repositioned or stirred every 5 minutes and it is advantageous to

COOKING CHICKEN	
Casseroles	30–40 minutes on HIGH for 1.5-kg (3-lb) bird cut up, three-quarters covered.
Pieces	2½–3½ minutes on HIGH per piece; 6–9 minutes for 4 pieces.
Whole	9 minutes per 450 g (1 lb) on MEDIUM or 6 minutes on HIGH. Cover loosely. It is better to cook for half the time on HIGH, then the remaining time on MEDIUM.
DUCK	
Portions	4 × 300-g (11-oz) joints on HIGH for 10 minutes or on LOW for 30 minutes.
Whole	10 minutes per 450 g (1 lb) on MEDIUM or 7 minutes on HIGH. Cover with greaseproof paper.
GOOSE	1–1¼ hours on HIGH for an average bird. Cook covered.
LIVERS, chicken and turkey	As per recipe. Prick or halve to prevent exploding.
POUSSIN	1 poussin 5 minutes on HIGH; 4 poussins 20 minutes on HIGH, turning over halfway through.
RABBIT	Cook as for chicken casseroles.
TURKEY	11–13 minutes per 450 g (1 lb) on MEDIUM or 9–11 minutes on HIGH. Cook in roasting bag.
VENISON	15 minutes for 4 cutlets on HIGH.

give the dish a quarter-turn occasionally. Microwave covered with greaseproof paper to avoid splattering.

Casseroles

Do not hesitate to cook chicken casseroles in the microwave oven. They will be as tender and juicy as when cooked conventionally. Although not always strictly necessary, many conventional recipes recommend that chicken pieces be browned before cooking in a casserole and if you prefer to brown the chicken first then do so either conventionally in a frying pan or if the chicken pieces are small they can be browned successfully in the browning dish. However many recipes will be equally succulent without pre-browning the chicken.

The cooking will be more even if the pieces are of equal size and thickness. Leg and side quarters are thicker than breast and wing quarters and will cook more evenly if they are cut into two pieces. Although the skin, wing tips and leg tips add to the quality of the gravy, producing a more jellied stock, you may prefer to remove these for the sake of appearance. The skin also produces extra fat and if you decide to leave it on you may have to skim the fat from the top of the casserole before serving.

Casseroles should be cooked covered and be stirred during cooking so that the uppermost and outer pieces do not become dry and overcooked. A chicken casserole may be microwaved on HIGH when cooked in a large amount of liquid. If there is little sauce then it is better to microwave on LOW; this will take more than twice as long but you can expect the flesh to be softer. When in a hurry for an almost instant meal, microwave on HIGH in half the given quantity of liquid or stock, adding the remainder after three-quarters of the cooking time. When casseroles are cooked in a small amount of liquid be careful to stir and scrape around the edges to prevent the sauce becoming lumpy and congealed

against the sides of the dish. Leave to stand covered for 10 minutes and stir thoroughly before serving.

On average a chicken casserole takes 30–45 minutes to cook. The flavour of all casseroles improves if the dish is cooled rapidly, refrigerated for 24 hours and then reheated before serving. Do not leave the casserole to cool at room temperature but immerse the base in ice cold water and stir to assist the cooling process. When reheating be sure that the mixture comes to boiling point. For variety, buy turkey pieces and casserole these in the same way.

Cooked chicken or turkey

Any recipe using cooked chicken or turkey must be reheated thoroughly. Add the chicken to the remaining ingredients halfway through cooking if there is a lot of sauce but three-quarters of the way through cooking if the sauce is minimal. Although most cooked chicken or turkey dishes are designed for using up leftovers, now that you have the microwave oven you can enjoy these dishes at any time by simply and quickly cooking the quantity that you require in the microwave oven prior to use. Be sure not to overcook the poultry as further cooking will take place during the time it takes to reheat it with the other ingredients. Cook the pieces thoroughly if they are going to be used in a cold dish such as Turkey and Ham terrine (see page 74).

Thawing Poultry

Frozen poultry must be completely thawed before cooking. If doing this in the microwave oven, defrost until just a few ice crystals remain inside. Finish thawing in a large bowl of cold clear water until no ice crystals are left.

Chicken livers

Frozen chicken livers are often sold in tubs or blocks. Because they deteriorate quickly after thawing, buy only the quantity you require.

Thaw chicken livers before cooking. To do this, remove the frozen block from the container and put into a dish. Cover with a thick wad of absorbent kitchen paper which will soak up some of the excess liquid during thawing. Do not place the frozen block on top of kitchen paper as the liver will stick to the paper. Thaw in the refrigerator or according to the chart opposite.

Because chicken livers are enclosed in a skin they will pop during cooking. Cut them in half to help avoid this and remove any pieces of white sinew. Always cook chicken livers covered. If they are cooked in liquid it does not matter whether you use a lid or vented cling film, but when sautéeing they should be covered with greaseproof paper. This prevents too much moisture being trapped, causing the livers to sweat rather than sauté.

The livers are ready when they are still just pink inside but no pink liquid runs. Stir frequently during cooking but do not overcook. Because they are so small cooking continues rapidly after the microwave oven is switched off.

Thawing Poultry and Game

THAWING CHICKEN	
Casseroles	15 minutes, on HIGH, three-quarters covered.
Drumsticks	4 minutes per 450 g (1 lb) on LOW placed on rack, then in cold water for 15 minutes.
Legs and thighs	4 minutes per 450 g (1 lb) on LOW, then in cold water for 15 minutes.
Wings	7 minutes per 450 g (1 lb) on LOW, then in cold water 15 minutes.
Whole	6 minutes per 450 g (1 lb) on LOW. Remove giblets and neck as soon as they are free (if they are inside the bird) and use them for making stock or gravy.
DUCK	
Portions	4 minutes per 450 g (1 lb) on LOW, then in cold water for 15 minutes.
Whole	6 minutes per 450 g (1 lb) on LOW. 30–40 minutes for an average sized bird.
GOOSE	5 minutes per 450 g (1 lb) on LOW. Average bird takes 45 minutes.
LIVERS, chicken and turkey	20 seconds on LOW, turn over then microwave for further 20 seconds. Leave to fully thaw at room temperature.
POUSSIN	1 × 400-g (14-oz) bird 6 minutes on LOW. Turn over halfway through. Immerse in cold water for 30 minutes. 4 × 400-g (14-oz) birds 4 minutes on LOW, turn over and reposition, microwave for further 4 minutes and reposition, then microwave for final 4 minutes. Immerse for 30–45 minutes in cold water.
RABBIT	10 minutes per 450 g (1 lb) on LOW, covered.
TURKEY	10–12 minutes per 450 g (1 lb) on LOW.
VENISON	10 minutes per 450 g (1 lb) on LOW.

Note On ovens with a 10% or WARM setting, almost double the thawing times, but the thawing will be more even (thawing should still be completed by immersing in cold water).

Thawing Whole Chicken or Duck

1

Cut away any metal clip and open the end of the wrapping. Make a slit in the bag along the back bone, under the bird, to let out the juices.

2

Put the bird breast-side up on an upturned, undecorated saucer or dish in a large shallow dish. Microwave on LOW or DEFROST for half the thawing time given on the chart (page 63).

3

Remove the wrappings and giblets as soon as they loosen. Drain any liquid from the dish. Turn the bird breast-side down and continue microwaving.

4

Feel the bird and shield with small, smooth pieces of foil any parts that are warm to touch, including wing tips and legs if their colour seems to be changing. Be careful that the foil does not touch lining of oven.

5

Continue microwaving until just a few ice crystals remain inside. Remove the foil and immerse the bird in a bowl of cold water until no ice crystals remain inside. To double test, insert a small, sharp knife into the thickest part of the thigh. If it goes in easily the bird is fully thawed.

Thawing Whole Turkey

1

Remove any metal clips or tags, slit the bag underneath the bird and place the bird on a rack in a shallow dish. Microwave on the lowest possible setting.

2

Turn the bird over and give the dish a quarter-turn several times during thawing so that it has an equal amount of time on breast, back and sides. Follow each defrosting period with a 10–20 minute rest.

3

Remove the bag of giblets and outer wrappings as soon as they loosen.

4

Microwave according to the chart until half thawed. If shielding warm parts with foil is necessary, overwrap with cling film to prevent the foil touching the oven lining.

5

When half thawed, leave the turkey at room temperature well away from any other meats (particularly cooked meats) and leave to finish thawing.

Giblets when being used for stock or soup may be cooked from frozen.

Thawing Poultry pieces

1

Remove from the packaging—do not thaw on a polystyrene container. Separate the pieces as soon as possible if they are stuck together.

2

Place on a plate or in a shallow dish, thick sides towards the outside.

3

Microwave on LOW or DEFROST according to the chart timing, turning the pieces over and repositioning two or three times during thawing.

4

Small single poultry joints must *not* be shielded with foil. Finish thawing in cold water. When thawing several pieces at the same time, shield any parts which feel warm with small pieces of smooth foil. Remove any thawed pieces as soon as they are ready.

Chicken and Mushroom Casserole (page 68) in a round Pyrex casserole, and *overleaf,* **Chicken Liver and Port Pâté (page 73)**

Coffee
Soup
Pizza
Beef
Whole
Pork C
Cod
Jacket
Omele
Scramb
Jam Pu

Roast Chicken in a Baking Dish

1

Thaw frozen poultry completely. Wash thawed, frozen or fresh bird inside and out, shake out excess water and dry with absorbent kitchen paper.

2

Season inside the cavity with salt and pepper and place half an onion inside, or stuff the neck end loosely.

3

Tuck the wings underneath and legs close to the sides of the chicken. Tie the legs together with string.

4

Rub with butter and paprika or Worcestershire sauce, gravy browning, tomato ketchup or gravy powder (or a specialist microwave browning agent).

5

Put the prepared chicken breast side down in large shallow dish. Cover with greaseproof paper.

6

Microwave on HIGH for half the cooking time. Give dish a half-turn halfway through the cooking period.

7

Turn the chicken breast side up, replace the greaseproof paper and microwave on MEDIUM or LOW for the remaining cooking time.

8

If preferred, insert a microwave thermometer into the thicker part of the thigh. An ordinary meat thermometer is not suitable.

9

Shield any less meaty parts such as leg and wing tips as soon as they are cooked, making sure the foil does not touch the oven lining.

10

As soon as the chicken is ready remove from the microwave oven and tent with foil. Leave to stand for 15 minutes.

Note This method is perfectly adequate for an everyday roast or when the meat is required subsequently in a made-up chicken dish.

Roast chicken using an upturned undecorated saucer: Cook as above but put the chicken on an inverted undecorated saucer in a shallow dish. This helps keep the chicken out of its cooking juices, encouraging it to roast rather than braise.

Roast chicken using a roasting rack: Cook as above but remove the chicken and rack halfway through cooking and pour away excess fat. Then replace the chicken and rack and continue cooking.

Cooking Poultry in a Roasting Bag

1

Place the chicken, breast side up, in the roasting bag.

2

Tie the end loosely with string or a large elastic band, leaving a gap at the top.

3

Microwave on HIGH for half the time and MEDIUM or LOW for the remaining time. Give the dish a quarter-turn four times during cooking.

Microwaving chicken with a temperature probe
Insert the probe through the roasting bag into the thickest part of the thigh. Follow the manufacturer's instructions for the recommended temperature setting.

Gravy for Turkey or Chicken

giblets from 1 turkey or
    chicken
15 ml (1 level tbsp) cornflour

1

Put the giblets in a 2.8-litre (5-pint) bowl with 450 ml ($\frac{3}{4}$ pint) water. If including the chicken livers, prick or halve first so that they do not explode. Three-quarters cover with cling film and microwave on HIGH for 30 minutes. Allow an extra 15 minutes if the giblets were still frozen. Strain.

2

Blend the cornflour with 15–20 ml (3–4 tsp) cold water. Mix into the freshly cooked stock and make up to 450 ml ($\frac{3}{4}$ pint) with juices from the cooked poultry.

3

Microwave on HIGH for 3 minutes or until the gravy thickens. Stir occasionally during cooking. To give added colour, add a few drops of gravy browning or a chicken stock cube.

Candida Chicken

1.6-kg ($3\frac{1}{2}$-lb) oven-ready chicken
40 g ($1\frac{1}{2}$ oz) butter, softened
$\frac{1}{2}$ green pepper, seeded and
    finely sliced
1 small onion, skinned and
    finely sliced
125 g (4 oz) courgettes,
    trimmed and thinly sliced
2 tomatoes, chopped
15 ml (1 level tbsp) tomato
    purée
25 g (1 oz) fresh breadcrumbs
pinch of dried marjoram
little beaten egg
salt and freshly ground pepper

1

Rub the chicken with 15 g ($\frac{1}{2}$ oz) of the butter. In a bowl mix the remaining butter with the green pepper, onion and courgettes. Cover and microwave on HIGH for 4 minutes or until the vegetables begin to soften. Stir occasionally during cooking.

2

Mix in the tomatoes, tomato purée, breadcrumbs, marjoram and enough egg to bind. Season to taste with salt and pepper.

3

Fill the neck with the stuffing and tuck the wings underneath. Place the chicken in an unsealed roasting bag in a large shallow dish. Microwave on HIGH for 12 minutes, giving the dish a quarter-turn four times during cooking.

4

Reduce the setting and microwave on LOW for 30 minutes or until the chicken is cooked.

5

Leave for 10 minutes, then slit the roasting bag and transfer the chicken to a carving dish. Carve the chicken and arrange it with the stuffing on a warmed serving dish.

Serves 4–6.

Chicken Divan

1.4-kg (3-lb) oven-ready chicken
2–3 large rosemary sprigs
salt and freshly ground pepper
25 g (1 oz) butter or block
    margarine
30 ml (2 level tbsp) plain flour
200 ml (7 fl oz) milk
grated rind and juice of $\frac{1}{2}$ lemon
1 egg yolk
75 ml (5 tbsp) mayonnaise
45 ml (3 level tbsp) grated
    Parmesan cheese
225–350 g (8–12 oz) frozen
    broccoli spears or florets of
    fresh broccoli

1

Put the chicken, rosemary sprigs, salt, pepper and 120 ml (8 tbsp) water into a large roasting bag and place in a large shallow dish.

2

Loosely close the roasting bag with a large elastic band, leaving a big opening. The bag need not be upright but must not touch the walls or top of the oven, which could tip it over.

3

Turn the bag over so that the chicken is breast side down and microwave on HIGH for 10 minutes, giving the dish a quarter-turn four times during cooking.

4

Using oven gloves carefully turn the bag over so that the chicken is breast-side up. Reduce the power and microwave on LOW for 25 minutes or until the chicken is cooked. Give the dish a quarter-turn four times during cooking.

5

Leave to stand for 10 minutes, then take the chicken carefully out of the bag. Strain the cooking liquid into a jug and skim the fat away from the surface.

6

Put the butter in a medium bowl and microwave on HIGH for 45 seconds. Stir in the flour and blend in the milk and 150 ml ($\frac{1}{4}$ pint) of the reserved cooking liquid. Beat in the lemon rind, juice, egg yolk, mayonnaise and the cheese. Microwave on HIGH, whisking vigorously every 30 seconds, for 3 minutes or until the sauce thickens.

7

Put the broccoli into the roasting bag with 45 ml (3 tbsp) water and microwave on HIGH for 4 minutes. Drain. Remove the bones and skin from the chicken and arrange the chicken pieces in the cooking dish.

8

Cover with the broccoli and pour the sauce over the top. Cover with the lid or cling film and microwave on HIGH for 4 minutes or until thoroughly hot. Give the dish an occasional turn and stir around the edges of the sauce during reheating.

Serves 4–6.

Crumbed Chicken

1 chicken quarter, skinned
salt and freshly ground pepper
plain flour
beaten egg
40 g (1$\frac{1}{2}$ oz) golden
    breadcrumbs
15 ml (1 tbsp) vegetable oil

1

Season the chicken with salt and pepper and coat with flour, shaking off the surplus.

2

Dip the floured chicken joint in the beaten egg, then coat with the breadcrumbs.

3

Put the oil in a shallow dish and microwave on HIGH for 30 seconds.

4

Put the chicken in the dish fleshy side down, cover with greaseproof paper and microwave on HIGH for 3 minutes.

5

Turn the chicken over, cover with the greaseproof paper and microwave on HIGH for 3 minutes or until cooked. The chicken should be tender when tested, with no pink near the bone.

Serves 1.

Marinated Chicken in Teriyaki Sauce

60 ml (4 tbsp) soy sauce
60 ml (4 tbsp) clear honey
90 ml (6 tbsp) dry sherry
1.25 ml ($\frac{1}{4}$ level tsp) ground ginger
1 small garlic clove, skinned and crushed
1.25 ml ($\frac{1}{4}$ level tsp) salt
1.6-kg ($3\frac{1}{2}$-lb) oven-ready chicken
30 ml (2 level tbsp) cornflour

1

Put the soy sauce, honey, sherry, ginger, garlic and salt in a large roasting bag and microwave on HIGH, unsealed and upright, for 1 minute or until the honey melts.

2

Using oven gloves, shake the bag gently to combine the ingredients.

3

Put the chicken in the bag and seal securely. Stand the bag in a shallow dish, turn the bag over once to coat the chicken with the marinade, then leave for 2 hours, turning the bag and the chicken occasionally to cover well.

4

Turn the roasting bag so that the chicken is breast side up and remove the seal. Replace with a large elastic band, leaving a big gap so that steam can escape. Microwave on HIGH for 20 minutes or until the chicken is cooked. Give the dish a half-turn halfway through cooking.

5

Leave to stand for 10 minutes, then test again to make sure that the chicken is completely cooked. A thermometer or sharp knife can be plunged through the roasting bag to do this.

6

Slit the bag down the centre and place the chicken in a warm serving dish.

7

Carefully remove the roasting bag, allowing the juices to run into the cooking dish. Remove surplus fat.

8

Mix the cornflour with 15 ml (1 tbsp) cold water. Stir into the juices in the dish. Microwave on HIGH for 2 minutes or until the sauce thickens, stirring vigorously once or twice. Pour the sauce over the chicken and serve hot.

Serves 4–6.

Chicken and Mushroom Casserole

2 medium onions, skinned and finely chopped
1 garlic clove, skinned and crushed
15 ml (1 tbsp) vegetable oil
25 g (1 oz) plain flour
1.6-kg ($3\frac{1}{2}$-lb) oven-ready chicken, skinned and cut into 8 or 12 pieces
300 ml ($\frac{1}{2}$ pint) red wine
225-g (8-oz) can tomatoes
175 g (6 oz) mushrooms, sliced
15 ml (1 tbsp) chopped fresh parsley
2 bay leaves
salt and freshly ground pepper

1

Put the onions, garlic and oil into a deep casserole and microwave on HIGH for 8 minutes or until the onions start to brown. Stir once or twice during cooking.

2

Stir in the flour then add the chicken and all the remaining ingredients.

3

Cover with a lid and microwave on HIGH for 25 minutes, repositioning the chicken twice during cooking.

4

Reduce power and microwave on LOW for 15 minutes or until the chicken is cooked. Reposition once during this cooking period. Leave to stand, covered, for 10 minutes before serving.

Serves 4–6.

Note It may be necessary to add more liquid halfway through the cooking period and it is a good idea to stir round the edges of the sauce when repositioning the chicken. At the end of the cooking time, if the sauce is too thin, thicken with 5 ml (1 level tsp) cornflour blended with 30 ml (2 tbsp) cold water, return the casserole to the microwave oven uncovered and microwave on HIGH until boiling.

Chicken in Barbecue Sauce

2-kg (4½-lb) oven-ready chicken

For the stuffing
knob of butter
1 small onion, skinned and
    finely chopped
½ celery stalk, trimmed and
    finely chopped
50 g (2 oz) sausagemeat
25 g (1 oz) cooking apple,
    peeled and chopped
25 g (1 oz) fresh breadcrumbs
5 ml (1 tsp) chopped fresh
    parsley
salt and freshly ground pepper
little beaten egg

For the sauce
75 ml (5 tbsp) red wine
60 ml (4 tbsp) chicken stock or
    water
5 ml (1 tsp) soy sauce
30 ml (2 tbsp) red wine vinegar
5 ml (1 tsp) Worcestershire
    sauce
15 ml (1 level tbsp) tomato
    purée
5 ml (1 level tsp) French
    mustard
15 ml (1 level tbsp) demerara
    sugar
5 ml (1 level tsp) cornflour

1

To make the stuffing, put the butter, onion and celery in a large bowl, cover and microwave on HIGH for 3 minutes or until the onions are soft but not coloured. Stir once during cooking.

2

Add the sausagemeat and cooking apple to the onion mixture, stir well, cover and microwave on HIGH for 2 minutes or until the apple is soft, and the sausagemeat partly cooked.

3

Mix in the breadcrumbs, parsley, salt, pepper and bind with the beaten egg.

4

Fill the neck of the chicken with the stuffing and tuck the wings underneath. Put the chicken breast side down in a shallow dish.

5

To make the sauce, combine all the ingredients in a large jug. Mix thoroughly, making sure that the cornflour does not stick on the bottom of the jug. Microwave on HIGH for 30 seconds, then stir and microwave on HIGH for 1 minute or until the sauce thickens slightly. Beat thoroughly.

6

Pour the sauce over the chicken, cover with a lid or greaseproof paper and microwave on HIGH for 15 minutes, giving the dish a quarter-turn every 3–4 minutes.

7

Turn the chicken over carefully and microwave on HIGH for 15 minutes, basting once during cooking. Give the dish a half-turn and reduce the setting, then microwave on LOW for 25 minutes or until the chicken is cooked.

8

Test, then tent with foil and leave for 10–15 minutes before serving.

9

Lift the chicken on to a serving dish and spoon away any surplus fat from the sauce. Reheat the sauce either in the cooking dish or in a jug, microwaving on HIGH for 1–2 minutes.

Serves 6–8.

Curried Chicken

2 large onions, skinned and
    finely chopped
60 ml (4 tbsp) vegetable oil
10 ml (2 level tsp) cumin
1.25 ml (¼ level tsp) cinnamon
10 ml (2 level tsp) cardamom
1.25 ml (¼ level tsp) ground
    bayleaves
freshly ground black pepper
1.25 ml (¼ level tsp) ginger
1 garlic clove, crushed
397-g (14-oz) can tomatoes
1.6-kg (3½-lb) oven-ready chicken,
    skinned and cut into 8 pieces
5 ml (1 level tsp) salt

1

To make the curry sauce, combine the onion, oil, spices and garlic in a large, deep casserole. Microwave on HIGH for 10 minutes or until the onion is just browning. Stir frequently during cooking.

2

Add the tomatoes and their juice, the chicken pieces and the salt.

3

Cover with the lid and microwave on HIGH for 25 minutes or until the chicken is tender. Stir and reposition the chicken at least twice during cooking.

4

Leave to stand, covered, for 10 minutes before serving.

Serves 4–6.

Note The flavour of curry improves if the dish is cooled quickly, refrigerated for 24 hours and reheated thoroughly before serving.

Italian Chicken

15 ml (1 tbsp) olive oil
15 g (½ oz) butter or block
    margarine
4 chicken joints, wiped
½ green pepper, seeded and
    sliced
½ red pepper, seeded and sliced
227-g (8-oz) can tomatoes
1 garlic clove, skinned and
    crushed
5 ml (1 level tsp) dried basil
90 ml (6 tbsp) red wine
salt and freshly ground pepper
15 ml (1 level tbsp) cornflour

1

Preheat the browning dish to
maximum, according to the
manufacturer's instructions,
adding the oil and butter for the
last 15 seconds.

2

Without removing the dish from
the oven, quickly place the chicken
pieces, skin side down, in the hot
butter mixture. Microwave on
HIGH for 3 minutes, then turn the
pieces over.

3

Stir in the peppers, tomatoes with
their juice, garlic, basil and red
wine. Cover with the lid and
continue to cook on HIGH for 12
minutes, repositioning the chicken
twice.

4

Reduce the setting to LOW and
cook for a further 10 minutes or
until the chicken is tender.

5

Remove the pieces to a warmed
serving dish. Blend the cornflour
to a paste with a little cold water
and stir into the juices. Microwave
on HIGH for 5 minutes, stirring
once. Pour over the chicken.

Serves 4.

Chicken and Mushroom Scallops

100 g (4 oz) mushrooms, finely
    sliced
30 ml (2 level tbsp) canned
    sweetcorn
25 g (1 oz) butter or block
    margarine
25 g (1 oz) plain flour
150 ml (¼ pint) chicken stock
45 ml (3 tbsp) double cream,
    whipped
225 g (8 oz) cooked chicken,
    finely chopped
salt and freshly ground pepper
450 g (1 lb) potato, cooked and
    mashed

1

Put the mushrooms and sweetcorn
on a plate or in a dish, cover and
microwave on HIGH for 3 minutes
or until the mushrooms are soft.

2

Put the butter in a medium bowl
and microwave on HIGH for 45
seconds or until melted. Stir in the
flour and gradually beat in the
stock.

3

Microwave on HIGH for 2–3
minutes, whisking after the first
minute then frequently until the
sauce is very thick.

4

Stir in the cream then mix in the
chicken, mushrooms and
sweetcorn, adding their cooking
liquid. Season to taste with salt and
pepper.

5

Divide the mixture between 4
scallop shells and pipe a decorative
border of mashed potato around
the edges. Reheat in the
microwave oven on HIGH for
about 5 minutes and brown under
the grill if you wish.

Serves 4 as a starter.

Chicken à la King

50 g (2 oz) butter or block
    margarine
¼ green pepper, seeded and
    finely chopped
¼ red pepper, seeded and finely
    chopped
40 g (1½ oz) plain flour
450 ml (¾ pint) milk
½ chicken stock cube, crumbled
10 ml (2 tsp) sherry
100 g (4 oz) button mushrooms,
    wiped and thinly sliced
salt and freshly ground pepper
225–350 g (8–12 oz) cooked
    chicken, cut in small pieces
30 ml (2 tbsp) double cream

1

Put the butter in a casserole and
microwave on HIGH for 1 minute
or until melted.

2

Stir in the green and red pepper.
Cover and microwave on HIGH for
2 minutes, stirring once during
cooking.

3

Stir in the flour, milk, crumbled
stock cube and sherry. Add the
mushrooms, three-quarters cover
with cling film and microwave on
HIGH for 4 minutes or until the
mushrooms are soft. Stir
occasionally during cooking.

4

Season to taste with pepper,
adding salt only if necessary. Stir in
the chicken and the cream. Three-
quarters cover and microwave on
HIGH for 5 minutes or until the
chicken is hot. Stir two or three
times through the gap in the cling
film during cooking, making sure
to draw any coagulating sauce away
from the sides and into the
mixture. Serve with boiled rice or
green tagliatelle.

Serves 4.

Walnut and Yogurt Chicken

1.4-kg (3-lb) oven-ready
    chicken, cut into 8 pieces, or
    4 chicken joints, halved
25 g (1 oz) wholemeal flour
15 g ($\frac{1}{2}$ oz) butter or block
    margarine
2.5 ml ($\frac{1}{2}$ level tsp) salt
1.25 ml ($\frac{1}{4}$ level tsp) pepper
150 ml ($\frac{1}{4}$ pint) natural yogurt
25 g (1 oz) shelled walnuts,
    finely chopped
10 ml (2 level tsp) paprika
pinch of garlic salt
15 ml (1 level tbsp) sesame
    seeds
watercress to garnish

1

Dip the chicken pieces in the flour and shake off the surplus.

2

Put the butter, salt and pepper in a large shallow dish and microwave on HIGH for 45 seconds or until the butter is melted. Stir to mix the seasoning evenly.

3

Put the chicken pieces into the melted butter and turn them over so that they are lightly coated.

4

Cover with greaseproof paper and microwave on HIGH for 20 minutes or until cooked. Reposition the chicken twice during cooking.

5

Combine the yogurt, walnuts, paprika, garlic salt and sesame seeds. Spoon over the chicken and microwave on LOW without covering, for 5 minutes or until hot. Give the dish a quarter-turn every minute during reheating.

6

Garnish with watercress and serve at once.

Serves 4.

Stuffed Chicken Thighs or Drumsticks

25 g (1 oz) dry stuffing mix
8 chicken thighs or drumsticks,
    skinned and boned
25 g (1 oz) butter or margarine,
    softened
5 ml (1 level tsp) paprika
2.5 ml ($\frac{1}{2}$ level tsp) salt
1.25 ml ($\frac{1}{4}$ level tsp) pepper

1

Reconstitute the stuffing according to the directions on the packet.

2

Divide the stuffing into equal portions and press onto each chicken piece. Press edges together and secure with cocktail sticks.

3

Mix together the fat, paprika, salt and pepper. Rub the chicken with the softened paprika butter and place the pieces, seam side down, in a shallow dish. Cover lightly with greaseproof paper and microwave on HIGH for 15 minutes or until cooked. Reposition the chicken pieces two or three times during cooking.

Serves 4.

Note Be sure to test for cooking on both sides of the poultry. A thermometer inserted into the stuffing may not give a true reading.

'Stir-fried' Turkey

225 g (8 oz) turkey fillet
15 ml (1 tbsp) vegetable oil
30 ml (2 tbsp) soy sauce
30 ml (2 tbsp) dry sherry
2.5 ml ($\frac{1}{2}$ level tsp) ground
    ginger
$\frac{1}{2}$ green pepper, seeded and
    sliced
4 spring onions, skinned and
    chopped
125 g (4 oz) beansprouts

1

Cut the turkey fillet into strips and put in a bowl. Add the oil, soy sauce and sherry and stir. Leave to marinate for about 30 minutes.

2

Preheat a browning dish to maximum according to the manufacturer's instructions. Stir in the turkey strips, then add the marinade and ginger and stir quickly to seal the meat. Add the pepper and onions and microwave on HIGH for 2 minutes.

3

Stir in the beansprouts and microwave on HIGH for a further 2 minutes. Serve at once with rice and soy sauce.

Serves 2.

Note This dish can also be made without a browning dish. Allow about 1–2 minutes extra cooking time and test the turkey for tenderness.

Duck à l'Orange

4 duck joints (each weighing
    about 400 g (14 oz))
vegetable oil

For the sauce
3 large oranges
about 75 ml (3 fl oz) red wine
15 ml (1 level tbsp) cornflour
30 ml (2 tbsp) orange
    marmalade
salt and freshly ground pepper

1

Place the duck skin side up on a
roasting rack in a large shallow
dish. For best results overlap the
legs and thicker parts of the joints.

2

Brush the skin lightly all over with
the vegetable oil. Cover with
greaseproof paper and microwave
on HIGH for 10 minutes, giving the
dish a quarter-turn three times
during cooking.

3

Re-arrange the duck pieces so that
the outer sides are in the middle,
then reduce the setting and
microwave on LOW for 30
minutes, repositioning the duck
pieces and giving the dish a quarter
turn three times during cooking.

4

Meanwhile, start to prepare the
sauce. Grate the rind from the
oranges, squeeze the juice from 2
of them and pour into a measuring
jug. Remove the peel and pith from
the other orange, cut into
segments and reserve for garnish.

5

Remove the duck pieces to a
flameproof serving dish, crisp
under a hot grill, and keep warm.

6

Remove the roasting rack. Tilt the
dish and pour away all but 15 ml
(1 tbsp) duck fat. Put this into a
.85 litre (1½-pint) bowl. Stir the
remaining duck juices into the jug
with the orange juice and make up
to 300 ml (½ pint) with red wine.

7

Stir the cornflour into the fat in
the bowl, add the orange juice and
wine mixture and marmalade and
microwave on HIGH for 5 minutes,
stirring occasionally. Season with
salt and pepper. Arrange the duck
on a hot serving dish, pour the
sauce over the top and garnish
with the orange segments.

Serves 4.

Note Duck joints must be
microwaved on a roasting rack
because of the large amount of fat
that comes from them. A 1.2-kg
(2¾-lb) duck can produce more
than 150 ml (¼ pint) fat.
   To separate the juices from the
fat most efficiently pour both into a
freezer or roasting bag. Hold the
bag so one corner is filled, then,
having a jug and a large bowl at the
ready, snip the tip off the filled
corner. Allow the juices which will
be in the bottom of the bag to run
into the jug. Quickly grasp the
open end before any fat escapes
and put the whole bag with the fat
into the bowl.

Pheasant in White Wine

1 brace oven-ready pheasants,
    cut in half along backbone
salt and freshly ground pepper
1 medium onion, skinned and
    finely sliced
1 orange, peeled and
    segmented, reserving the
    peel
300 ml (½ pint) dry white wine
30 ml (2 tbsp) brandy
30 ml (2 level tbsp) cornflour

1

Season pheasant halves with salt
and pepper and place skin side
down in a casserole. Arrange
thicker parts towards outside of
dish.

2

Cover with the onion slices and
orange segments. Gradually stir
the wine and brandy into the
cornflour so that it is evenly
blended, then pour over the
pheasants.

3

Cover with a lid and microwave on
HIGH for 10 minutes. Turn and
reposition the pheasant portions.

4

Meanwhile, pare the pith away
from the reserved orange peel and
cut the rind into matchstick strips.
Put these strips into a large jug,
cover with cold water and
microwave on HIGH for 1 minute
or until boiling. Drain, then repeat
and drain again.

5

Add the orange strips to the
casserole and microwave on HIGH
for 10 minutes or until the
pheasants are cooked. Give the
dish a quarter-turn four times
during cooking.

Serves 4.

Mustard Rabbit Casserole

1 rabbit, about 1 kg (2½ lb), jointed
30 ml (2 level tbsp) plain flour
salt and freshly ground pepper
2 medium onions, skinned and finely sliced
2 large carrots, peeled and sliced
30–45 ml (2–3 level tbsp) French mustard
300 ml (½ pint) chicken stock
150 ml (¼ pint) dry cider
5 ml (1 level tsp) dried thyme

1

Wash the rabbit joints well and pat dry with absorbent kitchen paper. Coat in the flour seasoned with salt and pepper.

2

Put the joints, onions and carrots in a 3-litre (6-pint) casserole. Stir the mustard into the stock and cider and pour over the rabbit. Sprinkle over the thyme. Cover the casserole.

3

Microwave on HIGH for 15 minutes, turning and repositioning the rabbit twice. Reduce the setting to MEDIUM and cook for a further 35 minutes or until the rabbit is tender. Reposition the rabbit joints twice during the cooking time. Serve with Red cabbage and apple casserole (see page 83).

Serves 4.

Note If time permits place the rabbit joints, onions, carrots, thyme, mustard, stock and cider in the casserole and marinate overnight. Blend the flour to a paste with a little water and add before cooking.

Chicken Liver and Port Pâté

450 g (1 lb) chicken livers
75 ml (5 tbsp) dry white wine
350 g (12 oz) butter
2.5 ml (½ level tsp) salt
1.25 ml (¼ level tsp) freshly ground black pepper
2.5 ml (½ level tsp) ground mixed spice
60 ml (4 tbsp) port
cherries to garnish

1

Rinse the chicken livers in cold water and cut in half to prevent popping.

2

Put the wine in a medium bowl and microwave on HIGH for 1½ minutes or until fully boiling.

3

Stir in the chicken livers and three-quarters cover with cling film. Microwave on HIGH, stirring occasionally, for 6 minutes or until the livers are just cooked but still pinky brown inside.

4

Transfer the livers to a blender or food processor using a slotted spoon and add 30 ml (2 tbsp) of the cooking liquor (save the remaining liquor for use in stocks and gravies).

5

Add 275 g (10 oz) of the butter, salt, pepper, mixed spice and the port and blend until smooth. Spoon into a 600-ml (1-pint) pâté dish. Chill until firm.

6

Put the remaining butter in a small dish and cover with greaseproof paper. Microwave on HIGH for 45 seconds or until melted.

7

Garnish the pâté with cherries. Being careful to exclude any sediment, strain the melted butter evenly over the top of the pâté. Chill until the butter is set.

Serves 8–12.

Note The pâté can be spooned into 8 individual ramekins if preferred.

Turkey and Ham Terrine

**225 g (8 oz) skinned cooked
   turkey**
225 g (8 oz) cooked ham
1 onion, skinned and minced
10 ml (2 tsp) chopped fresh sage
salt and freshly ground pepper
1 chicken stock cube, crumbled
30 ml (2 level tbsp) gelatine
**300 ml ($\frac{1}{2}$ pint) double cream,
   whipped**

For the topping
7.5 ml (1$\frac{1}{2}$ level tsp) gelatine
200 ml (7 fl oz) mayonnaise
**6–8 green olives, pitted and
   sliced**

1

Mince or finely chop the cooked turkey and cooked ham together. Thoroughly mix the onion and herbs into the meat mixture and season to taste with salt and pepper.

2

Heat 600 ml (1 pint) water either in the kettle or in a jug in the microwave oven on HIGH. When the water is very hot but not boiling, add the crumbled chicken stock cube, stir thoroughly then sprinkle the gelatine over the surface. Stir until dissolved. Leave to cool.

3

Pour the cooled stock into the turkey mixture and when it begins to thicken, fold in the whipped cream.

4

Spoon into a 28-cm (11-inch) loaf-shaped dish. Leave to set in the refrigerator.

5

Dip the base of the dish into hot water for a few seconds to release the terrine and turn it out on to a wire rack over a tray.

6

Put 75 ml (5 tbsp) water in a 600 ml (1 pint) jug and microwave on HIGH for 45 seconds or until nearly boiling. Remove from the microwave oven and sprinkle on the 7.5 ml (1$\frac{1}{2}$ level tsp) gelatine. Stir until dissolved. Leave to cool but not thicken.

7

Stir the cooled gelatine into the mayonnaise. Pour evenly over the terrine, allowing the surplus to drain into the tray.

8

Garnish with a line of green olives. Transfer to a serving dish and refrigerate until the mayonnaise coating is set.

Serves 12.

Chicken with Mushrooms and Almonds

50 g (2 oz) flaked almonds
**4 chicken breasts, weighing
   225 g (8 oz) each, skinned and
   boned**
25 g (1 oz) butter
**100 g (4 oz) mushrooms, wiped
   and sliced**
150 ml ($\frac{1}{4}$ pint) single cream
salt and freshly ground pepper

1

Spread the almonds in one layer on a pie plate and microwave on HIGH for 5 minutes or until golden brown. Move the almonds around on the plate twice during the cooking time to prevent them burning in the centre. Leave to cool.

2

Place the chicken breasts between sheets of greaseproof paper or foil and beat flat.

3

Put the butter in a shallow dish large enough to hold the chicken breasts in a single layer and microwave on HIGH for 45 seconds until melted.

4

Add the chicken breasts and turn over to coat in the butter. Cover with cling film and microwave on HIGH for 12 minutes or until tender.

5

Push the chicken to one side of the dish, add the mushrooms and stir to coat in the juices. Recover and microwave on HIGH for 3 minutes until the mushrooms are cooked. Add the cream, seasoning and the almonds and stir well. Cover and microwave on HIGH for 2 minutes until sauce is hot but not bubbling.

Serves 4.

CHAPTER SIX

Vegetables

Microwaved vegetables have a good texture and colour, are full of taste and retain more vitamins than when they are cooked conventionally. Vegetables also respond well to reheating in the microwave oven.

Pierce or score the skins of shiny vegetables such as aubergines, peppers or tomatoes and thoroughly prick potatoes when they are to be cooked in their jackets. Evenly sliced or diced vegetables will cook more uniformly than whole or mis-shapen pieces. For example, sliced carrots will cook more quickly and successfully than whole carrots. When vegetables are cooked whole, arrange the thinner parts towards the centre of the dish or overlap the thick and thin pieces to make an even layer. Vegetables cooked in water should be stirred or repositioned several times during cooking.

Never sprinkle salt directly on to raw vegetables before cooking. Salt distorts the microwave patterns and causes the vegetables to dry up. If appropriate, stir salt into the water before adding the vegetables.

Most fresh vegetables can be cooked on HIGH. High water content vegetables such as courgettes, marrow, mushrooms, spinach and tomatoes require no added liquid. Small podded vegetables such as peas, beans and corn kernels, require a small amount of water. Root vegetables require a larger amount of water and cooking times depend upon the age of the vegetable. Cauliflower is one of the most difficult vegetables to cook by microwave, since the stalk is much tougher than the florets. For best results break the cauliflower into separate florets and discard the tough stalk. However if cauliflower is required for soups or purées, it is quite in order to microwave it whole.

Fresh vegetables can be cooked very successfully in roasting bags, which must be only loosely sealed with a non-metallic fastening. Take care not to scald yourself when removing the vegetables from the roasting bag.

Blanching vegetables for the freezer

Use the microwave oven for blanching prior to freezing. A maximum of 450 g (1 lb) of prepared vegetables can be blanched at one time in 45–60 ml (4–5 tbsp) water without added salt. Microwave on HIGH for 2 minutes, then stir and microwave on HIGH for 1–2 more minutes or until the vegetable pieces are all equally hot. Drain and plunge vegetables into ice-cold water, then drain and pack. Cauliflower and brussel sprouts need extra attention when stirring to make sure that they are thoroughly heated through. Otherwise they will become musty during freezer storage.

Frozen vegetables

All frozen vegetables may be cooked on a HIGH setting. Single portions of small vegetables such as peas, beans or corn kernels can be cooked without added water, as can spinach and mushrooms, which contain sufficient water themselves. Larger amounts should be cooked in a few tablespoons of salted water. The exception is corn on the cob which requires only butter or margarine.

Canned vegetables

Canned vegetables require reheating only. Drain and reheat on HIGH. Cover, particularly when whole vegetables are mixed in a sauce (eg beans). General cooking instructions are given in the chart (overleaf) but cooking times vary depending upon the freshness, type, size, shape, dish and starting temperature of the canned vegetables.

Drying herbs

If you have no freezer or freezer compartment and you have bought or grown more herbs than you can use, the remainder can easily be dried in a microwave oven. Herbs dried this way keep their colour and flavour well.

Be sure to stir and mix frequently during drying—every 20 seconds during the first minute and every 5–10 seconds thereafter—to prevent burning.

For specific information on drying herbs, see page 78.

Cooking Fresh Vegetables

All times are given as a guide only, since variations in size and quality will affect cooking times. Try to choose even-sized vegetables. Unless otherwise stated cook covered in 75–90 ml (5–6 tbsp) salted water. Leave to stand for 3 minutes before draining off the water.

Vegetables	Preparation	Quantity	Approximate time on HIGH	Further instructions
Artichokes, globe	Wash and drain. Cut off stalk at base. Slice off upper tip and trim tips of leaves.	1 2 3	5–6 minutes 7–8 minutes 11–12 minutes	Place upright in covered dish.
Asparagus	Remove white woody part to give even length spears.	350 g (12 oz)	5–7 minutes	Place stalks towards outside of dish. Cooking time may vary with thickness and age.
Aubergines	Wash, slice, sprinkle with salt and leave for 30 minutes. Rinse and pat dry.	450 g (1 lb) (2 medium)	8–10 minutes	Stir or shake after 4 minutes.
Beans, broad	Shell.	450 g (1 lb)	6–8 minutes	Stir or shake after 3 minutes and test after 5 minutes.
Beans, green	String and slice or leave whole.	450 g (1 lb)	12–16 minutes	Stir or shake during cooking period. Time will vary with age and size.
Beetroot, medium, whole	Wash and pierce skin with fork.	4 medium	14–16 minutes	Re-arrange during cooking. Skin and remove stalks after cooking.
Broccoli	Wash, remove outer leaves and tough portion of stalk. Slit stem ends to speed up cooking.	450 g (1 lb)	10–12 minutes	Re-arrange during cooking.
Brussel sprouts	Discard outside wilted leaves. Trim and cut a cross in stalk end.	225 g (8 oz) 450 g (1 lb)	4–6 minutes 7–10 minutes	Stir or shake during cooking.
Cabbage, quartered shredded	Discard damaged and wilted leaves. Trim stalk.	450 g (1 lb) 450 g (1 lb)	10–12 minutes 9–11 minutes	Stir or shake during cooking.
Carrots	Scrape, or peel and slice.	225 g (8 oz) 450 g (1 lb)	7–8 minutes 10–12 minutes	Stir or shake during cooking.
Cauliflower	Whole. Trim, break into florets.	 225 g (8 oz) 450 g (1 lb)	12–16 minutes 7–8 minutes 10–12 minutes	Stir or shake during cooking. Do not sprinkle salt directly on to the vegetable.
Celery	Separate sticks and wash. Slice or cut into strips.	450 g (1 lb)	7–10 minutes	Stir or shake during cooking.
Corn-on-the-cob	Remove husk, wash and trim. Wrap individually in greased greaseproof paper. Do not add water.	2	6–8 minutes	Turn over after 3 minutes.
Courgettes	Wash, dry and slice. Do not peel. Do not add more than 30 ml (2 tbsp) water.	450 g (1 lb)	8–12 minutes	Stir or shake gently twice during cooking. Stand for 2 minutes before draining.

Vegetables	Preparation	Quantity	Approximate time on HIGH	Further instructions
Leeks	Wash very thoroughly, trim and slice.	450 g (1 lb)	10–12 minutes	Stir or shake during cooking.
Mushrooms	Trim stalks. Wipe. Do not add water. Add 25 g (1 oz) butter and a squeeze of lemon juice.	225 g (8 oz)	2–3 minutes	Time will depend on type, and whether whole or sliced. Stir or shake gently during cooking.
Onions	Peel, and slice or leave whole. Add only 60 ml (4 tbsp) water to whole onions.	225 g (8 oz) sliced 175 g (6 oz) whole	4–6 minutes 10–12 minutes	Stir or shake sliced onions and re-arrange whole onions during cooking.
Parsnips	Peel, remove hard core and cut into quarters or halves, depending on size and shape. Place thinner parts towards centre. Add knob of butter and 15 ml (1 tbsp) lemon juice with 150 ml ($\frac{1}{4}$ pint) water.	450 g (1 lb)	10–16 minutes	Turn dish during cooking and re-arrange.
Peas	Shell.	450 g (1 lb)	9–11 minutes	Time will vary with the age of the peas. Stir or shake during cooking.
Potatoes Baked, jacket	Wash and prick skin with fork. Place on absorbent kitchen paper or napkin. When cooking more than 2 at a time, arrange in a circle.	1 ×175 g (6 oz) potato 2 ×175 g (6 oz) potatoes 4 ×175 g (6 oz) potatoes	4 minutes 6–8 minutes 12–14 minutes	Turn over half-way through cooking period.
Boiled (old)	Wash and peel. Cut into 40 g (1½ oz) pieces. Add 150 ml ($\frac{1}{4}$ pint) water.	450 g (1 lb)	7–10 minutes	Stir or shake during cooking period.
Boiled (new)	Wash and scrub.	450 g (1 lb)	6–8 minutes	Do not overcook or new potatoes become spongy.
Sweet	Wash and prick skin with fork. Place on absorbent kitchen paper. Use even sized potatoes.	450 g (1 lb)	5 minutes	Turn over halfway through cooking period.
Spinach	Wash, remove wilted leaves and any tough stems. Do not add water. Best cooked in roasting bag.	450 g (1 lb)	6–7 minutes 5–5½ minutes	Turn dish during cooking.
Swede/turnip	Peel and dice.	450 g (1 lb)	10–15 minutes	Time will vary with age and quality. Stir or shake during cooking. Mash after standing.

Dried Herbs

Fresh herbs can be dried in the microwave oven and you will find the colour and the bouquet are superb. There is a substantial loss of weight when drying herbs so you may like to start off with quite a large quantity. For example 200 g (7 oz) parsley will weigh about 160 g (5¾ oz) after the stalks are removed and the weight will be only 15 g (½ oz) after drying. Store your dried herbs in small screw top jars in a cool, dark cupboard.

Dried Parsley
Chop the parsley finely before drying. Put 50 g (2 oz) chopped fresh parsley on a piece of absorbent kitchen paper, place in the microwave oven and microwave on HIGH for 5 minutes or until the parsley and the paper are dry. Stir the parsley several times during cooking (you will find this easier to do with your fingers than with a spoon or fork, as this does not disturb the paper).

Dried Rosemary
Remove the leaves from the stalk before drying. Put 25 g (1 oz) rosemary leaves on a piece of absorbent kitchen paper and microwave on HIGH for 2–2½ minutes or until the leaves are dry. Stir occasionally during cooking. When the leaves are dry, chop in a food processor or blender.

Dried Basil
Place 25 g (1 oz) basil leaves on a piece of absorbent kitchen paper and microwave on HIGH for 2½ minutes, stirring occasionally during drying until the leaves are brittle. Do not overcook as basil leaves tend to burn. When the leaves are dry, chop in a food processor or blender.

Fresh Coriander
Put the coriander sprigs on a piece of absorbent kitchen paper and microwave on HIGH for 1½ minutes or until dry. Remove the stalks and crush the dried leaves between folded kitchen paper.

Okra and Tomato Casserole

225 g (8 oz) okra
397-g (14-oz) can tomatoes
salt and freshly ground pepper
1 beef stock cube, crumbled
3 sprigs fresh thyme

1

Wash, top and tail the okra and put in a deep casserole with the tomatoes and their juice.

2

Season with salt and pepper and stir in the stock cube and the sprigs of thyme.

3

Three-quarters cover with cling film and microwave on HIGH for 12 minutes or until the okra is tender. Stir once or twice during cooking. Remove the sprigs of thyme just before serving.

Serves 4.

Aubergine and Butter Bean Casserole

450 g (1 lb) aubergine
salt and freshly ground pepper
1 medium onion, skinned and finely chopped
50 g (2 oz) butter or block margarine
15 ml (1 level tbsp) cornflour
300 ml (½ pint) tomato juice
½ beef stock cube, crumbled
10 ml (2 tsp) chopped fresh parsley
213-g (7½-oz) can butter beans, drained

1

Cut off the tops and slice the aubergines into 1-cm (½-inch) slices, then quarter each slice. Sprinkle liberally with salt and leave for 30 minutes. Rinse thoroughly and pat dry with absorbent kitchen paper.

2

Put the onion and butter in a 23-cm (9-inch) round shallow dish and microwave on HIGH for 6 minutes or until the onion begins to brown.

3

Stir in the aubergine and three-quarters cover with cling film. Microwave on HIGH for 6 minutes, stirring twice during cooking.

4

Blend the cornflour with the tomato juice and stir in the stock cube and parsley (the stock cube will not dissolve at this stage). Pour into the aubergine mixture and add the butter beans.

5

Mix the ingredients well together. Then microwave on HIGH for 7 minutes or until the sauce thickens and the aubergine is soft. Stir twice during cooking. Season to taste.

Serves 3 as a supper dish; 4 as a vegetable accompaniment.

Creamed Mushrooms and Prawns

450 g (1 lb) button mushrooms, wiped
40 g (1½ oz) butter or block margarine
30 ml (2 level tbsp) plain flour
salt and freshly ground pepper
2.5–5 ml (½–1 level tsp) dried rosemary, well crushed
150 ml (¼ pint) double cream
100 g (4 oz) cooked peeled prawns, thawed and well drained
15 ml (1 tbsp) lemon Juice
whole prawns for garnish

1

Cut the mushroom stalks level with the caps. Cut larger mushrooms into quarters.

2

Put the butter in a 2.8-litre (5-pint) ovenproof glass mixing bowl and microwave on HIGH for 45 seconds or until melted.

3

Add the mushrooms and stir well so that they are coated with the butter. Without covering, microwave on HIGH for 6 minutes or until the mushrooms are partially cooked and some liquid gathers in the bottom of the bowl. Stir occasionally during cooking.

4

Stir in the flour, then add salt, pepper and herbs to taste. Stir in the cream. Microwave on HIGH for 3 minutes or until the sauce is boiling rapidly, stirring once.

5

Taste the sauce and adjust the seasoning, then stir in the prawns. Microwave on HIGH for 2 minutes or until the prawns are heated through. Stir in the lemon juice. Serve hot in individual dishes; garnish with prawns.

Serves 6 as a starter.

Horsham Mushrooms

16 open flat mushrooms 5–6 cm (2–2½ inches) diameter
2 firm tomatoes
8 small bay leaves
salt and freshly ground pepper
15 g (½ oz) butter or block margarine

For the sauce
10 ml (2 level tsp) plain flour
15 g (½ oz) butter or margarine, softened
60 ml (4 tbsp) single cream
10 ml (2 tsp) sherry
15–30 ml (1–2 tbsp) milk, if needed

1

Cut the stalks level with the mushroom caps. (Discard the stalks or reserve for use in other dishes.) Remove a thin sliver from the top and bottom of the tomatoes and cut each tomato into 4 slices.

2

Arrange half the mushroom caps stalk-side up in a large shallow dish. Cover each cap with a tomato slice and a bay leaf leaving the stalk of the bay leaf protruding. Season with salt and pepper. Top with the remaining mushroom caps, stalk-side down, and dot with butter.

3

Cover and microwave on HIGH for 6 minutes or until the mushrooms are just tender. Reposition the mushrooms and give the dish a half-turn once during cooking.

4

Remove the mushroom sandwiches carefully with a slotted spoon and arrange on a warm dish; carefully remove the bay leaves. Cover and keep warm while making the cream sauce.

5

To complete the sauce, blend the flour and butter together to a soft paste and add to the juices remaining in the cooking dish. Stir thoroughly. Microwave on HIGH for 1 minute or until the sauce thickens, stirring occasionally.

6

Stir in the cream. Add any extra juices given off by the mushrooms, the sherry and the milk if the sauce is too thick. Microwave on LOW for 2 minutes.

7

Replace the mushrooms in the sauce or pour the sauce over the mushrooms on the warm dish. If too thick, thin with a little extra cream.

Serves 4 as an accompanying vegetable or as a starter.

Beans in Soured Cream Sauce

350 g (12 oz) frozen or fresh cut green beans
1 small onion, skinned and finely chopped
15 g ($\frac{1}{2}$ oz) butter or block margarine
2.5 ml ($\frac{1}{2}$ tsp) lemon juice
salt and freshly ground pepper
pinch of sugar
227-g (8-oz) can water chestnuts, drained and chopped
30 ml (2 tbsp) soured cream or natural yogurt

1

Cook the beans according to the chart on page 76.

2

Combine the onion and butter in a medium casserole and microwave on HIGH for 3 minutes or until the onion softens.

3

Add the lemon juice, salt, pepper and sugar and microwave on HIGH for 1 minute. Stir thoroughly.

4

Mix in the beans and water chestnuts. Cover and microwave on HIGH for 2 minutes or until the beans are hot. Stir once during reheating.

5

Mix in the soured cream, reduce the setting and microwave on LOW for 2 minutes, stirring twice during cooking. Serve hot or cold.

Serves 4.

Variation Use frozen peas and sweetcorn instead of the beans and water chestnuts.

Stuffed Onions

four 225-g (8-oz) Spanish onions, skinned
100 g (4 oz) unsmoked bacon, rinded
150 g (5 oz) lean minced beef
2 sprigs of parsley
1 garlic clove, skinned and crushed (optional)
salt and freshly ground pepper
15 ml (1 tbsp) bottled fruit sauce
1 egg, beaten
micro-fried breadcrumbs to garnish (see Kidneys in Madeira (page 57))

1

Remove a 1-cm ($\frac{1}{2}$-inch) slice from the stalk end of each onion and trim the base so that the onions will stand level.

2

Put the onions in a shallow dish. Cover and microwave on HIGH for 10 minutes or until the outsides yield to pressure. Leave to cool.

3

Using a grapefruit knife or spoon, scoop out the centres of the onions, leaving a sturdy shell.

4

Mince together the bacon, beef, parsley, garlic and half the scooped-out onion. Season with salt and pepper, mix in the sauce and bind with the egg.

5

Press the stuffing into the onion cavities. Replace the stuffed onions in the dish. Do not drain the cooking juices. Cover tightly and microwave on HIGH for 8 minutes or until the meat filling is cooked. Give the dish a quarter-turn three times during cooking. Leave to stand for 5 minutes before removing the cover. Sprinkle onions with breadcrumbs. Use up cooked chopped onions in soup.

Serves 4.

Lyonnaise Potatoes

1 medium onion, skinned and finely chopped
20 g ($\frac{3}{4}$ oz) butter or block margarine
60 ml (4 tbsp) double cream
450 g (1 lb) old potatoes, peeled and thinly sliced
salt and freshly ground pepper

1

Put the onion and butter in a 23-cm (9-inch) round shallow, flameproof dish and microwave on HIGH for 3 minutes or until the onion is soft. Stir once during cooking.

2

Stir in the cream, then add the potatoes, season well with salt and pepper and toss so that all the potato slices are well coated with the butter.

3

Cover the dish with cling film, pulling back one corner to vent, and microwave on HIGH for 12 minutes or until the potatoes are tender. Give the dish a half-turn once during cooking.

4

Leave to stand for 5 minutes, then carefully remove the cling film. Brown the top of the potatoes under the grill.

Serves 4.

Lyonnaise Potatoes, Stuffed Peppers and Beans in Soured Cream Sauce (pages 80–1)

Stuffed Peppers

1 small onion, skinned and
   chopped
15 ml (1 tbsp) vegetable oil
4 green or red peppers
225 g (8 oz) cooked rice
2 medium tomatoes, skinned
   and chopped
25 g (1 oz) pine kernels, grated
25 g (1 oz) currants
30 ml (2 tbsp) chopped fresh
   parsley
5 ml (1 level tsp) dried dill
   weed
100 g (4 oz) cooked minced
   lamb
salt and freshly ground pepper

1

Put the onion and oil in a 23-cm
(9-inch) shallow ovenproof dish
and microwave on HIGH for
3 minutes. Transfer onion to a
bowl.

2

Remove the cores from the
peppers. Cut in half lengthwise and
remove any further seeds. Put the
peppers in the dish with 60 ml
(4 tbsp) water. Cover with a lid and
microwave on HIGH for 6 minutes,
repositioning the peppers three
times during cooking. Leave
covered while preparing the filling.

3

To complete the filling, mix
remaining ingredients with the
onion, seasoning with salt and
freshly ground pepper to taste.

4

Remove the lid from the peppers
and drain away most of the water,
but do not wipe out the dish.

5

Stuff the peppers with the filling
and arrange in 2 layers in the dish,
separating the layers with a piece
of cling film.

6

Replace the lid and microwave on
LOW for 10 minutes or until the
peppers are cooked and the filling
thoroughly reheated. Give the dish
a quarter-turn three times during
the cooking period.

7

Serve the top 4 peppers first, then
remove the cling film before
serving the remainder. Serve with
Tomato Sauce (see page 94).

Serves 4.

**Quick Sautéed Vegetables
(page 83) in a Corningware
browning dish**

Colcannon

450 g (1 lb) potatoes, peeled
450 g (1 lb) cabbage, shredded
150 ml ($\frac{1}{4}$ pint) double cream
salt and freshly ground pepper
50 g (2 oz) Cheddar cheese,
   grated

1

Cut up the potatoes into even sized
pieces and place in a roasting bag
with 150 ml ($\frac{1}{4}$ pint) water. Seal
loosely with a non-metallic
fastening such as an elastic band.

2

Cook on HIGH for 7–10 minutes
until tender. Carefully remove the
potatoes from the roasting bag and
transfer to a large bowl and mash
well.

3

Place the cabbage in the roasting
bag and seal as above. Cook on
HIGH for 9–11 minutes until
tender. Drain well and add to the
mashed potato.

4

Mix in the cream and plenty of
seasoning and turn into an
ovenproof serving dish. Sprinkle
with cheese.

5

Without covering, microwave on
HIGH for 5 minutes or until
thoroughly reheated. Stir
occasionally during cooking.
Brown under the grill if wished, to
give a golden topping.

Serves 4.

Soft Sautéed Potatoes

25 g (1 oz) butter or block
  margarine
700 g (1½ lb) peeled potatoes,
  cut into 4-cm (1½-inch)
  chunks about 50 g (2 oz) each
15 ml (1 level tbsp) seasoned
  flour

1

Preheat a large browning dish to maximum according to the manufacturer's instructions, adding the butter during the last 30 seconds. While the browning dish is heating toss the potatoes in the seasoned flour.

2

When the browning dish is ready and the butter sizzling, toss in the potatoes and microwave on HIGH for 1 minute. Quickly turn the potatoes over and microwave on HIGH for a further minute.

3

Reposition the potatoes, cover with the lid and microwave on HIGH for 5 minutes, stirring and repositioning the potatoes once during cooking. Test by piercing with a fork. The potatoes should be almost tender.

4

Leave covered with the lid for 5 minutes before serving. (The potatoes will continue cooking during this time.)

Serves 4.

Ratatouille

350 g (12 oz) aubergines, cut
  into small chunks
salt and freshly ground pepper
30 ml (2 tbsp) vegetable oil
2 medium onions, skinned and
  finely chopped
4 medium tomatoes, skinned
  and chopped
½ small red pepper, seeded and
  thinly sliced
½ small green pepper, seeded
  and thinly sliced
2 medium courgettes, thinly
  sliced
1 garlic clove, skinned and
  crushed
30 ml (2 tbsp) tomato purée

1

Cut off the tops and slice the aubergines thickly. Cut into chunky pieces and place in a bowl. Sprinkle with salt and leave for 30 minutes. Drain and pat dry with absorbent kitchen paper.

2

Put the oil and onions in a 2.8-litre (5-pint) ovenproof glass bowl and microwave on HIGH for 3 minutes until the onion softens.

3

Stir in the remaining vegetables, garlic and tomato purée and mix well. Three-quarters cover with cling film and microwave on HIGH for 18 minutes or until the vegetables are tender. Stir two or three times during cooking.

4

Season to taste. Serve hot as an accompaniment to grilled meats or cold as a starter, with crusty French bread.

Serves 4.

Creamed Spinach

450 g (1 lb) fresh spinach
25 g (1 oz) butter or block
  margarine
150 ml (¼ pint) single cream
1.25 ml (¼ level tsp) ground
  nutmeg
salt and freshly ground pepper

1

Wash the spinach leaves in plenty of cold water and remove any coarse stems. Place the leaves in a large roasting bag and close loosely with an elastic band.

2

Place the bag upright on the oven shelf and microwave on HIGH for 6 minutes or until the spinach is packed down and cooked.

3

Carefully open the bag and tip the contents into a sieve. Push down with a wooden spoon to remove excess moisture, and chop the spinach roughly.

4

Put the butter and single cream in a 1.1-litre (2-pint) bowl and microwave on HIGH for 1 minute to melt the butter. Add the chopped spinach, nutmeg and salt and pepper. Reheat to serving temperature on HIGH for 1½–2 minutes.

Serves 4.

Red Cabbage and Apple Casserole

450 g (1 lb) red cabbage, finely shredded
225 g (8 oz) cooking apple, peeled, cored and sliced
60 ml (4 tbsp) red wine vinegar
50 g (2 oz) demerara sugar
10 ml (2 level tsp) French mustard
pinch ground cloves
salt and freshly ground pepper

1

Put the shredded cabbage and apple into a 2 litre (3½-pint) ovenproof glass casserole and mix together. Add the remaining ingredients and stir in well.

2

Cover the casserole and microwave on HIGH for 15 minutes, or until cooked, stirring three times during cooking. Check seasoning. Serve with pork or game dishes.

Serves 4.

Quick Sautéed Vegetables

15 g (½ oz) butter or block margarine
½ red, yellow or green pepper, seeded and sliced
1 large courgette, thinly sliced
50 g (2 oz) mushrooms, wiped and sliced
75 g (3 oz) broccoli florets
50 g (2 oz) spring onions, trimmed and finely sliced
salt and freshly ground pepper
soy sauce (optional)

1

Preheat the browning dish to maximum according to manufacturer's instructions, adding the butter during the last 30 seconds.

2

Add all the vegetables quickly to the sizzling butter and stir to coat. Microwave on HIGH for 2 minutes until the vegetables are slightly softened. Season well with salt and pepper and soy sauce to taste; serve hot.

Serves 2.

Note Vary the vegetables according to taste—use red pepper slices, carrot sticks, celery and fennel slices. Serve with soy sauce, if wished.

Curried Lentils

30 ml (2 tbsp) vegetable oil
1 medium onion, skinned and very finely chopped
1 garlic clove, skinned and crushed
15 ml (1 level tbsp) mild curry paste
175 g (6 oz) red lentils, rinsed and drained
5 ml (1 level tsp) salt

1

Put the oil in a 2.8-litre (5-pint) ovenproof glass bowl and stir in the onion and garlic. Microwave on HIGH for 3 minutes or until the onion is soft. Stir occasionally during cooking.

2

Stir in the curry paste and lentils and microwave on HIGH for 3 minutes, stirring occasionally.

3

Add the salt and 1 litre (1¾ pints) boiling water and stir thoroughly. Microwave on HIGH for 25 minutes or until the lentils are just tender, stirring occasionally during cooking.

4

Mash thoroughly or purée the lentils in a blender. Serve hot.

Serves 4.

Note Curry paste is easy to use but if you do not have it substitute 15 ml (1 level tbsp) curry powder.

CHAPTER SEVEN

Pasta, Rice and Grains

Cooking pasta

Because pasta is a dried product, it must be cooked in a considerable quantity of water and it must have sufficient time to absorb this water. There is therefore no saving in time when you cook pasta by microwave. On the other hand, the results are good and you may often find it convenient. It is also a much cleaner process than the conventional method—there is no contact between the bottom of the bowl and a direct heating element so that the pasta cannot stick on the bottom. To be sure that the pasta pieces do not stick together, add a little vegetable oil to the cooking water.

To cook pasta by microwave, the water must be fully boiling when the pasta is put in; it will then stay hot enough for cooking. Smaller pieces of pasta such as shells, elbow macaroni or spaghetti can be added all at once to the boiling water but larger pieces like lasagne must be added in two batches, bringing the water back to the boil after each batch of leaves is lowered in. If lasagne is not treated this way it will stick together as a solid mass.

Cooking times vary depending on the variety of the pasta. All dried pasta requires the same amount of cooking time but the standing time will vary.

Noodles require practically no standing time at all. Freshly made pasta, whether home-made or commercially prepared, is much softer than the dry, brittle type that we are accustomed to using and it is usually made with eggs rather than simply durum flour and water. It requires practically no cooking. Microwave this type of pasta for only 1 minute and do not give it a standing time, but drain and serve at once.

Cooked pasta can be reheated on HIGH unless mixed with a sauce that would be better reheated on LOW; cover while reheating. It can also be frozen and reheated in the microwave oven and, if you intend to do this, it is best to arrange it in a circle in the dish before freezing. It will not save any time to freeze and reheat, as it takes just as long to thaw and reheat as to cook from fresh, but it is a useful standby for other members of the household who may be either unwilling or unable to cook.

When reheating pasta in a sauce, either mix the sauce thoroughly with the pasta before freezing or arrange the pasta round the outside of the dish and the sauce in the middle.

Cooking rice

As for pasta, cooking rice by microwave saves no time over conventional methods. But the results are so good, with each grain tender and separate, that you may well prefer it.

The amount of rice that you can cook at any one time is in direct relation to the size of the container you use. You can cook about 450 g (1 lb) in a 2.8-litre (5-pint) ovenproof glass bowl or similar container. Traditional long grain rice can be cooked by the old-fashioned method of using lots and lots of boiling salted water; cook the rice uncovered, then pour into a colander, rinse and leave to drain. Or use the measured amount of water and salt recommended on the packet; it is usual to use double the volume of water to rice, add a measured amount of salt and cook, covered, until tender.

So many different kinds of rice are now obtainable that it is difficult to give precise recommendations for cooking times but I find that easy-cook rice takes just about the same length of time as untreated rice. The more pre-cooking that has taken place in manufacture, the less cooking time will be needed. Pudding rice is more difficult to tenderise, and when it is cooked in milk it is likely to boil over. If your microwave oven is fitted with a probe you can avoid this. In other cases either cook the rice in water before adding milk (evaporated is best for this because it is concentrated), or cook on a LOW setting. Cook brown rice in the same way as white rice but allow a longer cooking time.

Frozen rice thaws and heats very quickly. When reheating, add 5–10 ml (1–2 tsp) water so that a little steam is created and microwave on HIGH, breaking up the lumps as soon as it is possible. It is best to reheat uncovered to prevent overcooking.

To give extra flavour to boiled rice add a stock cube to the cooking water or cook the rice completely in freshly made stock.

Cooking Noodles

225 g (8 oz) pasta shapes such as tagliatelle, spaghetti, macaroni
10 ml (2 level tsp) salt
5 ml (1 tsp) vegetable oil

1

Boil 2 litres (3½ pints) water in a kettle and pour into a deep casserole or 2.8-litre (5-pint) ovenproof glass bowl. Add the salt and the oil.

2

Bring the water back to a full rolling boil in the microwave oven set on HIGH. Quickly lower in the pasta and without covering, microwave on HIGH for 5 minutes until partially cooked.

3

Remove from the oven, stir and cover. Leave to stand for 2–5 minutes until the pasta is firm to the bite. (Standing times vary according to the type of pasta eg stand tagliatelle for 2 minutes, spaghetti and macaroni for 5 minutes.) Drain and serve.

Serves 4.

Spaghetti Bolognese

450 ml (¾ pint) Bolognese sauce (see page 94)
225 g (8 oz) spaghetti

1

Prepare and cook the sauce.

2

Cook the spaghetti as directed left. Leave to stand.

3

During the standing time, reheat the sauce if necessary. Drain the spaghetti and serve with the sauce.

Serves 4.

Spaghetti Napolitana

450 ml (¾ pint) Tomato sauce (see page 94)
225 g (8 oz) spaghetti

1

Prepare and cook the sauce.

2

Cook the spaghetti as directed left. Leave to stand.

3

During the standing time, reheat the sauce if necessary. Drain the spaghetti and serve with the sauce.

Serves 4.

Macaroni Cheese

450 ml (¾ pint) Cheese sauce
    (see page 92)
175 g (6 oz) macaroni
60 ml (4 tbsp) milk
50 g (2 oz) Cheddar cheese,
    grated

1

Prepare and cook the sauce. Cover
and set aside while preparing the
pasta.

2

Cook the macaroni as directed on
page 8.

3

Drain the macaroni and return to
the casserole, bowl or an
ovenproof serving dish. Stir the
sauce and milk.

4

Sprinkle with the cheese, cover
and microwave on LOW until
reheated. Brown under the grill if
wished, to give a golden topping.

Serves 4.

Noodles with Prawn Sauce

300 ml (½ pint) Prawn sauce
    (see page 94)
225 g (8 oz) noodles

1

Prepare and cook the sauce. Cover
and set aside while preparing the
pasta.

2

Cook the noodles as directed on
page 84.

3

Reheat the sauce, if necessary.
Drain the noodles and serve with
the sauce.

Serves 4.

Tagliatelle with Walnut and Spinach Sauce

1 quantity Walnut and spinach
    sauce (see page 95)
125 g (4 oz) Tagliatelle or other
    pasta

1

Prepare and cook the sauce. Cover
and set aside while preparing the
pasta.

2

Cook the pasta as directed on
page 84. Leave to stand.

3

During the standing time, reheat
the sauce if necessary. Drain the
pasta and serve with the sauce. Top
with Parmesan cheese.

Serves 2.

Crispy-topped Creamed Spaghetti

4 rashers streaky bacon, rinded and finely chopped
40 g (1½ oz) fresh brown breadcrumbs
15 g (½ oz) butter
50 g (2 oz) butter or block margarine
1 small onion, skinned and finely chopped
25 g (1 oz) plain flour
salt and freshly ground pepper
150 ml (¼ pint) double cream
350 ml (12 fl oz) milk
175 g (6 oz) Cheddar, grated
175 g (6 oz) spaghetti, freshly cooked

1

First make the topping. Mix the bacon and breadcrumbs together in a large ovenproof glass bowl. Add the butter and microwave on HIGH for 4 minutes or until the bacon is crisp and the crumbs are golden brown and have absorbed all of the bacon fat. Stir occasionally during cooking. Turn out on to a plate and set aside.

2

Using the same bowl, put in the butter and onion. Microwave on HIGH for 3 minutes or until the onion is soft, stirring once.

3

Stir in the flour, salt and pepper. Then add the cream and milk. Stir thoroughly. Microwave on HIGH for 4½ minutes or until the sauce has thickened. Beat after each minute with a balloon whisk.

4

Stir the cheese into the sauce. Mix in the spaghetti and microwave on HIGH for 1 minute or until thoroughly reheated.

5

Turn the creamed spaghetti into a warmed serving dish and sprinkle the crispy bacon crumbs on top.

Serves 4.

Boiled Rice

450 g (1 lb) long grain rice
20 ml (4 level tsp) salt

1

Rinse the rice and put in a 2.8-litre (5-pint) ovenproof glass bowl with 2 litres (3½ pints) boiling water and the salt. Stir once.

2

Without covering, microwave on HIGH for 15 minutes or until a grain of rice can be broken when pressed with a fork. Stir once during cooking. Cover and leave to stand for 5 minutes. Drain through a colander under hot running water. If rice is to be served cold, drain under cold running water.

Serves 6.

Saffron Rice
To colour rice yellow, add a small pinch of saffron to the rice and water in Step 1.

Boiled Rice All-in-one Method

275 g (10 oz) long grain rice
7.5 ml (1½ level tsp) salt

1

Put the rice, salt and 750 ml (1¼ pints) boiling water in a large casserole, stir once, then cover with a lid.

2

Microwave on HIGH for about 15 minutes or until a grain of rice can be broken easily with the side of a fork. (Most of the water should have been absorbed. If the rice is dry but not quite cooked add 15–30 ml (1–2 tbsp) boiling water.)

3

Leave to stand, covered, for 8 minutes, by which time all the water should be absorbed and the rice tender.

Serves 4.

Note Various kinds of rice absorb different amounts of liquid, but as a rule put into a bowl the required quantity of rice and double the volume in water, adding salt to taste. For exact instructions follow the recommendations on the packet but add a few extra tablespoons of water.

Boiled Brown Rice

100 g (4 oz) brown rice
2.5 ml (½ level tsp) salt
boiling water

1

Put the rice, salt and 600 ml (1 pint) boiling water in a medium casserole. Stir once.

2

Cover with the lid and microwave on HIGH for 30 minutes or until the rice is nearly cooked and most of the water absorbed. Stir once during cooking.

3

Stir once after cooking, then replace the lid and leave to stand for 5 minutes or until the rice is fully cooked and all the liquid is absorbed. If on the first testing the liquid is absorbed but the rice is not yet cooked, add 75–90 ml (5–6 tbsp) boiling water.

Serves 2.

Note The volume of rice increases considerably when cooked, be sure to use a casserole that is big enough.

Brown Rice (Old-fashioned Method)

100 g (4 oz) brown rice
2.5 ml (½ level tsp) salt
1 litre (1¾ pints) boiling water

1

Combine the rice, salt and boiling water in a large ovenproof glass bowl and stir once.

2

Without covering, microwave on HIGH for 30 minutes, stirring occasionally.

3

Drain the rice through a colander, then put into a serving dish and cover. Leave to stand for 5 minutes.

Serves 2.

Note Any remaining droplets of water will be absorbed by the hot rice as it stands.

Chinese Fried Rice

40 g (1½ oz) butter or block margarine
30 ml (2 tbsp) chopped spring onions
400 g (14 oz) cooked long grain rice
30 ml (2 tbsp) soy sauce
100 g (4 oz) ham, cut into strips
4 eggs
freshly ground pepper

1

Put 25 g (1 oz) butter in a large bowl or suitable serving dish and microwave on HIGH for 45 seconds or until melted.

2

Stir in the spring onions and the rice and microwave on HIGH for 3 minutes or until thoroughly heated. Stir once during cooking.

3

Stir in the soy sauce and ham and microwave on HIGH for 2 minutes or until the mixture is thoroughly hot. Cover tightly while preparing the eggs.

4

Put the remaining 15 g (½ oz) butter in a bowl or jug and microwave on HIGH for 10 seconds or until the butter is very soft. Add the eggs, 60 ml (4 tbsp) water and a little pepper and beat thoroughly. Microwave on HIGH for 2½ minutes or until the eggs are just set but not completely cooked. Stir the mixture every 30 seconds during cooking, drawing the edges to the middle and making sure that no large lumps are left to set.

5

Stir the egg into the rice mixture and serve at once.

Serves 4–6.

Spicy Pilaff

40 g (1½ oz) butter or block
   margarine
175 g (6 oz) long grain rice,
   rinsed, drained and dried
40 g (1½ oz) mixed nuts, finely
   chopped
450 ml (¾ pint) hot chicken
   stock
2.5 ml (½ level tsp) salt
2.5 ml (½ level tsp) ground
   cardamom
2.5 ml (½ level tsp) ground
   turmeric
25 g (1 oz) sultanas
¼ red pepper, seeded and diced
60 ml (4 tbsp) frozen peas

1

Put the butter in a 1.7-litre
(3-pint) casserole and microwave
on HIGH for 45 seconds or until
the butter is melted.

2

Stir in the rice and microwave on
HIGH for 3 minutes, stirring once
during cooking.

3

Add the nuts and microwave on
HIGH for 2 minutes or until the
rice is a pale gold colour.

4

Stir in the remaining ingredients
and microwave on HIGH for 12
minutes or until the rice is just
tender and most of the liquid
absorbed. Stir the rice once
during cooking.

5

Stir lightly once again, then cover
tightly and leave for 5 minutes
during which time the liquid
should be absorbed.

6

Fork up the rice, then serve as a
light supper dish or vegetable
accompaniment to a main course.

Serves 3–4.

Barley and Mushroom Casserole

50 g (2 oz) butter or block
   margarine
1 medium onion, skinned and
   finely chopped
175 g (6 oz) pearl barley
225 g (8 oz) mushrooms, wiped
   and quartered
5 ml (1 level tsp) dried basil
salt and freshly ground pepper

1

Put the butter in a large casserole
and microwave on HIGH for 45
seconds or until melted.

2

Stir in the onion and microwave on
HIGH for 3 minutes or until soft.
Stir once during cooking.

3

Stir in the pearl barley and
microwave on HIGH for 5 minutes
or until a light golden colour (you
may see some brown flakes; this is
the onion frying further). Stir
twice during cooking.

4

Add 750 ml (1¼ pints) boiling water
and the mushrooms. Stir in the
basil and season with salt and
pepper. Cover with a lid and
microwave on HIGH for 30
minutes, stirring twice during
cooking. Leave to stand for 10–15
minutes until tender.

*Serves 4–6 as an accompanying
vegetable.*

Porridge

150 g (5 oz) porridge oats
5 ml (1 level tsp) salt

1

Combine the oats, salt and 900 ml
(1½ pints) water in a 2.8-litre
(5-pint) ovenproof glass bowl and
stir well. Microwave on HIGH for 5
minutes, stirring once during
cooking. Reduce the setting and
microwave on MEDIUM for 10
minutes or on LOW for 20
minutes, stirring once or twice to
break up any lumps that may form.

2

Stir, then cover and store in a cool
place overnight, if wished.

3

To reheat, three-quarters cover
the bowl with cling film and
microwave on HIGH for 6–8
minutes, stirring two or three
times during reheating. To reheat a
single bowl, microwave on HIGH
for about 1½ minutes, stirring once
during reheating and once again
before serving.

Serves 6.

Note Most porridge oats are now
quick cooking, made from rolled
oats which have been partially
cooked in manufacture. Porridge
improves if made the night before
then covered to prevent a crust
forming and stored in the
refrigerator or cool place until the
next morning. Thin down the
porridge with milk, cream or
water and serve with sugar or
extra salt if preferred.

Sauces

Cooking sauces by microwave is foolproof. Unlike conventional cooking, when the direct contact between the base of the pan and the heat can cause lumps and burning, in the microwave oven the heat is created within the food so these are less likely to occur. All you need is a long-handled wooden spoon, a balloon whisk and a cooking bowl.

Roux-based sauces

Sauces based on a roux, that is, when the flour and butter are cooked together before the liquid is added, are simply marvellous cooked in a microwave oven. Once you have made a sauce this way you will never do it any other way. This method includes Basic white sauce, Béchamel sauce and many variations.

Brown sauces

You can achieve brown sauces in the microwave oven, too. Use a deep bowl or dish and be sure that your container is made of a material that will withstand the temperature of the very hot fat. Cook the onion in butter or oil until it is brown, then stir in the flour and allow this to cook for a little while before adding further ingredients. Alternatively mix an equal volume of vegetable oil and flour in a deep dish and microwave on HIGH for 5–10 minutes until brown. Add the onion, which will immediately sizzle and brown, and then add hot stock and any other ingredients.

Sauces that are cooked by reduction, such as Tomato sauce, should be cooked uncovered. They must be stirred frequently because the boiling bubbles will burst and splatter as the sauce thickens.

Thickening sauces

Take care when cooking sauces that are thickened with eggs. These are the sauces that are normally cooked in the top half of a double saucepan. Practise cooking these sauces on LOW and you will soon find that you are able to achieve a good result when cooking on HIGH, which will be much quicker. It is imperative to whisk every few seconds and not to overcook.

When cooking sauces thickened with cornflour or arrowroot and including no butter or eggs, make sure that the starch is blended thoroughly with cold liquid before adding hot liquid. When whisking these sauces the whisk must reach right to the bottom of the bowl.

In meat sauces made with fresh raw mince, either brown the meat conventionally, or in a browning dish, or cook on a roasting rack in a shallow dish so that the fat can be poured off.

Freezing sauces

Most sauces can be made in advance and many can be frozen. But sauces containing cream, soured cream, yogurt or egg must not be boiled. If you intend to reheat these sauces, omit these ingredients and add them after reheating just to boiling point.

White sauces

The basic white sauce is the foundation for any number of variations. It is used as a pouring or coating sauce and when very thick as a panada for soufflés. If a white sauce is not to be served immediately it is better to make it fairly thin because sauces thicken as they cool and during prolonged standing time. The basic white sauce can be made in advance and stored in the refrigerator. Cover the surface of the sauce with a piece of damp greaseproof paper or cling film to prevent a skin forming on top.

The Basic White Sauce recipe (opposite) freezes well. When cold pour into a rigid container, seal and freeze. Thaw in the microwave oven for about 5 minutes then tip into a larger bowl so that the sauce can be beaten smooth and heated to the required temperature.

Basic White Sauce

20 g ($\frac{3}{4}$ oz) butter or block
   margarine
20 g ($\frac{3}{4}$ oz) flour
300 ml ($\frac{1}{2}$ pint) milk or milk and
   stock
salt and freshly ground black
   pepper

1

Put the butter in a bowl and microwave on HIGH until melted.

2

Stir in the flour and microwave on HIGH for a few seconds to help the flour to cook and avoid an uncooked starchy taste.

3

Gradually mix in the liquid (this is usually milk but it can be milk and stock combined). Microwave on HIGH for the time stated in the chart, then whisk thoroughly with a balloon whisk to prevent lumps forming.

4

Continue microwaving on HIGH, whisking every 30 seconds until the sauce thickens. Thicker sauces cook slightly more quickly than thin sauces. Add seasoning to taste. Add additional ingredients such as parsley, cheese and egg just before serving.

Makes 300 ml ($\frac{1}{2}$ pint) pouring sauce.

Basic White Sauce

(All microwave cooking on HIGH)

	Butter or margarine		Flour		Liquid (cold)		Final cooking period,
	Quantity	Time to melt	Quantity	Time to cook	Quantity	Time to cook	
		(Step 1)		mixed with butter (Step 2)	(stirred in gradually)	(Step 3)	whisking every 30 seconds (Step 4)
Pouring sauce	20 g ($\frac{3}{4}$ oz)	20 secs	20 g ($\frac{3}{4}$ oz)	20 secs	300 ml ($\frac{1}{2}$ pt)	1 min	2 mins
	40 g (1$\frac{1}{2}$ oz)	45 secs	40 g (1$\frac{1}{2}$ oz)	30 secs	600 ml (1 pt)	1$\frac{1}{2}$ min	3$\frac{1}{2}$ mins
Coating sauce	25 g (1 oz)	30 secs	25 g (1 oz)	30 secs	300 ml ($\frac{1}{2}$ pt)	45 secs	1$\frac{3}{4}$ mins
	50 g (2 oz)	1 min	50 g (2 oz)	45 secs	600 ml (1 pt)	1 min	3 mins
Panada (thick)	25 g (1 oz)	30 secs	25 g (1 oz)	30 secs	150 ml ($\frac{1}{4}$ pt)	$\frac{1}{2}$ min	1 min

Note Allow extra time for larger quantities, eg 1.1 litre (2 pints) sauce takes 6$\frac{1}{2}$ minutes on HIGH. If the liquid is warm when added, reduce the cooking time. White sauce thickens on standing, so it may be necessary to thin it down with a little extra liquid on reheating.

Cheese Sauce

20 g (¾ oz) butter or margarine
20 g (¾ oz) flour
300 ml (½ pint) milk
60 ml (4 level tbsp) grated
   cheese (hard cheese is best)
1.25 ml (¼ level tsp) prepared
   mustard
pinch of salt
shake of cayenne pepper

1

Put the butter in a bowl and microwave on HIGH until melted.

2

Stir in the flour and microwave on HIGH for a few seconds to help the flour to cook and avoid an uncooked starchy taste.

3

Gradually mix in the milk. Microwave on HIGH for the time stated in the chart (page 91), then whisk thoroughly.

4

Continue microwaving on HIGH, whisking every 30 seconds until the sauce thickens. Stir in the grated cheese, mustard, salt and cayenne pepper. Reheat if necessary, but do not boil.

Makes 300 ml (½ pint) pouring sauce.

Parsley Sauce

20 g (¾ oz) butter or margarine
20 g (¾ oz) flour
300 ml (½ pint) milk
10 ml (2 tsp) chopped fresh
   parsley
salt and freshly ground pepper

1

Put the butter in a bowl and microwave on HIGH until melted.

2

Stir in the flour and microwave on HIGH for a few seconds to help the flour to cook and avoid an uncooked starchy taste.

3

Gradually mix in the milk. Microwave on HIGH for the time stated in the chart (page 91), then whisk thoroughly.

4

Continue microwaving on HIGH, whisking every 30 seconds until the sauce thickens. Add the parsley during the last 2 minutes of the cooking period. Season with salt and pepper.

Makes 300 ml (½ pint) pouring sauce.

Egg Sauce

20 g (¾ oz) butter or margarine
20 g (¾ oz) flour
300 ml (½ pint) milk
1 hard-boiled egg, chopped
salt and freshly ground pepper

1

Put the butter in a bowl and microwave on HIGH until melted.

2

Stir in the flour and microwave on HIGH for a few seconds to help the flour to cook and avoid an uncooked starchy taste.

3

Gradually mix in the milk. Microwave on HIGH for the time stated in the chart (page 91), then whisk thoroughly.

4

Continue microwaving on HIGH, whisking every 30 seconds until the sauce thickens. Add the hard-boiled egg during the last 30 seconds of the cooking period. Season with salt and pepper.

Makes 300 ml (½ pint) pouring sauce.

Quick Tomato Sauce

20 g (¾ oz) butter or margarine
20 g (¾ oz) flour
150 ml (¼ pint) milk
150 ml (¼ pint) chicken stock
60 ml (4 tbsp) tomato ketchup
salt and freshly ground pepper

1

Put the butter in a bowl and microwave on HIGH until melted.

2

Stir in the flour and microwave on HIGH for a few seconds to help the flour to cook and avoid an uncooked starchy taste.

3

Gradually mix in the milk and stock combined. Microwave on HIGH for the time stated in the chart (page 91), then whisk thoroughly.

4

Continue microwaving on HIGH, whisking every 30 seconds until the sauce thickens. Add the tomato ketchup and microwave for 1 minute more. Season with salt and pepper.

Makes 300 ml (½ pint) pouring sauce.

Béchamel Sauce

300 ml (½ pint) milk
1 bay leaf
1 thyme sprig
1 parsley sprig, roughly
  chopped
1.25 ml (¼ level tsp) grated
  nutmeg
small piece onion
small piece carrot
25 g (1 oz) butter
25 g (1 oz) plain flour
salt and freshly ground pepper

1

Put the milk in a large jug. Add the herbs, nutmeg and vegetables. Without covering, microwave on HIGH for 1½ minutes or until the milk begins to steam.

2

Cover the jug and set aside for 15–30 minutes (the longer you leave it the better the flavour of the sauce will be). Strain the milk into a large jug or lipped bowl.

3

Put the butter in a medium bowl and microwave on HIGH for 30 seconds or until melted.

4

Stir in the flour and microwave on HIGH for 20 seconds or until the mixture puffs up slightly.

5

Gradually add the infused milk to the roux mixture, beating vigorously with a balloon whisk. Microwave on HIGH for 2 minutes or until the sauce thickens. Whisk frequently during cooking. Season to taste with salt and freshly ground black pepper.

Makes 300 ml (½ pint) coating sauce.

Note To make a pouring sauce, double the quantity of milk. To make a thick sauce for use in hot soufflés, halve the quantity of milk.

Tomato Sauce

25 g (1 oz) butter or block
  margarine
1 medium onion, skinned and
  finely chopped
1 garlic clove, skinned and
  crushed
397-g (14-oz) can tomatoes
30 ml (2 tbsp) tomato purée
5 ml (1 level tsp) dried basil
pinch of sugar
salt and freshly ground pepper
15 ml (1 level tbsp) arrowroot
45 ml (3 tbsp) red wine

1

In a 2.8-litre (5-pint) ovenproof
glass bowl, heat the butter on
HIGH for 15 seconds or until
melted. Stir in the onion and garlic
and microwave on HIGH for
6 minutes or until the onion starts
to brown.

2

Add the tomatoes, 300 ml ($\frac{1}{2}$ pint)
water, tomato purée, basil, sugar
and seasoning and microwave on
HIGH for 15 minutes or until the
sauce reduces and thickens. Stir
occasionally during cooking.

3

Blend the arrowroot with the
wine, pour into the sauce and
microwave on HIGH for 3 minutes
until boiling. Stir every minute
during cooking.

4

Allow to cool for about 10 minutes
then purée in a blender. Adjust the
seasoning to taste.

5

To reheat, three-quarters cover
with cling film and microwave on
HIGH to serving temperature.

Makes about 600 ml (1 pint).

Prawn Sauce

5 ml (1 tsp) olive oil
1 small garlic clove, skinned
  and crushed
100 ml (4 fl oz) tomato juice
50 ml (2 fl oz) tomato purée
45 ml (3 tbsp) red wine
15 ml (1 tbsp) chopped parsley
2.5 ml ($\frac{1}{2}$ level tsp) sugar
2.5 ml ($\frac{1}{2}$ level tsp) dried
  tarragon
1.25 ml ($\frac{1}{4}$ level tsp) salt
1.25 ml ($\frac{1}{4}$ level tsp) freshly
  ground black pepper
225 g (8 oz) cooked shelled
  prawns

1

Put all the ingredients, except
the prawns, in a medium
ovenproof glass bowl or a
casserole. Stir well, then
microwave on HIGH for 5 minutes
or until the sauce is bubbling
around the edges. Stir once, then
microwave on HIGH for a further 2
minutes.

2

Stir in the prawns. Three-quarters
cover with cling film, and
microwave on HIGH for 3 minutes
or until the prawns are fully
heated. Stir once during cooking.

Makes about 450 ml ($\frac{3}{4}$ pint).

Bolognese Sauce

1 medium onion, skinned and
  very finely chopped
30 ml (2 tbsp) olive oil
225 g (8 oz) fresh minced lamb
  or beef
2.5 ml ($\frac{1}{2}$ level tsp) ground bay
  leaves
2.5 ml ($\frac{1}{2}$ level tsp) dried basil
5 ml (1 level tsp) dried parsley
salt and freshly ground black
  pepper
45 ml (3 tbsp) red wine
15 ml (1 tbsp) tomato purée
397-g (14-oz) can tomatoes,
  crushed with their juice

1

Combine the onion and oil in a
2.8-litre (5-pint) ovenproof glass
bowl and microwave on HIGH for
7 minutes or until the onion is
browned. Stir occasionally during
cooking.

2

Stir in the meat and microwave on
HIGH for 5 minutes, stirring once
during cooking.

3

Add the herbs, seasoning, wine,
tomato purée and the tomatoes.
Stir thoroughly so that no lumps
of meat are sticking together and
microwave on HIGH for 10
minutes or until the sauce is thick.
Stir occasionally during cooking.

Enough for 3–4 servings of pasta.

Note Fresh ripe tomatoes can be
used when they are in season. You
will require about 900 g (2 lb).
The tomatoes should be skinned
and chopped.

Walnut and Spinach Sauce

100 g (4 oz) streaky bacon, rinded and chopped
15 ml (1 tbsp) vegetable oil
1 medium onion, skinned and finely chopped
1 garlic clove, skinned and crushed
450 g (1 lb) fresh spinach, cooked and chopped or 227-g (8-oz) packet frozen chopped spinach, thawed and drained
150 ml (¼ pint) single cream
50 g (2 oz) shelled walnuts, coarsely chopped
25 g (1 oz) Parmesan, grated

1

In a 1.5-litre (2-pint) ovenproof pan or bowl microwave the bacon and oil on HIGH for 2 minutes or until cooked, covered with a piece of absorbent kitchen paper to minimise splattering.

2

Stir in the onion and garlic. Microwave uncovered on HIGH for 2 minutes until soft. Stir in the spinach and cream and continue to microwave on HIGH for 5 minutes or until well heated, stirring halfway through cooking time. Stir in the walnuts.

Serves 2 as a main dish with freshly cooked pasta or rice and top with Parmesan cheese.

Rich Brown Sauce

75 ml (5 tbsp) vegetable oil
50 g (2 oz) plain flour
1 large onion, skinned and finely chopped
1 garlic clove, skinned and crushed
2 celery stalks, finely chopped
2 rashers back bacon, rinded and finely chopped
1 medium carrot, peeled and grated
15 ml (1 tbsp) chopped fresh parsley
1 bay leaf
salt and freshly ground pepper
15 ml (1 level tbsp) tomato purée
60 ml (4 tbsp) red wine
900 ml (1½ pints) strong hot beef stock

1

Blend the oil and flour together in a large deep casserole or 2.8-litre (5-pint) bowl. Microwave on HIGH for 7 minutes or until fudge coloured. Stir once during cooking (the flour and oil will appear sandy and rough).

2

Stir in the onion and garlic and microwave on HIGH for 3 minutes. Add the celery, bacon and carrot and microwave on HIGH for 2 minutes.

3

Add the remaining ingredients, three-quarters cover with cling film and microwave on HIGH for 20 minutes or until the sauce has thickened. Stir occasionally during cooking.

4

Remove the bay leaf, allow to cool a little and purée the sauce in a blender. Adjust the seasoning. Reheat if necessary.

Makes 900 ml (1½ pints).

Note This sauce is good with many meat dishes and can be added to soups for extra flavour. The sauce thickens considerably as it cools. Store in the freezer in the quantities you are most likely to require for use in recipes.

Hollandaise Sauce

3 egg yolks
30 ml (2 tbsp) lemon juice
1.25 ml ($\frac{1}{4}$ level tsp) salt
pinch of white pepper
100 g (4 oz) unsalted butter, cut
 into 4 pieces

1

Beat the egg yolks, lemon juice, salt and pepper together in a small bowl.

2

Put the butter in a large bowl and microwave on HIGH for 1 minute or until just melted.

3

Stir the egg yolk mixture into the melted butter, then whisk thoroughly with a balloon whisk. Microwave on HIGH for 45 seconds or until the sauce is just thick enough to coat the back of a spoon, whisking every 15 seconds during cooking.

4

Remove from the oven and continue whisking for about 20 seconds to thicken the sauce further. Serve hot. If serving cold, cover the surface with cling film and leave until cold. Stir before serving.

Makes 300 ml ($\frac{1}{2}$ pint).

Note The sauce can be reheated gently on LOW, whisking often. Do not reheat on HIGH.

Sauce fines herbes
Add 2.5 ml ($\frac{1}{2}$ tsp) chopped fresh parsley and 5 ml (1 tsp) chopped fresh tarragon.

Cucumber Sauce

$\frac{1}{2}$ cucumber
3 egg yolks
30 ml (2 tbsp) lemon juice
1.25 ml ($\frac{1}{4}$ level tsp) salt
pinch of white pepper
100 g (4 oz) unsalted butter, cut
 into 4 pieces

1

Peel and purée the cucumber in a blender. Set aside.

2

Beat the egg yolks, lemon juice, salt and pepper together in a small bowl.

3

Put the butter in a large bowl and microwave on HIGH for 1 minute or until just melted.

4

Stir the egg yolk mixture into the melted butter, then whisk thoroughly with a balloon whisk. Microwave on HIGH for 45 seconds or until the sauce is just thick enough to coat the back of a spoon, whisking every 15 seconds during cooking.

5

Remove from the oven and continue whisking for about 20 seconds to thicken the sauce further. Stir in the puréed cucumber. Serve hot or cold with fish.

Makes about 300 ml ($\frac{1}{2}$ pint).

Sauce Raifort

3 egg yolks
30 ml (2 tbsp) tarragon vinegar
1.25 ml ($\frac{1}{4}$ level tsp) salt
pinch of white pepper
100 g (4 oz) unsalted butter, cut
 into 4 pieces
45 ml (3 level tbsp) grated
 horseradish

1

Beat the egg yolks, vinegar, salt and pepper together in a small bowl.

2

Put the butter in a large bowl and microwave on HIGH for 1 minute or until just melted.

3

Stir the egg yolk mixture into the melted butter, then whisk thoroughly with a balloon whisk. Microwave on HIGH for 45 seconds or until the sauce is just thick enough to coat the back of a spoon, whisking every 15 seconds during cooking.

4

Remove from the oven and continue whisking for about 20 seconds to thicken the sauce further. Stir in the grated horseradish. Serve hot or cold with smoked mackerel.

Makes about 300 ml ($\frac{1}{2}$ pint).

Tagliatelle with Walnut and Spinach Sauce (page 86) in a Corningware vision range saucepan.

Thick Mayonnaise Sauce

3 eggs
30 ml (2 tbsp) lemon juice
1.25 ($\frac{1}{4}$ level tsp) salt
pinch of white pepper
100 g (4 oz) unsalted butter, cut into 4 pieces
75 ml (5 tbsp) double cream, whipped
75 ml (5 tbsp) mayonnaise

1

Beat the egg yolks, lemon juice, salt and pepper together in a small bowl.

2

Put the butter in a large bowl and microwave on HIGH for 1 minute or until just melted.

3

Stir the egg yolk mixture into the melted butter, then whisk thoroughly with a balloon whisk. Microwave on HIGH for 45 seconds or until the sauce is just thick enough to coat the back of a spoon, whisking every 15 seconds during cooking.

4

Remove from the oven and continue whisking for about 20 seconds to thicken the sauce further. Fold in the whipped cream and the mayonnaise. Cover the surface with cling film and leave until cold. Serve with cold chicken.

Makes about 450 ml ($\frac{3}{4}$ pint).

Strawberry Cheesecake (page 104)

Butterscotch Almond Sauce

50 g (2 oz) flaked almonds
100 g (4 oz) soft dark brown sugar
175 g (6 oz) golden syrup
50 g (2 oz) butter
170-g (6-oz) can evaporated milk
30 ml (2 tbsp) lemon juice

1

Spread the almonds evenly in a pie plate and microwave on HIGH for about 5 minutes or until browned. Watch as they brown very fast in the centre, so stir several times to obtain even browning. Cool.

2

Combine the sugar, syrup and butter in a medium 1.1-litre (2-pint) bowl and microwave on HIGH for 2 minutes until melted. Add the evaporated milk, beating until smooth, then beat in the lemon juice. Stir in the almonds. To serve hot, reheat on HIGH for about 2 minutes. Serve hot or cold, spooned over sponge puddings or ice cream.

Makes 450 ml ($\frac{3}{4}$ pint).

Note The sauce can be stored in the refrigerator for 3–4 days. Add a little extra evaporated milk if it appears too thick after storing.

Sabayon Sauce

75 g (3 oz) granulated sugar
4 egg yolks
75 ml (5 tbsp) Madeira

1

Put the sugar in a .85 litre (1$\frac{1}{2}$-pint) bowl. Beat the egg yolks and Madeira in a small jug.

2

Strain the egg yolk mixture into the sugar and microwave on HIGH for 1$\frac{1}{4}$ minutes or until the sugar has dissolved. Whisk twice. Continue to cook on LOW for 1$\frac{1}{2}$ minutes until the sauce thickens. Using a balloon whisk, whisk every 30 seconds during cooking.

3

Remove from the microwave oven. If serving hot, use immediately with sponge fingers or over sponge pudding. To serve cold, cover the surface with cling film and leave to cool. Stir before serving. Goes well with fresh fruit.

Makes 175 ml (6 fl oz).

Chocolate Mocha Sauce

50 g (2 oz) granulated sugar
100 g (4 oz) cooking chocolate drops or cooking bar chocolate, broken up
2.5 ml ($\frac{1}{2}$ level tsp) instant coffee
5 ml (1 level tsp) cornflour
15 ml (1 tbsp) milk
2.5 ml ($\frac{1}{2}$ tsp) vanilla flavouring

1

Mix 150 ml ($\frac{1}{4}$ pint) water and the sugar together in a large measuring jug and microwave on HIGH for 3 minutes or until a thin syrup is formed. Stir every minute.

2

Stir in the chocolate and instant coffee. Microwave on HIGH for 30 seconds then stir well.

3

Blend the cornflour, milk and vanilla flavouring together and stir into the sauce. Microwave on HIGH for 3 minutes or until the mixture boils and thickens. Stir once during cooking and once at the end of cooking. Cover with cling film and leave to cool.

Makes 200 ml (7 fl oz).

Marshmallow Sauce

125 g (4 oz) sugar
pinch of salt
8 large marshmallows
2.5 ml ($\frac{1}{2}$ tsp) vanilla flavouring
1 egg white

1

Combine the sugar, salt and 75 ml (2$\frac{1}{2}$ fl oz) water in a 1.1-litre (2-pint) ovenproof glass bowl. Microwave on HIGH for 3 minutes or until a thin syrup is formed and all the sugar is dissolved. Stir every minute during cooking.

2

Add the marshmallows and microwave on HIGH for 45 seconds or until the marshmallows melt. Stir in the vanilla flavouring.

3

Whisk the egg white until soft peaks form, then whisk into the marshmallow mixture, adding flavouring and colouring. Beat well before serving as this sauce tends to separate. Serve over ice cream.

Makes 450 ml ($\frac{3}{4}$ pint)

Fruit Marshmallow Sauce
Fold 450 g (1 lb) puréed raspberries, strawberries or blackberries into the sauce before serving over ice cream.

Peppermint Sauce

125 g (4 oz) sugar
pinch of salt
8 large marshmallows
2.5 ml ($\frac{1}{2}$ tsp) vanilla flavouring
1 egg white
few drops of peppermint flavouring
few drops of green food colouring

1

Combine the sugar, salt and 150 ml ($\frac{1}{4}$ pint) water in a 1.1-litre (2-pint) ovenproof glass lipped bowl. Microwave on HIGH for 3 minutes or until a thin syrup is formed and all the sugar is dissolved. Stir every minute during cooking.

2

Add the marshmallows and microwave on HIGH for 45 seconds or until the marshmallows melt. Stir in the vanilla flavouring.

3

Whisk the egg whites until soft peaks form, then whisk into the marshmallow mixture. Stir before serving over chocolate ice cream.

Makes 450 ml ($\frac{3}{4}$ pint).

Note Peppermint flavourings vary widely in strength—peppermint extract and peppermint oil, for instance, are far more concentrated than peppermint 'flavouring'.

Orange Sauce

25 g (1 oz) unsalted butter
15 ml (1 level tbsp) cornflour
30 ml (2 level tbsp) sugar
75 ml (3 fl oz) concentrated
  canned orange juice
15 ml (1 tbsp) rum

1

Put the butter in a 1.1-litre
(2-pint) ovenproof glass bowl and
microwave on HIGH for 30 seconds
or until melted.

2

Add the cornflour and sugar and
blend thoroughly. Gradually mix
in the orange juice and 200 ml
(7 fl oz) water and stir thoroughly.
Microwave on HIGH for 4 minutes
or until the sauce boils up and
thickens. Whisk every minute
during cooking.

3

Stir in the rum. Serve warm with
sponge puddings or gingerbread or
cover and leave to cool and serve
with ice cream, fresh strawberries
or canned pears.

Makes 300 ml (½ pint).

Flambé Fruit Sauce

376-g (13¼-oz) can crushed
  pineapple or other fruit in
  syrup
15 ml (1 level tbsp) cornflour
2 pinches of ground ginger
120 ml (8 tbsp) apricot jam
50 g (2 oz) butter, cut into 4
  pieces
60 ml (4 tbsp) brandy

1

Empty the pineapple and its syrup
into a large ovenproof glass bowl.
Stir in the cornflour, ginger, jam
and butter.

2

Microwave on HIGH for 3 minutes.
Stir and microwave on HIGH for a
further 3 minutes or until the
sauce thickens, stirring every 30
seconds during this part of the
cooking period.

3

Purée in a blender if wished. Pour
into an ovenproof glass jug and
microwave on HIGH for 2 minutes
until hot.

4

Put the brandy into a small bowl or
glass and microwave on HIGH for
5 seconds to warm. Pour over the
sauce and light with a taper. Stir
in before serving. Serve with ice
cream or hot puddings.

Makes 450 ml (¾ pint).

Piquant Plum Sauce

75 ml (5 tbsp) red wine vinegar
15 ml (1 tbsp) Worcestershire
  sauce
45 ml (3 level tbsp) plum jam
5 ml (1 level tsp) French
  mustard
30 ml (2 level tbsp) demerara
  sugar

1

Mix all the ingredients together in
a large ovenproof glass measuring
jug and microwave on HIGH for 3
minutes or until boiling rapidly.
Stir thoroughly.

2

Press the sauce through a sieve or
purée in a blender.

Makes 75 ml (3 fl oz).

Note Serve with microwaved
pork chops. Serves 4.

CHAPTER NINE

Puddings and Desserts

The microwave oven can be used for a whole range of desserts, from gooey, warming suet puddings with sticky sauces to simple fruit compotes. Use it for fast baking of egg custards and rice puddings or to prepare the sauces for a fruit fondue. It is also useful for quick thawing of fruits from the freezer—whether they are to be cooked or eaten raw. For thawing times, see the chart at the bottom of this page.

Making sponge puddings

A basic sponge pudding with a syrup or jam topping is ready with the help of a microwave oven in less than 10 minutes. And the result will be as soft and light as you could wish. To cook it, grease a pudding basin just as you would for cooking in a conventional oven, but cover the pudding with cling film. Making a very loose tent of the film, wrapping it close to the sides of the basin but pulling it up high in the centre so that there is room for the pudding to rise. Do the same for a suet pudding.

Always leave a standing time before turning out puddings cooked in a basin. The shape of the basin traps moisture in the lower part of the mixture and slows down cooking in that area. Leaving the pudding to stand for 5 minutes (or as directed in the recipe), allows it to finish cooking without becoming dry and overcooked on top. Beware particularly of overcooking suet puddings, as they quickly become dry and rather unpalatable.

Any fruit can be cooked in the microwave oven whether fresh, frozen or dried. The fruit retains its colour and flavour and will cook to perfection whether you require large crunchy pieces or soft stewed purée. The speed of cooking can be quite amazing.

Piercing skinned fruits

All fruit and vegetables enclosed in a skin are likely to burst when cooked in the microwave oven because there is no external dry heat to soften the skins first. So, after coring score round the waist of whole shiny fruits such as cooking apples to allow the steam to escape and if you pierce fruit such as gooseberries, it will help the fruit to keep its shape during cooking. Plums and greengages do not require piercing but they should be cooked covered as the skins will pop during cooking.

Stewing fruit

When stewing high water content fruits, such as rhubarb, provided the dish is covered completely no extra water is needed. The full flavour of the fruit is therefore undiluted in the finished dish. Small berries such as blackcurrants and redcurrants will be more tender if enough water is added to just cover them. Dried fruits need no soaking before cooking in the microwave oven but enough water must be added to allow for absorption without overcooking.

Thawing and blanching fruit

Use the microwave oven to thaw frozen fruit even if you intend to eat it raw. But do this on LOW so that the pieces remain whole. You run the risk of par-cooking if you thaw on HIGH. Partially thaw and follow by a standing time at room temperature to complete the process. Use the microwave oven for blanching fruit for the freezer, too. It is particularly useful for fruit such as apple slices which discolour quickly.

Cook fruit in the microwave oven for purées, fools and crumbles and if you want to make a traditional fruit pie, cook the fruit in the microwave oven first and then combine it with the pastry, and finish in the conventional oven. When making crumble use a deep rectangular dish because with this shape the steam escapes more easily from the boiling fruit syrup.

Thawing frozen fruit

Fruit	Time on LOW: 450 g (1 lb)
Apples, sliced	6 minutes
Apricots, halved	6 minutes plus 20 minutes standing time
Berries, soft	6 minutes
Currants, black and red	6 minutes
Gooseberries	8 minutes
Peaches, whole	6 minutes plus 20 minutes standing time
Plums	8 minutes plus 10 minutes standing time
Rhubarb	4 minutes (on HIGH)

Basic Sponge Pudding

100 g (4 oz) softened butter or
soft margarine
100 g (4 oz) soft light brown
sugar
2 eggs, beaten
100 g (4 oz) self raising flour
1.25–2.5 ml ($\frac{1}{4}$–$\frac{1}{2}$ tsp) vanilla
flavouring
15 ml (1 tbsp) milk

For the syrup topping
30 ml (2 tbsp) jam

1

Grease a .85-litre (1$\frac{1}{2}$-pint)
ovenproof glass pudding basin.
Beat the butter or margarine and
sugar together until light and fluffy.

2

Add a little of the beaten egg and
15 ml (1 level tbsp) of the flour and
beat again. Then beat in the
remaining egg.

3

Fold in the rest of the flour, blend
the vanilla flavouring and milk
together and gently stir into the
mixture to form a heavy batter.

4

Put the jam into the base of the
greased basin and spoon the batter
on top. Cover the basin very
loosely with cling film, pressing it
close in at the sides of the basin but
pulling it high above the centre of
the pudding so that it is very loose
and wrinkly.

5

Microwave on HIGH for 3 minutes
or until the pudding is just dry on
top and shrinks away from the
sides of the basin. Leave to stand
for 5 minutes or until cooked
underneath, then remove the cling
film carefully and turn the pudding
out on to a warm dish.

Serves 4.

Fruity Sponge Pudding

100 g (4 oz) softened butter or
soft margarine
100 g (4 oz) soft light brown
sugar
2 eggs, beaten
100 g (4 oz) self-raising flour
15 ml (1 tbsp) milk
30–45 ml (2–3 tbsp) raisins or
sultanas

1

Follow Steps 1 and 2 of Basic
Sponge Pudding. Add the raisins or
sultanas and fold in the remaining
flour.

2

Stir the mixture together to
evenly distribute the fruit.

3

Spoon the butter into the prepared
basin. Cover loosely with cling film
as in Step 4 of the Basic Sponge
Pudding. Complete the cooking as
in Step 5.

Spicy syrup pudding
Add ground ginger and warmed
jam to the mixture before cooking.

**Basic sponge pudding with
sweet sauce**
Omit the toppings and serve with a
plain sweet sauce.

Chocolate Banana Pudding

100 g (4 oz) softened butter or
soft margarine
100 g (4 oz) caster sugar
100 g (4 oz) banana, freshly
mashed
100 g (4 oz) self raising flour,
sifted
2 eggs, beaten
1.25–2.5 ml ($\frac{1}{4}$–$\frac{1}{2}$ tsp) vanilla
flavouring
100 g (4 oz) cooking chocolate
banana slices to decorate

1

Grease a 1.1-litre (1$\frac{3}{4}$-pint) pudding
basin. Beat the butter and the
sugar together until light and
fluffy. Mix in the banana and 15 ml
(1 level tbsp) of the flour.
Gradually beat in eggs and vanilla,
then fold in remaining flour.

2

Put the mixture in the basin and
cover loosely with cling film,
pressing it close in at the sides but
pulling it high above the centre of
the pudding to allow for rising.
Microwave on HIGH for 4 minutes
or until the mixture is just dry on
top. Leave for 5 minutes, then turn
out on to a serving dish.

3

Meanwhile, break up the chocolate
and put it in a basin. Microwave on
HIGH for 2$\frac{1}{2}$ minutes or until the
chocolate begins to melt. Stir well.
Pour the chocolate over the hot
pudding, spreading it smoothly.
Decorate with a few slices of
banana just before serving.

Serves 4–6.

Layered Fruit Suet Pudding

1 small orange
25 g (1 oz) dried apricots, chopped
25 g (1 oz) sultanas
25 g (1 oz) currants
25 g (1 oz) soft light brown sugar
15 ml (1 tbsp) golden syrup
150 g (5 oz) self raising flour
75 g (2½ oz) shredded suet
50 g (2 oz) soft light brown sugar
pinch of salt
1 egg, beaten
45 ml (3 tbsp) milk

1

Lightly grease a 85-litre (1½-pint) pudding basin.

2

To make the filling, grate the orange rind then peel and segment the orange over a bowl to catch the juices. Cut the segments in half. Mix the juice and orange segments with the remaining filling ingredients and set aside while making the pastry.

3

To make the pastry lightly mix the flour, suet, sugar and salt together, then add the beaten egg and sufficient milk to form a soft but not sticky dough.

4

Turn out on to a lightly floured board and shape into a cylinder wider at one end than the other. Divide into 3 equal lengths.

5

Shape the smallest piece into a round to fit into the bottom of the pudding basin. Put the pastry in the basin and cover with half the filling.

6

Shape the middle section of the pastry to fit and cover the fruit layer and place in the basin.

7

Cover with the remaining fruit, then top with the last piece of pastry, shaped to fit comfortably on top.

8

Cover the basin with a piece of cling film which should fit tightly round the sides of the basin but be slack enough in the centre to allow for rising. Microwave on HIGH for 4½ minutes or until the pastry is risen and just dry on top. Give the dish a half-turn once during the cooking period.

9

Leave for 5 minutes, then remove the cling film carefully, taking care not to burn yourself. Turn the pudding out on to a heated serving dish. Serve at once with custard or fruit sauce.

Serves 4–6.

Note Suet puddings should be served hot, preferably when they are fresh. On cooling they become hard but will soften again if reheated briefly.

Golden Pudding

30 ml (2 tbsp) golden syrup
75 g (3 oz) self raising flour
75 g (3 oz) fresh white breadcrumbs
75 g (3 oz) shredded suet
pinch of salt
50 g (2 oz) caster sugar
finely grated rind of ½ lemon
about 150 ml (¼ pint) milk

1

Grease a .85-litre (1½-pint) pudding basin and spoon in the syrup.

2

In a bowl, mix together the flour, breadcrumbs, suet, salt, sugar and lemon rind. Stir enough milk into the mixture to make a soft dropping consistency.

3

Turn the mixture into the prepared basin and cover loosely with cling film, pressing it around the sides of the basin and making sure that there is sufficient cling film in the centre to allow for rising.

4

Microwave on HIGH for 4½ minutes or until the pudding is just set on top.

5

Leave to stand for 5 minutes then carefully remove the cling film. Turn the pudding out on to a heated serving dish. Serve at once with custard.

Serves 4.

Suet Sponge Marmalade Pudding

75 g (3 oz) plain flour, sifted
75 g (3 oz) fresh breadcrumbs
5 ml (1 level tsp) baking
    powder
2.5 ml (½ level tsp) salt
40 g (1½ oz) caster sugar
75 g (3 oz) shredded suet
50 g (2 oz) sultanas
1 egg, beaten
60–75 ml (4–5 tbsp) milk

For the sauce
60 ml (4 tbsp) marmalade
5 ml (1 tsp) orange flavoured
    liqueur or brandy

1

Grease a .85-litre (1½-pint) pudding basin. Mix the flour, breadcrumbs, baking powder, salt, sugar and suet together with a fork. Stir in the sultanas.

2

Beat the egg with 60 ml (4 tbsp) milk, add to the mixture and mix as quickly and lightly as possible to a soft consistency that drops easily from a spoon. Add the remainder of the milk if necessary.

3

Spoon the mixture into the prepared basin and cover loosely with cling film, pressing it around the sides of the basin and making sure that there is sufficient cling film to dome high above the pudding to allow for rising.

4

Microwave on HIGH for 3½ minutes or until the pudding is just set on top. Leave for 5 minutes before carefully removing the cling film and turning the pudding out on to a serving plate.

5

While the pudding is standing, prepare the sauce. Put the marmalade and 30 ml (2 tbsp) water in a glass measuring jug and microwave on HIGH for 10 seconds or until the marmalade is melted. Stir, then microwave on HIGH for 30 seconds or until the liquid boils. Stir in the liqueur or brandy and pour the marmalade sauce over the hot pudding.

Serves 4–6.

Baked Egg Custard

450 ml (¾ pint) milk
3 eggs, lightly beaten
40 g (1½ oz) caster sugar
1.25 ml (¼ tsp) vanilla
    flavouring
pinch of ground nutmeg

1

Put the milk in a large measuring jug and microwave on HIGH for 1½ minutes or until it is warm to the touch.

2

Add the beaten eggs, sugar and vanilla flavouring and beat well. Strain the mixture into a 900-ml (1½-pint) undecorated soufflé dish. Sprinkle over the nutmeg.

3

Three quarters cover the dish with cling film. Reduce the setting and microwave on LOW for 12 minutes or until the outside of the custard is set and the centre is still wobbly. Give the dish a quarter-turn three times during the cooking period.

4

Leave to stand for 10 minutes, still covered, then remove the cling film and leave to cool. The custard will continue thickening during the cooling time. Chill before serving.

Serves 4.

Strawberry Cheesecake

75 g (3 oz) butter
175 g (6 oz) digestive biscuits, finely crushed
225 g (8 oz) cream cheese
225 g (8 oz) curd or cottage cheese
100 g (4 oz) caster sugar
10 ml (2 level tsp) grated lemon rind
7.5 ml ($1\frac{1}{2}$ tsp) lemon juice
3 eggs, beaten
$\frac{1}{4}$ packet strawberry jelly
225 g (8 oz) fresh strawberries, sliced
whipped cream (optional)

1

Put the butter in a 23-cm (9-inch) round shallow dish and microwave on HIGH for about 45 seconds until melted. Mix in the crumbs and press the mixture thoroughly into the base and sides.

2

Microwave on HIGH for 1–$1\frac{1}{2}$ minutes to set the crust.

3

Beat the cheeses, sugar, lemon rind and juice and eggs thoroughly together and pour evenly into the crumb base in the dish. Microwave on HIGH for 3 minutes, giving the dish a half-turn after $1\frac{1}{2}$ minutes.

4

Reduce the setting and microwave on LOW for 14 minutes or until the centre is almost set. Give the dish a quarter-turn every 2 minutes during cooking.

5

Remove from the microwave oven and loosely tent with foil, leaving a gap to prevent condensation. Cool.

6

When the cheesecake is cool, transfer to the refrigerator and chill for at least 3 hours. If you wish to turn the cake out before decorating, freeze until hard then dip the base of the dish into warm water and unmould.

7

Meanwhile prepare the decoration. Put the jelly in a glass measuring jug and make up to 75 ml ($2\frac{1}{2}$ fl oz) with cold water. Microwave on HIGH for 1 minute or until the water is hot. Stir thoroughly to dissolve the jelly, then make up to 90 ml ($3\frac{1}{2}$ fl oz) with cold water. Leave until beginning to set.

8

Arrange the sliced strawberries on the cheesecake and pour the jelly over just before it begins to set. Refrigerate until set.

9

When the jelly is set pipe rosettes of whipped cream around the edges, if you wish.

Serves 6–8.

Rice Pudding

50 g (2 oz) pudding rice
25 g (1 oz) caster sugar
7 g ($\frac{1}{4}$ oz) butter or block margarine
568 ml (1 pint) milk
2.5 ml ($\frac{1}{2}$ level tsp) grated nutmeg

1

Mix all the ingredients thoroughly together in a 2.8-litre (5-pint) mixing bowl.

2

Microwave on HIGH for 8 minutes or until the mixture begins to boil. Stir twice during cooking.

3

Reduce the setting and microwave on LOW for 35 minutes or until the rice is soft and the pudding creamy. Stir four times during cooking. Serve hot or cold.

Serves 4.

Note Rice pudding thickens as it cools and if you prefer to eat it cold, you will find it much improved the second day. Keep in the refrigerator. A creamier rice pudding can be made using evaporated milk, combining equal quantities of milk and water.

Mandarin Orange Rice

**227-g (8-oz) can mandarin
  oranges**
225 ml (8 fl oz) evaporated milk
50 g (2 oz) pudding rice
25 g (1 oz) caster sugar
**1.25 ml ($\frac{1}{4}$ level tsp) grated
  nutmeg**
25 g (1 oz) desiccated coconut
**45 ml (3 tbsp) double cream,
  whipped**

1

Drain the mandarin oranges,
reserving the juice. Make up the
juice to 350 ml (12 fl oz) with water.

2

Combine the evaporated milk, juice
and water in a 2.8-litre (5-pint)
bowl and stir in the rice, sugar and
nutmeg. Three-quarters cover
with cling film and microwave on
HIGH for 5 minutes or until the
mixture is boiling.

3

Reduce the setting and microwave
on LOW for 20 minutes.

4

Stir in the desiccated coconut.
Microwave on LOW for 15–20
minutes, stirring twice during
cooking. Leave until cold.

5

Mix half the mandarin oranges and
all of the cream into the rice
pudding. Turn into a serving dish
and decorate with the remaining
mandarin oranges.

Serves 4–6.

Chocolate, Rum and Sultana Pudding

568 ml (1 pint) milk
40 g (1$\frac{1}{2}$ oz) semolina
50 g (2 oz) caster sugar
**15 g ($\frac{1}{2}$ oz) butter or block
  margarine**
50–75 g (2–3 oz) sultanas
**50 g (2 oz) cooking chocolate,
  roughly chopped, or cooking
  chocolate drops**
15 ml (1 tbsp) dark rum

1

Put the milk in a 2.8-litre (5-pint)
bowl and microwave on HIGH for
5 minutes or until boiling.

2

Add the semolina, sugar and
butter, stir and microwave on
HIGH for 7 minutes or until the
mixture thickens to the
consistency of a pouring sauce. Stir
twice during the first minute and
twice during the remainder of the
cooking time.

3

Add the sultanas and microwave on
HIGH for 1 minute.

4

Add the chocolate and stir until
melted, then stir in the rum. Pour
into individual dishes and serve hot
or cold.

Serves 4.

Note The pudding thickens and
the sultanas soften additionally
during cooling.

Bread and Butter Pudding

**40 g (1$\frac{1}{2}$ oz) butter or block
  margarine**
**4 thin slices wholemeal bread,
  about 25 g (1 oz) each**
40 g (1$\frac{1}{2}$ oz) demerara sugar
**75 g (3 oz) mixed sultanas and
  currants**
300 ml ($\frac{1}{2}$ pint) milk
2 eggs
**1.25 ml ($\frac{1}{4}$ level tsp) ground
  cinnamon**
**1.25 ml ($\frac{1}{4}$ level tsp) grated
  nutmeg**

1

Butter the bread and cut each slice
into quarters diagonally.

2

Place 15 g ($\frac{1}{2}$ oz) sugar and half the
fruit in the base of a lightly oiled
85 litre (1$\frac{1}{2}$-pint) pie dish. Then
cover with half the bread, butter
side up and overlapping the pieces.

3

Cover with the remaining sugar
and fruit and top with the rest of
the bread (also butter side up).

4

Put the milk in a jug and
microwave on HIGH for 45 seconds
or until warm to the touch. Beat
the eggs and spices together and
stir in the milk.

5

Pour the milk mixture over the
bread and microwave on LOW for
12 minutes or until the centre is
nearly set. Give the dish a quarter-
turn three times during cooking.

6

Brown under a hot grill (this is
only possible if the pie dish is
flameproof).

Serves 4.

Fruit Fondue

a selection of fresh fruit
  (allowing 1 fruit per person):
  apples, bananas, pears, pineapple, oranges or satsumas,
  strawberries, peaches,
  apricots, kiwi fruit, mangoes
lemon juice
Marshmallow sauce (page 98)
225 g (8 oz) raspberries or
  blackberries, puréed
green food colouring
peppermint flavouring
Sabayon sauce (page 97)
Orange sauce (page 99)
Chocolate mocha sauce (page
  98)

1

Prepare the fruit, peeling and
coring where necessary. Peel and
divide the oranges into segments
but do not remove the membranes.
Leave strawberries whole. Cut
large fruit into bite-size chunks.
Toss fruit that might discolour in
lemon juice. This includes apples,
pears and bananas.

2

Arrange the fruit on a large round
dish in a decorative cartwheel
shape, mixing so that pale colours
are beside the more strident
colours. Cover with a few sheets of
absorbent kitchen paper to mop up
any excess moisture.

3

Into half the Marshmallow sauce
stir the puréed raspberries or
blackberries. Leave one-quarter of
the sauce plain and flavour the
remainder with 1 drop of green
colouring and 1–2 drops of
peppermint flavouring.

4

Put the 6 sauces into separate
serving bowls and arrange them in
a semi-circle round the fruit
platter. Intersperse them with
bundles of cocktail sticks arranged
in small glasses or serviette rings.
Have plenty of serving spoons
ready beside the sauces.

Fresh Pineapple Flambé

25 g (1 oz) unsalted butter or
  block margarine
4 medium-thick slices fresh
  pineapple, trimmed
15 g ($\frac{1}{2}$ oz) icing sugar
45 ml (3 tbsp) kirsch

1

Put the butter in a shallow
ovenproof serving dish and
microwave on HIGH for 45 seconds
or until melted.

2

Add the pineapple slices and turn
so that they are coated on both
sides. Sift the icing sugar over the
buttered pineapple.

3

Microwave on HIGH for 2 minutes,
then turn the pineapple pieces
over and stir any unmixed sugar
into the butter. Microwave on
HIGH for 1 minute. Remove the
dish from the microwave oven.

4

Put the kirsch in a cup or glass and
microwave on HIGH for 5 seconds
or until warm. Pour the kirsch
evenly over the pineapple and
flambé immediately. Serve hot.

Serves 4.

Note It is safer to use a lighted
taper rather than a match to
ignite the kirsch.
  You can prepare other fruits to
flambé such as peaches or apricots
in brandy, thick apple slices in
apple brandy, pear quarters or
halves in orange flavoured liqueur,
cherries in cherry brandy.

Orange Sorbet

300 ml ($\frac{1}{2}$ pint) unsweetened
  orange juice
juice of $\frac{1}{2}$ lemon
75 g (3 oz) granulated sugar
1 egg white

1

Put the orange juice in a .55-litre
(1-pint) ovenproof glass measuring
jug and add the lemon juice. Stir in
the sugar. Microwave on HIGH for
3 minutes or until the sugar is
dissolved, stirring from time to
time.

2

Cover the jug and put into the
freezer. Turn out the orange
mixture when firm but not frozen.
Beat thoroughly until opaque.

3

Whisk the egg white until stiff.
Fold into the half frozen orange
mixture and pour into a freezer
container. Seal the container and
return to the freezer.

4

Soften in the refrigerator for 30
minutes before serving.

Serves 8.

Dried Fruit Compote

350 g (12 oz) mixed dried fruits
(apricots, apples, pears,
peaches, small prunes and
quartered figs)
75 g (3 oz) seedless raisins or
sultanas
30 ml (2 tbsp) clear honey
30 ml (2 tbsp) lemon juice
600 ml (1 pint) water

1

Put all the fruit into a large
casserole and add water.

2

Cover with the lid and microwave
on HIGH for 10 minutes or until
almost tender, stirring once during
cooking.

3

Stir in the honey and lemon juice,
then replace the lid and leave to
stand for 30 minutes. Serve warm
or cold.

Serves 4.

Note If preferred, omit the honey
and add 25–50 g (1–2 oz) brown or
white sugar to the fruit.

Stewed Dried Fruit

Put the fruit, water and sugar if used in a dish making sure that there is
sufficient water for the fruit to absorb. Cook covered, stirring during
cooking. Allow a standing time before uncovering.

	Figs whole	Figs cut up	Apricots, Peaches and Pears	Prunes
Quantity	450 g (1 lb)	450 g (1 lb)	225 g (8 oz)	450 g (1 lb)
Pre-soak	Yes—cover with water in deep dish and leave for 2 hours	No	No	No
Sugar	Add to taste after soaking	Only add if required	Add towards end of cooking time	Add half-way through cooking time
Water	No extra required	600 ml (1 pint)	600 ml (1 pint)	600 ml (1 pint)
Microwave on HIGH	10 minutes, stir occasionally	10 minutes, stir occasionally	20 minutes, covered, stir frequently	15 minutes, three-quarters cover. Stir 3 times
Standing time	—	30 minutes	10 minutes	15 minutes

RAISINS AND SULTANAS—To plump before using in cakes put in a bowl,
barely cover with water or fruit juice, cover and microwave on HIGH for
5 minutes. Stir and leave to stand for 5 minutes.

Apple and Blackberry Crunch

350 g (12 oz) cooking apples, peeled, cored and sliced
225 g (8 oz) blackberries
50 g (2 oz) sugar

For the topping
25 g (1 oz) butter or block margarine
30 ml (2 tbsp) golden syrup
25 g (1 oz) cornflakes
150 ml ($\frac{1}{4}$ pint) whipping cream

1

Put the sliced apples, the blackberries and sugar in a large ovenproof glass bowl, three-quarters cover with cling film and microwave on HIGH for 5 minutes or until the fruit is soft. Stir occasionally during the cooking time.

2

Purée the fruit in a blender, then divide between 4 individual dishes or glasses and leave until cool.

3

Put the butter and golden syrup in an ovenproof glass bowl and microwave on HIGH for 45 seconds or until melted. Stir thoroughly. Stir in the cornflakes but do not crush them.

4

Whip the cream until stiff. Cover the puréed fruit with the cream and top with the cooled cornflake topping mixture.

Serves 4.

Apple Crumble

175 g (6 oz) plain flour
pinch of salt
75 g (3 oz) butter or block margarine
100 g (4 oz) granulated or demerara sugar
700 g (1$\frac{1}{2}$ lb) cooking apples
ground cloves

1

Sift the flour and salt into a mixing bowl and rub in the butter until the mixture resembles fine breadcrumbs. Stir in 40 g (1$\frac{1}{2}$ oz) of the sugar.

2

Peel, core, quarter and thinly slice the apples and spread evenly in a deep dish. Add 50 g (2 oz) sugar and ground cloves to taste.

3

Cover and microwave on HIGH for 5 minutes or until the apples begin to soften.

4

Top with the crumble mixture, pressed well down, and sprinkle with the remaining 10 g ($\frac{1}{2}$ oz) sugar and a pinch of ground cloves. Without covering, microwave on HIGH for 10–12 minutes or until just set. Give the dish a quarter-turn every 3 minutes during cooking. Do not overcook. Allow several minutes longer cooking time if the crumble topping has been taken direct from the freezer and the fruit is frozen or cold.

Serves 4.

Note The apple may bubble up while the crumble is cooking but will settle again, leaving the crumble intact when cooking is finished.

Summer Sponge Pudding

225 g (8 oz) black cherries, stoned, fresh or frozen
350 g (12 oz) blackberries, fresh or frozen
125 g (4 oz) raspberries, fresh or frozen
50–75 g (2–3 oz) caster sugar
whipped cream to serve

For the sponge cake lining
3 eggs, size 2
75 g (3 oz) caster sugar
few drops of vanilla flavouring
15 ml (1 tbsp) vegetable oil
75 g (3 oz) plain flour

1

Grease a .85-litre (1$\frac{1}{2}$-pint) pudding basin. Mix the cherries, blackberries, raspberries and sugar together in an ovenproof glass bowl. Three-quarters cover with cling film and microwave on HIGH for 5 minutes or until the fruit juices run (the fruit should not be cooked). Set aside while preparing the sponge mixture.

2

Cut two 30.5-cm (12-inch) circles from greaseproof paper and grease on one side. Take out the oven shelf unless it is fixed and put the paper on it, or put the greaseproof paper on a piece of cardboard or suitable tray that will fit into the oven cavity comfortably.

3

Whisk the eggs, sugar and vanilla flavouring together until pale and mousse-like; a fork drawn through the mixture should form a trail. Sprinkle the oil over the surface and fold in lightly.

4

Sift half the flour over the mixture and fold in, then sift the remaining flour over the mixture and fold in lightly and rapidly.

5

Pour the sponge mixture on to 1 piece of prepared paper to reach within 5 cm (2 inches) of the edge. Lift the shelf, turntable or cardboard with the sponge topped greaseproof paper still in position and put it into the microwave oven. If cardboard has been used slip this out carefully.

6

Microwave on HIGH for 3 minutes, then cover the sponge with the other paper circle, greased side against the sponge, and microwave on HIGH for 2 minutes or until the top is dry (the outside edges may still be slightly moist but do not cook further).

7

Remove the shelf or turntable from the oven and take off the paper cover. Slide a long palette knife between the cake mixture and the paper to make sure that it will come away easily. Cut out a wedge (about $\frac{1}{3}$–$\frac{1}{4}$ of the cake), then using your hands, lift the cake disc carefully and fit into the prepared pudding basin to line it. Push the edges to ease the cake into the base.

8

Reserve 150 ml ($\frac{1}{4}$ pint) of the fruit juices and a little of the fruit, then pour the remainder of the fruit into the basin. Cover the middle with the cut-out cake wedge and fold the edges of the cake lining over to completely enclose the fruit. Using a jug, pour the reserved fruit juice over the top and around the sides of the pudding so that it is completely soaked.

9

Cover the basin loosely with cling film and press a saucer on the top. Place a heavy weight on top of the saucer, then put the basin in a cool place or refrigerate at least 12 hours or overnight.

10

Loosen the pudding with a knife and turn out on to a serving dish. Pour the reserved juices and fruit over the pudding, making sure that any unsoaked parts are covered, and serve with whipped cream.

Serves 4–6.

Note To speed up the whisking of the eggs and sugar, take the chill off the eggs by putting them in the microwave oven for 5 seconds only, set on HIGH; take the chill off the sugar by placing the mixing bowl in the microwave oven on HIGH for 2 minutes. If the mixture is still too slow to thicken, microwave the foamy egg and sugar mixture on DEFROST for 20 seconds before continuing to whisk. This is the equivalent of whisking over hot water in the conventional way.

Traditional Summer Pudding can be made using the fruits as given in the Summer Sponge Pudding, increasing the sugar to 100 g (4 oz). Take 100–175 g (4–6 oz) bread slices and cut off the crusts. Trim the bread to line the base and sides of the pudding basin. Fill with most of the fruit and the juice. Cover the fruit with bread.

Cover loosely with cling film, put a saucer and weights on top and refrigerate for at least 12 hours. Turn out and serve with the reserved fruit and juices and cream.

CHAPTER TEN

Baking

There are many advantages in using the microwave oven for baking. There is no waste of valuable fuel, such as occurs when a large conventional oven has to be heated for just one cake and neither is preheating required. There are no baked-on tins to scour and the cakes are ready in no time at all.

But microwave baking has its limitations. Because of the nature of microwaves it is only possible to either bake crisp throughout or soft throughout; you cannot get a crisp crust and a soft centre. The moist heat obtained by microwaves keeps the crust soft and, incidentally, gives cakes a higher rise. Make sure that your cake containers are large enough to allow for this extra rising and only half-fill them. Any mixture that rises more than 1 cm ($\frac{1}{2}$ inch) above the container will spill over.

The shape of the container is important in baking. The use of a ring mould ensures an even overall texture. Round dishes should not be more than 23 cm (9 inches) in diameter and choose square dishes with rounded corners to prevent overcooking in the angles.

Shallow containers cook faster than deep and two shallow cakes cooked separately will take about the same time as one deep cake.

Cakes baked in loaf-shaped dishes tend to cook first at the ends before the centre is ready. When the ends are cooked, cover them with smooth pieces of foil and continue microwaving until the middle has caught up. Bake small cakes in double paper cases or in specialist bun tins.

Since browning doesn't occur in the microwave oven use dark coloured ingredients such as dark brown sugar, malt extract, treacle or dark coloured spices to darken baked mixtures. Chocolate cakes, ginger cakes and similar items require no embellishment but lighter cake mixtures must be iced or decorated in some way. When time is short freshly whipped cream is an excellent disguise.

Preparation of Containers
Generally speaking plastic re-usable containers designed for microwave cooking need no greasing unless the mixture contains only a small amount of fat. Ovenproof glass dishes do need greasing and it is always a good idea to line the base of a cake dish with a circle of greaseproof paper in addition to greasing it all over to allow the rising cake to climb easily up the sides.

Cake containers may also be loosely lined with cling film unless hot syrups or sugar mixtures are being baked in the base; this gives a cake a very smooth, shiny appearance. If a cake is being iced this is of no importance but if you find the shiny finish ugly, pare away the outer layer with a knife.

The outer layer of a cake is usually very soft on removal from the microwave oven. Do not overcook cakes, puddings or other baked items or they will harden very quickly. If they have been overcooked there is no remedy except to break them up and use them in trifles or similar dishes.

Turn out the cake immediately after the standing time to prevent it from sticking to the container. Cakes should be wrapped in cling film as soon as they are cool and similarly wrap the remainder if only a few pieces have been cut.

Biscuits
Although biscuits can be cooked in the microwave oven the traditional crisp type do not turn out well, so it seems more sensible to use your conventional oven for these. However, when a mixture is baked in one piece and subsequently cut into bars, such as flapjacks or bar cookies, the microwave oven is efficient. This type of biscuit usually has a high sugar content and will burn easily so do not overcook; burning begins in the centre and you may not see it until it is too late.

Pastry
Pastry tends to be tough and dry if cooked in the microwave oven. It is much better to cook pastry flan cases conventionally, then fill and cook the filling by microwave. For top crust pies, cook the filling by microwave first then cover with pastry and finish cooking in the conventional oven.

Bread
Bread is not good cooked by microwave, but the microwave oven is useful for refreshing stale loaves. Likewise it does wonders for a plain cake that is past its best.

Frangipane Tart

For the pie crust
**50 g (2 oz) butter or block
 margarine**
**100 g (4 oz) sweet biscuits,
 finely crushed**

For the filling
**30–45 ml (2–3 tbsp) raspberry
 jam**
**50 g (2 oz) butter, softened, or
 soft margarine**
50 g (2 oz) caster sugar
grated rind of 1 lemon
50 g (2 oz) fresh breadcrumbs
50 g (2 oz) ground almonds
2 eggs, beaten
**2.5 ml ($\frac{1}{2}$ tsp) almond
 flavouring**

For the topping
**about 100 g (4 oz) icing sugar,
 sifted**
red food colouring

1

Put the butter in an 18-cm (7-inch) round cake dish (measuring diameter across the top); the depth of the baked tart is about 3 cm (1$\frac{1}{4}$ inches). Microwave on HIGH for 45 seconds or until the butter is melted.

2

Mix in the biscuit crumbs thoroughly, using a fork, and press into the base and sides of the cake dish. Microwave on HIGH for 1 minute to set the mixture.

3

After a few minutes cover the base of the tart shell with a layer of raspberry jam (do not drag the jam across the surface or it will break up the shell). If necessary warm the jam for 5–10 seconds in a bowl in the microwave oven.

4

To make the filling, beat the butter and caster sugar together until the mixture is light and fluffy.

5

Stir in the lemon rind, fresh breadcrumbs and ground almonds, then beat in the eggs and almond flavouring.

6

Spread the filling evenly over the jam and microwave on HIGH for 2 minutes giving the dish a quarter-turn three times during cooking.

7

Reduce the setting and microwave on LOW for 5 minutes or until the centre of the cake is set. Give the dish a quarter-turn three times during cooking.

8

Leave the tart in the cake dish until cool but not cold and turn out carefully on to a large plate. Immediately reverse on to a similar sized plate (do not use a wire rack). If any of the crumb crust crumbles away, it can be easily pushed back using a warm table knife.

9

Mix the icing sugar with 10–15 ml (2–3 tsp) water to form a thick pouring consistency. Pour evenly over the tart.

10

Dip a skewer in the red food colouring and, just before the icing sets, draw the skewer in straight lines about 2.5 cm (1 inch) apart across the surface.

11

Leave for a few minutes for the colouring to set, then draw the cleaned skewer through the icing at right angles and at the same intervals as before but the lines should be drawn in alternate directions so that a feathering effect is achieved (for the best results hold the skewer at as flat an angle as possible). Leave until the icing has set firmly before serving. Store in an airtight container, if you wish.

Serves 8.

Rum and cherry truffles

10 glacé cherries
30 ml (2 tbsp) rum
75 g (3 oz) cooking chocolate
50 g (2 oz) caster sugar
50 g (2 oz) butter or block
 margarine
1 egg, lightly beaten
2.5 ml ($\frac{1}{2}$ tsp) vanilla flavouring

65 g (2$\frac{1}{2}$ oz) plain flour
2.5 ml ($\frac{1}{2}$ level tsp) baking
 powder
25 g (1 oz) ground almonds
30–45 ml (2–3 level tbsp)
 apricot jam
100 g (4 oz) chocolate
 vermicelli

1

Put the cherries and rum in a small bowl or glass and leave to soak while making the cake mixture.

2

Put the chocolate and sugar in a mixing bowl and if using chocolate chips stir before cooking. Microwave on HIGH for 2 minutes or until the chocolate begins to melt. Stir once during cooking. If necessary microwave on HIGH for a few more seconds until the chocolate is fully melted.

3

Add the butter and beat until it melts and blends with the melted chocolate.

4

Add the egg, vanilla flavouring, flour, baking powder and almonds and mix thoroughly. Microwave on HIGH for 1 minute, then stir to mix the half-cooked batter. Microwave on HIGH for 2$\frac{1}{2}$ minutes or until the mixture is dry on top.

5

Strain the rum from the cherries over the mixture and add the jam. Beat thoroughly while hot.

6

Leave to cool slightly, then divide the mixture into 10 and form 1 at a time into balls, tucking a cherry into the centre of each. *Do not overwork the mixture.* As each ball is shaped toss in a very small bowl quarter-filled with chocolate vermicelli, swirling the bowl to produce even-shaped cakes. Remove carefully with a spoon, place on a dish or plate and refrigerate.

Makes 10.

Variations Use small pieces of pineapple for stuffing and flavour the mixture with kirsch, or small pieces of partly cooked dried apricots and orange-flavoured liqueur. The truffles may also be made without stuffing, putting chopped raisins or sultanas into the mixture after it is cooked.

Marble Ring Cake

175 g (6 oz) soft light brown
 sugar
175 g (6 oz) butter or
 margarine, softened
175 g (6 oz) plain flour
5 ml (1 level tsp) baking
 powder
3 eggs, beaten
30 ml (2 level tbsp) cocoa
 powder, sifted
grated rind of 1 lemon

1

Beat the sugar and butter together until the mixture is light and fluffy. Sift together the flour and baking powder. Mix 15 ml (1 level tbsp) of the sifted flour into the butter mixture, then add the eggs gradually, beating all the time. Add remaining flour and fold in quickly.

2

Transfer half the mixture to another bowl and mix the cocoa into this. Stir in the grated lemon rind.

3

Spoon half the plain mixture into a 1-litre (1$\frac{3}{4}$-pint) plastic ring mould, then cover with half the chocolate mixture. Repeat, finishing with chocolate mixture.

4

Without covering, microwave on HIGH for 4 minutes or until the cake is just dry on top. Give the dish a quarter-turn four times during cooking. Leave for 3–4 minutes.

Serves 8.

Note Wrap in cling film as soon as it is cool. Ring moulds other than the soft white plastic specialist microware should be well greased before filling.

Lemon Ginger Cake

100 g (4 oz) butter, softened, or soft margarine
100 g (4 oz) soft dark brown sugar
225 g (8 oz) self raising flour
10 ml (2 level tsp) ground ginger
2 eggs, beaten
2.5 ml ($\frac{1}{2}$ level tsp) bicarbonate of soda
10 ml (2 tsp) milk
30 ml (2 tbsp) black treacle

For the topping
350 g (12 oz) icing sugar, sifted
30 ml (2 tbsp) lemon juice
15 g ($\frac{1}{2}$ oz) butter, softened, or soft margarine
pared rind of 1 lemon, cut into thin strips

1

Grease and base line either an 18-cm (7-inch) ovenglass dish, or (measuring diameter across the top) a 20.5-cm (8-inch) or an 18-cm (7-inch) round cake dish.

2

Beat the butter and sugar until light and creamy. Sift together the flour and ginger and add in alternate spoonsful to the creamed mixture with the beaten egg.

3

Blend the bicarbonate of soda with the milk and stir in to the cake mixture. Add the treacle and beat thoroughly to the consistency of a heavy batter.

4

Pour the cake mixture into the prepared dish and microwave on HIGH for 5 minutes or until the cake is only just dry on top. Give the dish a quarter-turn three times during cooking and reposition on the turntable. Leave for 5 minutes before turning out. Cool on a wire rack over a dish or plate. Decorate when cool.

5

To make the decoration blend the icing sugar with the lemon juice and about 30 ml (2 tbsp) water to form a thick coating icing. Add the butter and microwave on HIGH for 30 seconds or until the butter is melted, stirring occasionally during cooking.

6

Put the lemon rind strips into a glass measuring jug, just cover with water and microwave on HIGH for 4 minutes or until the water boils. Drain. Cover the lemon strips with fresh cold water and microwave on HIGH for 3 minutes or until the water reboils, then drain again. Cool.

7

Pour the icing over the cake, allowing it to dribble down the sides, and sprinkle the top of the cake with the lemon strips.

Serves 8–10.

Cinnamon Crumble Cake

25 g (1 oz) butter or block margarine
50 g (2 oz) plain flour
10 ml (2 level tsp) demerara sugar
12.5 ml (2$\frac{1}{2}$ level tsp) ground cinnamon
125 g (4$\frac{1}{2}$ oz) plain flour
pinch of salt
5 ml (1 level tsp) baking powder
125 g (4$\frac{1}{2}$ oz) light soft brown sugar
125 g (4$\frac{1}{2}$ oz) butter, softened
2 eggs, lightly beaten
15 ml (1 tbsp) orange cordial

1

Grease and base line an 18-cm (7-inch) ovenproof glass dish or (measuring diameter across top) an 18-cm (7-inch) round cake dish.

2

Rub the butter into the flour. Mix in the sugar and the cinnamon. To make the cake, sift together the flour, salt and baking powder. Beat the sugar and butter together until light and fluffy.

3

Add the eggs to the mixture with the flour, salt and baking powder and orange cordial. Beat thoroughly for 30 seconds.

4

Pour the mixture into the prepared dish. Microwave on HIGH for 3 minutes or until the cake is almost but not quite set. Give the dish a quarter-turn three times during cooking.

5

Sprinkle the crumble topping evenly over the cake and microwave on HIGH for 2 minutes or until the topping is cooked. Leave for 4 minutes, then turn out on to a wire rack and quickly reverse on to a second wire rack.

Serves 8.

Note This plain cake improves if kept for up to 3 days before cutting. Store it well wrapped.

Flapjacks

75 g (3 oz) butter or block
   margarine
75 g (3 oz) demerara sugar
30 ml (2 tbsp) golden syrup
150 g (6 oz) porridge oats

1

Put the butter and sugar in a
1.1-litre (2-pint) bowl and
microwave on HIGH for 1 minute
until melted. Stir in the golden
syrup and porridge oats and mix
until well blended.

2

Spread the mixture in a 24 × 19 cm
($9\frac{1}{2}$ × $7\frac{1}{2}$ inch) oblong flan dish and
level the surface.

3

Microwave on LOW for 6 minutes,
quarter-turning the dish three
times during the cooking time.
Mark into bars before the mixture
cools. When cold cover tightly
with cling film.

Makes 14 bars.

Note The flapjacks will soften on
storage and therefore are best
eaten fresh.

Brownies

75 g (3 oz) butter or block
   margarine
90 ml (6 level tbsp) cocoa
   powder
100 g (4 oz) caster sugar
2 eggs, beaten
30 ml (2 tbsp) milk
2.5 ml ($\frac{1}{2}$ level tsp) vanilla
   flavouring
100 g (4 oz) self raising flour
50 g (2 oz) walnuts, roughly
   broken

1

Put the butter and cocoa powder
in a 1.1-litre (2-pint) bowl and
microwave on HIGH for $1\frac{1}{2}$
minutes or until melted. Mix until
well blended.

2

Stir in the sugar, then add the eggs,
milk, vanilla flavouring, flour and
walnuts and beat well.

3

Pour into a 24 × 19 cm ($9\frac{1}{2}$ × $7\frac{1}{2}$
inch) oblong flan dish. Microwave
on HIGH for 5 minutes, quarter-
turning three times during
cooking. Cool. Cover with cling
film if the brownies are to be
stored.

Makes 16 squares.

Chocolate
Biscuit Cake

100 g (4 oz) butter or block
   margarine
30 ml (2 tbsp) golden syrup
25 g (1 oz) caster sugar
100 g (4 oz) plain chocolate
175 g (6 oz) digestive biscuits,
   roughly broken
25 g (1 oz) raisins
25 g (1 oz) flaked almonds
50 g (2 oz) glacé cherries

1

Put the butter, golden syrup, sugar
and chocolate into a 1.1-litre
(2-pint) ovenproof glass bowl and
microwave on HIGH for 2 minutes
or until the fat and chocolate have
melted. Stir well.

2

Add the rest of the ingredients and
mix well to coat them with the
chocolate mixture.

3

Place an 18-cm (7-inch) plain flan
ring on a flat serving plate and
spoon in the biscuit mixture. Press
down evenly and chill in the
refrigerator for about 8 hours or
overnight. Remove the flan ring.

Serves 8.

Malt Soda Bread

2.5 ml ($\frac{1}{2}$ tsp) malt extract, to glaze
100 g (4 oz) plain flour
125 g ($4\frac{1}{2}$ oz) wholemeal flour
2.5 ml ($\frac{1}{2}$ level tsp) salt
2.5 ml ($\frac{1}{2}$ level tsp) bicarbonate of soda
15 g ($\frac{1}{2}$ oz) softened butter or soft margarine
30 ml (2 tbsp) malt extract
200 ml (7 fl oz) buttermilk
flour for shaping

1

First prepare the glaze. Put the 2.5 ml ($\frac{1}{2}$ tsp) malt extract in a small bowl and add 2.5 ml ($\frac{1}{2}$ tsp) water. Microwave on HIGH for 20 seconds and stir well.

2

Mix the flours, salt and bicarbonate of soda thoroughly together in an ovenproof glass mixing bowl and microwave on HIGH for 20 seconds to warm slightly.

3

Add the butter, remaining malt extract and buttermilk and mix to a soft, sticky dough.

4

Shape on a lightly floured work surface to a 15-cm (6-inch) round and, using a long sharp knife, make a deep cross on the top.

5

Place a sheet of absorbent kitchen paper on a microwave roasting rack and gently put the dough on top. Microwave the bread on HIGH for 4 minutes.

6

Brush the top of the bread with the glaze then microwave on HIGH for 2 minutes or until risen and dry on top. Test with a wooden cocktail stick or skewer, which should come out clean.

7

Remove the rack from the microwave oven, then lift the bread and carefully peel away the kitchen paper (it will be hot but will stick if not removed at once). Leave the bread on the rack to cool, then serve fresh, with butter.

Makes 1 loaf.

Black Forest Cherry Cake

75 g (3 oz) golden syrup
75 g (3 oz) soft dark brown sugar
75 g (3 oz) butter or block margarine
100 g (4 oz) self raising flour
40 g ($1\frac{1}{2}$ oz) cocoa powder, sifted
1 egg, beaten
60 ml (4 tbsp) milk
425-g (14-oz) can stoned black cherries
300 ml ($\frac{1}{2}$ pint) double cream, whipped
15 g ($\frac{1}{2}$ oz) plain chocolate, grated

1

Grease and base line an 18-cm (7-inch) ovenproof glass dish or a round cake dish.

2

Place the golden syrup, brown sugar and butter in a 2.0-litre (5-pint) ovenproof glass bowl and microwave on HIGH for 2 minutes or until melted. Stir well.

3

Add the flour and cocoa and beat well. Beat in the egg and milk. Pour into the prepared dish and microwave on HIGH for 5 minutes. Turn three times during cooking.

4

Leave to stand for 5 minutes before turning out on to a wire rack. When cold, cut in half horizontally and place the base of the cake on a serving plate. Drain the black cherries and spoon a little of the cherry juice over the base.

5

Spoon half the whipped cream over the base and scatter the cherries over the cream. Top with the other cake layer. Pipe rosettes of cream around the edge of the cake and fill with grated chocolate.

Serves 6–8.

CHAPTER ELEVEN

Confectionery

Making chocolates, sweets and candies is more of a leisure pursuit than a necessity, but commercial sweetmeats are very expensive and the high prices result more from labour costs than the price of the ingredients. Home-made confectionery is relatively cheap, and perhaps purer because less chemical ingredients are used. Many people are put off confectionery-making by the thought of sticky pans, burnt-on caramel and the disappointment of failure. The microwave oven will give you more successful results than a conventional cooker because there is no direct contact between the sugary ingredients and the heat source.

Burning can still occur, but this does not happen unless the sugary ingredients are over-cooked; little can go wrong in the initial stages. Do not leave the kitchen while sweetmeats are cooking in the microwave oven. Because sugar syrups reach a very high temperature you must take the same precautions as you would when cooking conventionally. Make sure you have a good pair of non-slip oven gloves, a dry heatproof surface, wooden spoons with long handles and large cooking containers that can resist the very high temperatures. A 2.8-litre (5-pint) ovenproof glass bowl is indispensable and large glass measuring jugs or lipped measuring bowls should be included in your list of equipment.

Start with the easiest process, which is melting chocolate. You will find that you are able to dip all kinds of fruit and fillings into the chocolate to produce a variety of instant sweetmeats. After very little practice you will be able to determine when the chocolate is sufficiently softened to melt with just a stir or two. Plain chocolate melts more easily than milk chocolate and becomes thinner. Cooking chocolate sold either in bars or as chocolate dots contains additional fat and although it is not really chocolate, but a chocolate-flavoured coating, it is nevertheless extremely good for chocolate-making by microwave. It does not form such a hard coating. When used for dipping, chocolates made with this should be kept in a very cool place or refrigerator.

One final tip—save all your old chocolate boxes and chocolate papers. These will come in useful when making boxes of assorted sweets and chocolates for giving as presents.

Melting chocolate

Break up the chocolate unless using chocolate chips and put into a bowl. Use a jug if the chocolate is to be poured, such as over a cake. If chocolate is being melted for dipping centres, choose a narrow diameter bowl so that the melted chocolate will be sufficiently deep to minimise the need for turning.

Microwave only until the chocolate is soft and glossy on top, then stir until melted. If by accident you overheat the chocolate and it becomes set and grainy, quickly beat in 2.5 ml ($\frac{1}{2}$ tsp) blended white vegetable fat. Butter is not suitable for this purpose.

Block cooking chocolate heats more quickly than chocolate chips. As a guide, 100 g (4 oz) cooking chocolate takes about 3 minutes on HIGH; 100 g (4 oz) dessert chocolate takes about 4 minutes on LOW. The melting times vary according to the type of material and shape of container used, so it is advisable to check every 1 minute during melting. Take care not to overcook or the melted chocolate may scorch.

Orange Rind Snakes

2 medium oranges
100 g (4 oz) plain dessert
   chocolate

1

Put the oranges on a wooden board or work surface. Using a sharp knife and following the contour of the orange, pare away the rind and only a thin layer of the pith. Cut the rind into strips no more than 0.5 cm ($\frac{1}{4}$ inch) wide and about 6.5 cm (2$\frac{1}{2}$ inches) long.

2

Put the orange strips into a large glass measuring jug and just cover with cold water. Microwave on HIGH for 3 minutes or until boiling, then drain.

3

Cover with fresh cold water and microwave on HIGH for 2$\frac{1}{2}$ minutes or until boiling once more. Drain thoroughly. Spread the orange strips out on absorbent kitchen paper to absorb any remaining moisture.

4

Break up the chocolate and put into a small bowl. Microwave on LOW for 4 minutes or until the chocolate is shiny and just begins to lose its shape. Stir until melted, microwaving for a little longer if necessary. Do not overcook or the chocolate will burn.

5

Dip the orange strips into the melted chocolate one at a time and spread out on non-stick paper. Leave until cold.

Makes about 225 g (8 oz).

Note The orange rind snakes store well in the refrigerator for a few days. This is a good way of using up the peel when you want oranges for another recipe or to eat fresh.

Marzipan Chocolate

150 g (5 oz) block marzipan, cut into 12 pieces approximately 2.5 ×1 ×2 cm (1 ×$\frac{1}{2}$ ×$\frac{3}{4}$ inch)
100 g (4 oz) cooking chocolate, melted
6 whole almonds, lightly roasted and split in half lengthwise (see note)

1

Using a fork or skewer, dip the pieces of marzipan individually into the chocolate, scooping the melted chocolate over the marzipan with a table knife.

2

Lift carefully out of the bowl and place on a sheet of non-stick paper. Immediately top the chocolate with half an almond, browned side up.

3

Dip all the remaining marzipan pieces, topping with the almonds. Leave to cool. Trim off any jagged pieces of chocolate with a sharp knife (these can be remelted if more chocolate is required).

Makes 12 pieces.

Note Should the chocolate begin to set before all the marzipan pieces are dipped, replace the bowl in the microwave oven for a few seconds only, set on HIGH.
25 g (1 oz) almonds spaced out on a plate on the microwave oven shelf will take 1 minute on HIGH to lightly roast. Stir twice during cooking.

Handmade Chocolate Truffles

45 ml (3 tbsp) double cream
7.5 ml (1½ tsp) rum
2 egg yolks
two 150-g (5-oz) bars plain dessert chocolate

1

Put the cream in a small bowl and microwave on HIGH for about 20 seconds or until boiling. Leave to cool slightly, then stir in the rum and egg yolks.

2

Put half the chocolate in a larger bowl and microwave on HIGH for 3 minutes or until melted (the chocolate is ready as soon as it becomes shiny and some of the pieces lose their shape).

3

Stir in the egg and cream mixture and beat thoroughly. Microwave on HIGH for 30 seconds, then beat again. If the mixture is not obviously thickened, microwave for a further 30 seconds, then beat again vigorously.

4

Put the bowl in the refrigerator and leave until the mixture is firm enough to mould. Beat the mixture once during cooling.

5

When the mixture is ready, using your hands, roll into small even-sized balls.

6

To coat, break up the remaining chocolate and put into a small bowl. Microwave on LOW for 4 minutes or until the chocolate begins to lose its shape, then stir until melted.

7

Drop the truffles one at a time into the melted chocolate and turn so that they are completely coated. Lift out with the curved part of a fork and put, spaced out, on a dish lined with non-stick paper. Refrigerate until the chocolate coating is set.

Makes 24 truffles, 175 g (6 oz).

Peanut Brittle

175 g (6 oz) caster sugar
75 ml (5 tbsp) glucose syrup
25 g (1 oz) butter or block margarine
150 g (5 oz) salted peanuts
5 ml (1 level tsp) bicarbonate of soda
1.25 ml (¼ tsp) vanilla flavouring

1

Place a sheet of waxed or non-stick paper on a heatproof surface. Oil a palette knife.

2

Place the sugar, glucose syrup and 30 ml (2 tbsp) water in a large ovenproof glass bowl. Microwave on HIGH for 2 minutes until dissolved. Using a wooden spoon, stir in the butter. Microwave on HIGH for 1 minute until melted.

3

Stir in the peanuts and microwave on HIGH for 6 minutes until light brown. Do not stir while the peanuts are cooking.

4

Meanwhile mix the bicarbonate of soda, vanilla flavouring and 5 ml (1 tsp) cold water together. As soon as the peanut mixture is ready, pour in the soda mixture and beat thoroughly with a wooden spoon for 2 minutes until the mixture 'honeycombs' throughout. If the mixture is not stirred sufficiently the peanut brittle will turn tacky, not brittle.

Turkish Delight

25 g (1 oz) cornflour
175 g (6 oz) granulated sugar
few drops of red or green
   edible food colouring
7.5–10 ml (1½–2 tsp) rose water
   or a few drops of crème de
   menthe flavouring
extra cornflour for the mould

For coating
30 ml (2 level tbsp) cornflour
30 ml (2 level tbsp) icing sugar

5

Smooth the mixture over the paper with the palette knife to 0.5 cm (¼ inch) thickness. Leave for 3 minutes as the brittle is too hot to handle.

6

Turn the mixture over on the paper while it is still pliable and leave until cool enough to touch. Pulling from the edges, stretch the brittle until the peanuts stand out of the mixture and it measures about 28 × 20.5 cm (11 × 8 inches). Pull the brittle in stages.

7

Leave until cold then break up into pieces and store in an airtight tin. It will keep for 1–2 weeks.

Makes 275 g (10 oz).

1

Blend the cornflour with 75 ml (2½ fl oz) water in a small bowl and set aside.

2

Combine the sugar with 225 ml (7½ fl oz) water in a large ovenproof glass bowl and microwave on HIGH for 3 minutes. Then stir until the sugar has dissolved.

3

Add the cornflour mixture to the sugar syrup and microwave on HIGH for 6 minutes, stirring every minute. Add either red colouring and rose flavouring, or green colouring and crème de menthe flavouring. Microwave on HIGH for 3 minutes or until the mixture is the consistency of thick jelly and will not drop easily from a spoon. Stir every minute during cooking.

4

While the Turkish delight is cooking, rub a 19 × 8 cm (7½ × 3½ inch) container (see note) lightly with oil, put in a generous quantity of cornflour making sure that it coats not only the base but also the sides. Spoon the thick mixture as evenly as possible into the container and leave until cool.

5

Sift together the cornflour and icing sugar on to a sheet of non-stick paper. Turn the set Turkish delight on to it.

6

Cut the Turkish delight into approximately 21 squares and generously coat the cut surfaces with the cornflour and icing sugar mixture. Leave until cold then toss in the cornflour mixture again. Leave uncovered for several hours until the jellies are crusty outside. Store in a box with the remainder of the cornflour and icing sugar (this is to make sure that the Turkish delight keeps dry).

Makes 21 pieces.

Note Make sure that the Turkish delight mixture is fully cooked and really thick. If it is too soft when poured into the mould, it will not harden sufficiently to make it manageable. The Turkish delight dries out and becomes much firmer after about 12 hours. A foil dish is an ideal container for setting. Cut down the sides of the dish with scissors and flatten before turning out the Turkish delight.

Pineapple Chocolates

2 fresh pineapple slices
100 g (4 oz) cooking chocolate, melted
silver sugar balls

1

Remove the centre core from fresh pineapple slices and cut the rings into bite-sized wedges. Pat very thoroughly with absorbent kitchen paper to remove excess moisture.

2

Using a fork or skewer dip the pineapple pieces one at a time in the melted chocolate, scooping the chocolate over with a table knife to make sure the pineapple is completely covered.

3

Put the chocolates, spaced out, on a sheet of non-stick paper and place a silver ball on each before the chocolate has set.

4

Trim the chocolates with a sharp knife when the chocolate is firm, so that they look neat. Store in the refrigerator.

Makes about 20.

Creamy Vanilla Fudge

25 g (1 oz) butter
225 g (8 oz) granulated sugar
75 ml (5 tbsp) condensed milk
2.5 ml ($\frac{1}{2}$ tsp) vanilla flavouring

1

Lightly oil a small rectangular foil dish or suitable mould.

2

Put the butter into a 2.8-litre (5-pint) ovenproof glass bowl and microwave on HIGH for 30 seconds or until the butter is only just melted.

3

Stir in the sugar, milk, 60 ml (4 tbsp) water and the vanilla flavouring and continue stirring for 1 minute until the sugar is almost dissolved. Microwave on HIGH for 2 minutes then, using oven gloves, give the bowl a gentle shake.

4

Microwave on HIGH for 6 minutes or until a spoonful of the mixture forms a soft ball when dropped into cold water.

5

Carefully remove the bowl from the microwave oven and beat constantly until the mixture is thick and creamy and tiny crystals form (do not continue beating after this or the fudge will become candy-like and granular).

6

Pour the fudge immediately into the prepared dish. Allow to cool; refrigerate overnight until cold, then turn out and cut into squares. These creamy fudges improve if stored, uncovered, in the refrigerator for 24 hours.

Makes about 350 g (12 oz), or 25

Note For a variation make marshmallow fudge. When the mixture is removed from the microwave oven, quickly add 50 g (2 oz) chopped marshmallows, then beat until cool and continue as before. For fruit fudge, add 50 g (2 oz) chopped seeded raisins, sultanas, chopped glacé cherries or dates. For nut fudge, add 50 g (2 oz) any chopped nuts. For ginger fudge, add 25 g (1 oz) finely chopped preserved ginger.

Summer Sponge Pudding (pages 108–109)

above **Chocolate Truffles (page 118),
Creamy Vanilla Fudge (page 120) and
Coconut Ice (page 121)**

left **Cinnamon Crumble Cake (page 113)
and Frangipane Tart (page 111)**

Coconut Ice

225 g (8 oz) granulated sugar
pinch of cream of tartar
30 ml (2 tbsp) condensed milk
75 g (3 oz) desiccated coconut
2 drops of red food colouring
2 drops of rose water

1

Have ready a small rectangular dish or suitable mould. Put the sugar, cream of tartar, 45 ml (3 tbsp) water and the condensed milk into a large ovenproof glass bowl (it boils up considerably). Stir well; microwave on HIGH for 1 minute.

2

Shake the bowl gently to help the sugar dissolve but do not stir. Microwave on HIGH for 2 minutes or until a spoonful of the syrup forms a soft ball when dropped into cold water. Test at frequent intervals after the first 2 minutes if the syrup needs further cooking.

3

Using oven gloves, remove the bowl from the microwave oven and stir in the desiccated coconut. Beat thoroughly until the mixture thickens, then pour half of the mixture into the dish or mould.

4

Beat the colouring and flavouring into the remaining mixture and spread on top, smoothing with a palette knife. Leave until set, then cut into bars.

Makes 350 g (12 oz), about 8–16 bars.

Orange Marmalade (page 124),
Blackberry Jam (page 123),
Lemon Curd (page 125) and
Strawberry Jam (page 124).

Chocolate Peppermint Creams

225 g (8 oz) icing sugar, sifted
1 egg white
peppermint flavouring
green food colouring
225 g (8 oz) cooking chocolate

1

Put the icing sugar in a large bowl and mix in only sufficient of the egg white to form a stiff paste.

2

Add a few drops of peppermint flavouring and the colouring (take care not to add too much flavouring or colouring as this could ruin the peppermint creams).

3

Knead the paste in the bowl with the fingers until it becomes sufficiently manageable to roll, firm but pliable.

4

Roll out to 0.5 cm ($\frac{1}{4}$ inch) thick between 2 sheets of non-stick paper (use the rolling pin on the paper and not directly on to the sugar mixture).

5

Remove the top sheet of paper and cut out 2.5 cm (1 inch) circles of peppermint creams using a plain cutter. Continue kneading the cut out scraps and rolling out as before until all the paste is used. Leave to dry for 12 hours.

6

Put the chocolate into a bowl, breaking up the pieces if you are using block chocolate, and microwave on HIGH for 4 minutes or until the chocolate is just melted. Stir thoroughly.

7

Half-dip the peppermint creams in the chocolate and place on non-stick paper until dry.

Makes about 30 pieces.

CHAPTER TWELVE

Jams and Preserves

Making jams, preserves and chutneys in the microwave oven is easy. The colours and flavours are excellent and the process is far less trouble than the conventional methods. When using conventional methods it isn't worth making a small quantity of jam or chutney if you have to get out a large preserving pan and scour it afterwards. But with the microwave oven the preserve is made in an ordinary ovenproof glass mixing bowl and sticking is infinitesimal. Microwaved jams and chutneys are completely successful provided you follow the rules for their preparation.

Fruit
Fruit with a high pectin content will be the easiest to cope with so, when first making jam, choose blackcurrants, redcurrants, gooseberries, plums or apples. This does not mean that low pectin fruits such as strawberries are less successful, but it is essential to add lemon juice or commercial pectin to these to help them to set. Jams made from soft fruits thicken on storage, so do not overcook. Either fresh or frozen fruit can be used successfully. See page 100 for instructions on thawing fruit, and remember to include the juices.

Sugar
Choose either preserving sugar or granulated sugar for jams. Preserving sugar gives a clearer, brighter jam but granulated is cheaper and its use does not affect flavour or setting. The fruit must be soft before the sugar is added and the sugar must be well dissolved before the jam is boiled. As a rule the liquid is sufficiently hot after the fruit has been cooked to dissolve the sugar without further cooking at this stage. It helps if you warm the sugar first. To do this put the sugar in its opened bag or in a bowl, preferably lipped, and microwave on HIGH for 3–4 minutes.

Potting
Jams, curds and chutneys should be potted in hot, sterilised jars. Quarter-fill the jars with water and bring to a full boil in the microwave oven. Four jars will take about 1½ minutes, but they will not all come to the boil at the same time. Remove each one as soon as it is ready, using oven gloves, and empty out the water.

For long term potting use traditional jam pot seals and covers. For short term potting you can use freezer quality cling film and store in the refrigerator.

Fruit curds
Made with eggs and butter as well as fruit and sugar, curds are not a true 'preserve' and should only be made in small quantities and eaten quickly. They will keep for up to a month in a cupboard or for up to 3 months in the refrigerator. Lemon curd is particularly easy to make in the microwave oven, and a couple of jars can be made in just a few minutes. Substitute oranges or grapefruit for a change.

Chutneys
The high acid content in chutneys cannot affect an ovenproof glass bowl as it does some metal pans and the mixture is far less likely to burn in the microwave oven than when cooked conventionally as there is no direct contact of heat with the base of the bowl.

The fruits and/or vegetables for a chutney should be finely chopped, sliced or minced. Bruised and poorly-shaped ingredients can very often be used as their appearance in the finished preserve is of no account. They are cooked to a pulp with vinegar, sugar, spices and salt. Chutneys do have to be cooked until of a very thick consistency and you must stir frequently during the last minute of cooking. The chutney is ready when no excess liquid remains and the mixture is the consistency of a thick sauce. Never use a metal lid for storing chutneys as the acid will corrode the lid, making the chutney unsafe to eat. Chutneys should be stored in a cool, dry, dark place and allowed to mature for 2–3 months before eating.

Marmalade
With the help of a food processor, marmalade can be made successfully in the microwave oven. Drawing the pectin out of the pips and pith used to require long, slow cooking. Chopping up the pips in the food processor overcomes this, making marmalade as quick to cook as jam.

Blackberry Jam

225 g (8 oz) sugar
225 g (8 oz) fresh or frozen
blackberries, prepared or
thawed

1

Put the sugar in a 2.8-litre (5-pint) ovenproof glass mixing bowl and microwave on HIGH for 2 minutes or until the sugar is just warm.

2

Add the blackberries, stirring thoroughly.

3

Microwave on HIGH for 3 minutes, stirring every minute to dissolve the sugar (make sure that you stir to the bottom of the bowl). Microwave on HIGH for 5 minutes, by which time the mixture should be boiling rapidly.

4

Stir, then test for setting; 5 ml (1 tsp) of the syrup when dropped on to a chilled plate should wrinkle slightly when pushed with a finger.

5

Pot in hot sterilised jars and cover and label in the usual way.

Makes about 450 g (1 lb).

Note The jam thickens further as it cools. Do not overcook.

Strawberry Jam Using Frozen Fruit

450 g (1 lb) frozen strawberries
30 ml (2 tbsp) lemon juice
450 g (1 lb) sugar
knob of butter

1

Thaw the strawberries on LOW for 8–10 minutes. Drain the liquid into a 2.8-litre (5-pint) ovenproof glass mixing bowl and set the strawberries aside.

2

Stir the lemon juice into the strawberry liquid and microwave on HIGH for 2 minutes or until the mixture is boiling.

3

Stir in the sugar and microwave on HIGH for 7 minutes or until the sugar is dissolved. Stir every 2 minutes during cooking.

4

Add the drained strawberries and microwave on HIGH for 5 minutes. Stir in the butter.

5

Microwave on HIGH for 5 minutes, stirring occasionally, and test for setting; 5 ml (1 tsp) jam when dropped on to a chilled plate should wrinkle when pushed with finger. Pot in hot sterilised jars and cover and label in the usual way.

Makes 700 g (1½ lb).

Note Do not overcook strawberry jam as it becomes firm on cooling. A weak wrinkle test is generally adequate.

Strawberry Jam Using Fresh Fruit

450 g (1 lb) fresh strawberries, hulled
450 g (1 lb) sugar
30 ml (2 tbsp) lemon juice
knob of butter

1

Gently mix the strawberries, sugar and lemon juice together in a 2.8-litre (5-pint) ovenproof glass mixing bowl. Cover tightly and leave to stand for 6–8 hours until the strawberries soften and a syrup is formed.

2

Microwave on LOW for 15 minutes or until the sugar is completely dissolved. Stir very gently twice during cooking.

3

Raise the setting and microwave on HIGH for 25 minutes. Test for setting; 5 ml (1 tsp) syrup should wrinkle when dropped on to a chilled plate and pushed with a finger. Pot in hot sterilised jars and cover and label in the usual way.

Makes 700 g (1½ lb).

Orange Marmalade

900 g (2 lb) Seville or sweet oranges
2 lemons
900 g (2 lb) sugar
knob of butter

1

Wash and dry the fruit and pare away the thin rind, avoiding the white pith.

2

Shred or chop the rind, cover and set aside.

3

Chop up the fruit including the pith, flesh and the pips, which must be broken. A food processor is useful for this.

4

Put the chopped mixture into a 2.8-litre (5-pint) ovenproof glass mixing bowl and add 900 ml (1½ pints) boiling water. Without covering, microwave on HIGH for 15 minutes.

5

Strain the mixture into another large ovenglass bowl and press the cooked pulp until all the juice is squeezed out. Discard the pulp. Stir the shredded rind into the hot juice and microwave on HIGH for 15 minutes or until the rind is tender. Stir twice during cooking. Stir in the sugar until fully dissolved. Half cover the bowl with cling film and microwave on HIGH for 10 minutes.

6

Stir in the butter and microwave on HIGH for 5–6 minutes. Stir once during cooking. Test for setting. 5 ml (1 tsp) marmalade should wrinkle when dropped on to a chilled plate. Pot in hot sterilised jars and cover and label in the usual way.

Makes 1.1 kg (2½ lb).

Blackcurrant Jam

450 g (1 lb) fresh or frozen
   blackcurrants, prepared or
   thawed
450 g (1 lb) sugar

1

Place the blackcurrants in a
2.8-litre (5-pint) ovenproof glass
mixing bowl. Stir in 450 ml ($\frac{3}{4}$ pint)
water and three-quarters cover
with cling film. Microwave on
HIGH for 15 minutes or until the
fruit is very soft, stirring
occasionally during cooking.
(Allow an extra 10 minutes if the
fruit is frozen.)

2

Put the sugar in another bowl and
microwave on HIGH for 3 minutes
or until the sugar is warm. Add the
sugar to the jam and stir until it has
completely dissolved.

3

Without covering, microwave on
HIGH for 20 minutes or until 5 ml
(1 tsp) of the liquid wrinkles when
dropped on to a chilled plate and
pushed with a fingertip. Stir three
or four times during cooking.

4

Remove from the microwave oven
carefully, using oven gloves. Leave
to cool for 5 minutes then stir
thoroughly. Pot in hot sterilised
jars, cover and label.

Makes about 700 g (1$\frac{1}{2}$ lb).

Note Do not overcook
blackcurrant jam or it will darken
and develop a caramel flavour. The
jam thickens during cooling.

Lemon Curd

4 large lemons
4 eggs, beaten
225 g (8 oz) caster sugar
125 g (4 oz) unsalted butter

1

Finely grate the rind from the
lemons and place in a 2.8-litre
(5-pint) ovenproof glass mixing
bowl. Squeeze the juice from the
lemons and add to the beaten eggs.
Strain into the bowl.

2

Stir in the sugar, then add the
butter, cut into 4 or 6 pieces.
Microwave on HIGH for 1 minute,
stir, then microwave for 5 minutes
or until the lemon curd is thick.
Whisk well every minute (this is
important to avoid curdling).

3

When the lemon curd is thick,
remove the bowl from the
microwave oven using oven gloves
and continue whisking until the
mixture is cool. Lemon curd
thickens on cooling.

4

Pot in hot sterilised jars, cover,
label and store in the refrigerator.

Makes 900 g (2 lb).

Note Lemon curd will keep for
about 1 month, after which it
begins to deteriorate.

Tomato Chutney

700 g (1$\frac{1}{2}$ lb) firm, greenish-red
   tomatoes
225 g (8 oz) cooking apples,
   peeled and cored
1 medium onion, skinned
125 g (4 oz) soft dark brown
   sugar
125 g (4 oz) sultanas
5 ml (1 level tsp) salt
200 ml (7 fl oz) malt vinegar
15 g ($\frac{1}{2}$ oz) ground ginger
1.25 ml ($\frac{1}{4}$ level tsp) cayenne
   pepper
2.5 ml ($\frac{1}{2}$ level tsp) mustard
   powder

1

Put the tomatoes in a 2.8-litre
(5-pint) ovenproof glass bowl and
just cover with boiling water.
Microwave on HIGH for 4 minutes,
then lift out the tomatoes one by
one using a slotted spoon or fork
and remove the skins.

2

Mince the apple and onion or chop
finely in the food processor to a
thick paste. Roughly chop the
tomatoes.

3

Mix all the chutney ingredients
together in a 2.8-litre (5-pint)
ovenproof glass mixing bowl.
Three-quarters cover with cling
film and microwave on HIGH for
45 minutes or until the mixture is
thick and all the liquid absorbed.
Stir every 5 minutes during
cooking and take particular care,
stirring more frequently, during
the last 5 minutes.

4

Leave to stand for 10 minutes, then
stir, pour into hot sterilised jars,
cover and label. Store for at least
2 months before using.

Makes 900 g (2 lb).

Index

Apple and Blackberry Crunch 108
Apple Crumble 108
Aubergine and Butter Bean Casserole 78

Bacon
  cooking 45–7
  and egg recipes 27
  Rolls with Sausage 59
Baked Eggs with Frankfurters and Mushrooms 28
Baking 110–15
Banana and Chocolate Pudding 101
Barley and Mushroom Casserole 89
Beans in Soured Cream Sauce 80
Béchamel Sauce 93
Beef, cooking 43–4
Beefburgers 53
Beef stock 19
Beef Stroganoff 51
Beverages 17
Biscuits 110, 114
Blackberry and Apple Crunch 108
Blackberry Jam 123
Blackcurrant Jam 125
Black Forest Cherry Cake 115
Blanching vegetables 75
Boiled Rice 87
  Brown 88
Boiling 9
Boil-in-the-bag fish 31
Bolognese Sauce 94
Bread, Malt Soda 115
Bread and Butter Pudding 105
Brownies 114
Browning 9, 12
  recipes 27, 34, 58
Brown Sauce 90, 95
Butter Bean and Aubergine Casserole 78
Butterscotch Almond Sauce 97

Cake making 110, 112–15
  tips 8
Candida Chicken 66
Cauliflower, cooking 75
Cheese
  cooking 25
  Crispy Hot Sandwich 30
  and Ham Snack 30

Sauce 92
  Welsh Rarebit 28
Cheesecake, Strawberry 104
Chicken, cooking 60–3, 65–6
  gravy for 66
  stock 19
Chicken livers
  and Port Pâté 73
  thawing 62
Chicken recipes
  à la King 70
  in Barbecue Sauce 69
  Candida 66
  Chicken Divan 67
  Chinese Chicken and Mushroom Soup 24
  Crumbed 67
  Curried 69
  Italian style 70
  marinated in Teriyaki Sauce 68
  with mushrooms and almonds 74
  and Mushroom Casserole 68
  Mushroom and Sweetcorn Scallops 70
  stuffed thighs and drumsticks 71
  Walnut and Yogurt 71
Chilli Con Carne 52
Chinese Chicken and Mushroom Soup 24
Chinese Fried Rice 88
Chocolate
  Banana Pudding 101
  Biscuit Cake 114
  Marzipan 119
  melting 8, 116
  Mocha Sauce 98
  Peppermint Creams 121
  Rum and Sultana Pudding 105
  Truffles 118
Chocolates, Pineapple 120
Chops cooking 44, 46, 47–8, 50
  recipes for 54–6
Chutneys 122, 125
Cinnamon Crumble Cake 113
Coconut Ice 121
Coffee, heating 17
Colcannon 81
Compote, Dried Fruit 107
Confectionery 116–21

Containers, choosing 12–15
  for baking 110
Courgette soup, puréed 23
Cream of Mushroom Soup 22
Croûtons, Golden 24
Crumbed Chicken 67
Crumbed fish 31, 35
Crumble, Apple 108
Cucumber Sauce 96
Curried Chicken 69
Curried Lentils 83
Custard, Baked Egg 103
Custards, cooking 25

Duck, cooking 60–3
Duck à l'Orange 72

Eel, Smoked 33
Egg and Bacon recipes 27
Egg Custard, Baked 103
Egg Sauce 92
Eggs 25–30

Fish 31–42
Fish Balls in Cucumber Sauce 40
Fish Fingers 35
Flambé Fruit Sauce 99
Flapjacks 114
Fondue, Fruit 106
Frangipane Tart 111
Frankfurters, Baked with Egg and Mushroom 28
French Onion Soup 23
Fried eggs 25, 27
Frozen foods, defrosting 16
Fruit
  cooking technique 100
  Fondue 106
  for jams 122–3
Fruit, dried 107
Fruit curds 122, 125
Fruit Sauce, Flambé 99
Frying 9
  simulating for fish 31
Fudge, Creamy Vanilla 120

Game
  cooking techniques 60–3
  Mustard Rabbit Casserole 73
  Pheasant in White Wine 72

Gammon Steaks 58
Golden Pudding 102
Goose, cooking 61, 63
Gravy
    meat 49
    for Turkey or Chicken 66
Grilling 9

Halibut, Aromatic Poached Steaks 39
Ham
    and Cheese Snack 30
    and Turkey Terrine 74
Ham joints, cooking 45
Herbs, drying 78
Herring, Soused 37
Hollandaise Sauce 96
Horsham Mushrooms 79

Italian Chicken 70
Italian Meat Balls 52

Jams 122–5
    tips 8
Joints, roasting 43, 46, 47–8

Kebabs 53
Kidneys
    cooking 45–7
    in Madeira 57
Kipper Pâté 36
Kippers, Baked 33

Lamb
    and Artichoke Gratin 54
    Aubergine and Red Pepper Kebabs
        53
    Chops Paprika 54
    cooking techniques 44
Lemon Curd 125
Lemon Ginger Cake 113
Lemon Sole, Baked 32
Lentils, Curried 83
Liver
    chicken and turkey 61, 63
    cooking 45–7
    and Onions 58
Lobster, cooking 31
Lobster Thermidor 40
Lyonnaise Potatoes 80

Macaroni Cheese 86
Mackerel
    à l'Orange 36
    Smoked 33
Mandarin Orange Rice 105
Marble Ring Cake 112
Marinated Chicken in Teriyaki Sauce
        68
Marmalade 122, 124
Marshmallow Sauce 98
Marzipan Chocolate 119
Mayonnaise, making 8
Mayonnaise Sauce, Thick 97
Meat 43–59
Meat Balls 45, 52
Meat Loaf, Tomato with Rich Brown
        Sauce 51
Milk, heating 17
Mince, cooking 44, 49
Minestrone 22
Mushrooms
    Baked, with Frankfurters and Eggs
        28
    and Barley Casserole 89
    Cream of Mushroom Soup 22
    Chinese Chicken and Mushroom
        Soup 24
    and Chicken Casserole 68
    Creamed, with Prawns 79
    Horsham 79
Mustard Rabbit Casserole 73

Noodles, cooking 85
Noodles with Prawn Sauce 86

Offal, cooking 45
Okra and Tomato Casserole 78
Omelettes 29
Onions
    French soup 23
    with Liver 58
    stuffed 80
Orange Marmalade 124
Orange Rind Snakes 117
Orange Sauce 99
Orange Sorbet 106

Parsley Sauce 92
Pasta 84–9

Pâtés
    Chicken Liver and Port 73
    Kipper 36
Peanut Brittle 117
Peppermint Creams, Chocolate 121
Peppermint Sauce 98
Pheasant in White Wine 72
Pineapple
    Chocolates 120
    fresh flambéd 106
Plaice
    Baked Whole 32
    Rolled Fillets in Lemon and Caper
        Sauce 38
Plum Sauce, Piquant 99
Poached Eggs 25–6
Poached Fish 34
Poaching 9
Pork
    cooking 44
    Chop recipes 55–6
    Escalopes 57
    Fillet with Cashew Nuts 54
Porridge 89
Potatoes, cooking 80–2
Poultry 60–74
Poussin, cooking 61, 63
Prawn Sauce 94
Prawns
    and Creamed Mushrooms 79
    with Smoked Salmon and Cucumber
        on toast 41
Puddings 100–9
Puréed Courgette Soup 23

Rabbit
    cooking 61, 63
    Mustard Casserole 73
Ratatouille 82
Red Cabbage and Apple Casserole 83
Rice
    boiled 87
    brown 88
    Chinese Fried 88
    cooking 84
    Mandarin Orange 105
    Pudding 104
    Spicy Pilaj 89
Roast chicken, cooking 60, 65

Roasting bag, cooking in 66
Roasting meat 43–4
Roux sauces, technique 90
Rum and Cherry Truffles 112

Sabayon Sauce 97
Salmon
　fresh, with Sauce Maltaise 38–9
　smoked on toast 41
Sauce Fines Herbes 96
Sauce Raifort 96
Sauces 90–9
　freezing 90
　making tips 8, 9
Sausage and Bacon Rolls 59
Sausages
　browning 58
　cooking 45–7
　with Green Beans 59
Sautéed Potatoes, Soft 82
Scampi Walewska 41
Scrambled Eggs 25–6
Shellfish 40–1
　cooking techniques 31
Smoked fish
　à la Creme 37
　Baked Cod 33
　Baked Haddock 33
Smoked Salmon, Cucumber and Prawn
　　Toasts 41
Sorbet, Orange 106
Soups 19–24
Spaghetti, Crispy Topped Creamed 87
Spaghetti Bolognese 85
Spaghetti Napolitana 85
Spanish Omelette 29
Spicy Pilaj 89
Spinach
　creamed 82
　Soup 20
Sponge puddings 100–1, 103, 108–9
Steaks, cooking 44, 46–8, 51
Steaming 9
Stewed Dried Fruit 107
'Stir-fried' Turkey 71
Stocks 19
Strawberry Cheesecake 104
Strawberry Jam 123–4
Stuffed Chicken Thighs, Drumsticks 71

Stuffed Onions 80
Stuffed Peppers 81
Suet Pudding, Layered Fruit 102
Suet Sponge Marmalade Pudding 103
Sweetbreads, cooking 45
Sweets see Confectionery

Tagliatelle with Walnut and Spinach
　Sauce 86
Tomato
　Chutney 125
　Meat Loaf with Rich Brown Sauce 51
　and Okra Casserole 78
　Soup 21
Tomato Sauce 93, 94
Tongue, cooking 45
Trout
　with Almonds 42
　Smoked 33
Truffles
　Handmade Chocolate 118
　Rum and Cherry 112
Turkey
　cooking 61–4
　gravy for 66
　and Ham Terrine 74
　'stir-fried' 71
Turkish Delight 119

Veal
　cooking 44, 46–7
　Escalopes 56–7
Vegetables 75–83
Venison, cooking 61, 63
Vichyssoise 24

Walnut and Spinach Sauce 95
Walnut and Yogurt Chicken 71
Welsh Rarebit 28
White sauces 90–1

ACKNOWLEDGEMENTS

The author would like especially to thank her husband, Laurie, for all his support; Jenny Pouncett, who typed the manuscript, and Claudette McIntosh, for all her help with the preparation of recipes for this book.

The Publishers would also like to thank Corning, the manufacturers of Pyrex, for supplying items from their ranges of cookware for use in the photographs and line drawings.

Line drawings by John Woodcock.